# MOUNTBATTEN
## & THE MEN OF THE 'KELLY'

# MOUNTBATTEN
## & THE MEN OF THE 'KELLY'

**William Pattinson**
**Foreword by H.R.H. THE PRINCE OF WALES**
Preface by Philip Ziegler

Patrick Stephens, Wellingborough

**Picture Credits**
Roy Craine 14, 15; William Dunn 103, 104; Fleet
Photographic Unit 121; Grigson Studios 148;
Hawthorn Leslie 35, 36, 40; *Illustrated*, 62, 64, 141
bottom, 144; Imperial War Museum 37 top, 41, 80,
100, 101, 108, 109; Manuscript 96; Mirror Group
Newspapers 12, 13; *News Chronicle* 142, 143; Pattison
& Maughan 182, 183, 184, 185; Photographic Section
HMS *Osprey* 150, 151, 152, 153; Royal Navy Public
Relations Office 176; *The Shields Gazette* 146; Thames
Television 156, 157, 158; Bernard Tyrer 133, 137,
138, 139, 140, 141 top, 144, 146 top, 149 bottom,
164, 166, 167, 168, 171, 172, 178, 179, 180; T. Viney
149 top.

First published in 1986


*British Library Cataloguing in Publication Data*

Pattinson, William
    Mountbatten and the men of the 'Kelly'.
    1. Kelly, *Ship*    2. World War, 1939–1945—
    Naval operations, British
    I. Title
    940.54'5941        D772.K4

    ISBN 0-85059-768-4




*Patrick Stephens Limited is part of the
Thorsons Publishing Group*


Photoset in 11 on 12 pt Goudy Old Style
by Avocet Marketing Services, Aylesbury, Bucks.
Printed in Great Britain on 135 gsm Fineblade
coated cartridge, and bound, by
Butler & Tanner, Frome, Somerset,
for the publishers, Patrick Stephens Limited,
Denington Estate, Wellingborough, Northants, NN8 2QD,
England.

# Contents

# *Foreword by HRH The Prince of Wales* KG, KT, GCB

Although for a long time to come it is likely that many writers will be researching the life of Earl Mountbatten of Burma, this book is one which I think he would have welcomed and enjoyed.

Of all the aspects of his immensely varied and illustrious career I believe he would have said that his long service in the Royal Navy came first. His love of ships and in particular his love of destroyers is renowned, and of all the warships in which he served during and between the two World Wars his deepest affection was for his Flotilla Leader HMS *Kelly*, of which he declared: 'To me she was quite unlike any other ship I served in ... I knew and loved her from the time of her birth when her keel was laid until the keel was the last thing visible as she sank beneath the waves'.

Lord Mountbatten's regard for *Kelly* went with his esteem for his shipmates, more than half of whom were lost in the Battle for Crete, and those fortunate ones who survived with him and who came to know their Captain even better through the HMS *Kelly* Reunion Association.

It is a wonderful tribute to their Captain's memory that 45 years after the famous warship perished, and more than six years after his death, members of *Kelly's* crew, including officers, should go on remembering Lord Mountbatten and still refer to him as 'The Captain'.

Long before I had the opportunity of meeting members of the Reunion Association Lord Mountbatten had told me about *Kelly* and her crew. He often used to mention some of their names and some of the stories about them; about colleagues like Rocky Wilkins, 'Scrounger' Scorer, Sid Mosses and Ted West. It was Rocky and company who founded the *Kelly* Association and they invited me to one of their famous dinners while I was still on active service in the Royal Navy.

As my great uncle Lord Mountbatten assured me I would, I found them a splendid bunch of men and I readily realized how this respect between a Captain and his crew was mutual. The survivors of the *Kelly*, those who are left today, officers and men, have left me in no doubt that Lord Mountbatten's leadership, example and concern for them, profoundly affected them for the rest of their lives and long after they left the Service they all loved.

It was a surprise and an honour, therefore, when some months after

Lord Mountbatten had been killed, I was invited to succeed him as President of the *Kelly* Reunion Association.

No one could ever properly succeed such a man in such a unique organization. But I am delighted to join former *Kelly* men in remembering a truly remarkable great uncle, of whom I am inordinately proud.

Lord Mountbatten encouraged his former ratings to reminisce. He enjoyed reading their own unembellished accounts of what life was like on *Kelly's* messdecks. He endeavoured to keep his Ship's Company as fully in the picture as he could. Knowing him there were probably few 'secrets' kept from him. Nevertheless there were some surprises when he received their personal stories for his archives at Broadlands and he regularly wrote to Rocky Wilkins with that refreshing, engaging frankness which was one of his hallmarks.

Bill Pattinson, who served in destroyers and Combined Operations in Mediterranean landings, has spent some years talking with *Kelly* personnel and he has been able to capture some of the remarkable rapport that went on between Captain and crew in *Kelly*. Indeed the same spirit went on in other ships of the Royal Navy. It so happened that a Commanding Officer with Lord Mountbatten's personality made sure that *Kelly's* story became fully available.

I am glad that former *Kelly* men are still being given the opportunity of going to sea in HM ships to see the modern Navy and tell their own stories of what it was like almost half a century ago. Indeed, I have been able to arrange a few visits for them myself. Pat Quail, a *Kelly* signalman, is still going around dinners in New Zealand telling the 5th Flotilla story and he is very popular with Kiwis who fought at Crete. Others are retelling the *Kelly* story in Canada, Australia, the United States and Malta, telling of their own friendships with Lord Mountbatten.

The unique aspect of The HMS *Kelly* Association is that it still endures despite the departure of the Ship's Captain. The Association flourishes because the children, and now the grandchildren, of the Ship's Company are determined to keep it going. It is a wonderful example of the strength of human relationships which can be forged during the vicissitudes of war and which can continue into the future because the spirit of a ship lives on to inspire the descendants of those who served in her.

Charles .

# *Preface by Philip Ziegler*

Leadership, like the related quality of charm, is easy to recognize yet remarkably difficult to define. It is the ability to command loyalty, to inspire enthusiasm, to ensure that everybody does his best not merely in moments of crisis but over a long and wearisome haul. A great leader can accept responsibility for a school, a prison, an army, a nation, and transform its spirit overnight; he can take over a team of mediocre players, a cast of indifferent actors, and weld them into a unit far more formidable than the sum of their parts. He can make, not bricks without straw, but extraordinary bricks from ordinary straw.

Mountbatten was such a man. He has been justly — and unjustly — criticized on many counts, but about his qualities as a leader there is only one opinion. He was, at the lowest, superlative; at the highest he was in a class literally by himself.

This is the story of HMS *Kelly*, of the men who sailed in her, of her triumphs and disasters, of the *Kelly* Reunion Association which today still unites the survivors from her crew. Above all, it is the story of her Captain. Without Mountbatten there would still have been a *Kelly*, there might have been a Reunion Association, but it is his contribution that has made the spirit of HMS *Kelly* burn so bright and endure so long. The story of the *Kelly* is the story of leadership carried to its highest level, of a Captain who gained the devotion of his men and demanded from himself as well as from his crew total dedication to the task in hand. And it is the story of men who gave him all he asked for, without question and without regret.

A true leader must do more than just give orders and set a good example; he must identify himself totally with his followers and care about them with such intensity that he is in a sense as much their servant as their master. These pages are filled with testimonies to Mountbatten's preoccupation, obsession almost, with the well-being of his men. 'He believed,' wrote Rocky Wilkins, who in 1985 still keeps fresh the memory of the *Kelly* and presides over its Reunion Association, 'that if a man had problems at home it affected his life aboard the ship and he worried about that. He thought that if a man had a happy homelife he would be all right aboard ship.' When Wilkins' house was bombed and his wife left homeless, Mountbatten not only granted immediate compassionate leave, but did not let the matter rest until he was sure that all problems of money and accommodation had been resolved. He would have done as much for anybody else on his ship.

He was determined to know, and to know about, every man who served under him. Whenever he took over a new ship he laboured to learn the names and faces of everyone aboard; when his responsibilities became too great to allow such blanket coverage he still made a point of finding out about any officer or man whom he encountered personally and retaining that knowledge in a card-index or, more often, his phenomenal memory. If he saw a face at a *Kelly* dinner which he did not immediately recognize, he would first check up on all the details and then make a point of talking personally to the man before the evening was over. He would never need to ask the name a second time. His men mattered to him, and he made them feel that they mattered. 'He made me feel like an admiral,' said Ordinary Seaman Ron Hall. It was a trick of public relations perhaps, but such a trick could not have worked unless it had been based on genuine interest in and concern for all those he worked with.

Unlike many Naval officers he made it his object to keep his men as fully in the picture as could be managed. 'Obviously for security reasons he could not tell us certain things,' wrote Wilkins, 'but if we put to sea and we were going on an engagement or expected action, then he would tell us exactly where we were going, what the ship hoped to do and what we were expected to do. We were not like most ships where the lower deck was kept in the dark about it.' Whatever he asked them to do, he would do himself and more. As a result they found themselves doing things which under another Captain they might have found impossible or inexpedient. When war broke out *Kelly* still needed much work doing on her before she was ready for battle. 'The Captain was certainly some guy,' recorded Sid Mosses. 'He cleared lower deck, gave us a pep talk and explained the situation and how we were going to do in three days what would normally take three weeks. Some hopes! He must be quite good. We did it.'

The loyalty that Mountbatten expected from his men was repaid in full measure. Once a man had served with Mountbatten a tie existed between them which would only be cut by death. 'One always felt one wouldn't be out of order at all to write to him,' wrote his gunnery officer, Alastair Robin. 'The personal relationship he established with everybody was such that if you had a crisis it was quite in order that you could put extra weight on him, such as a bit of help with the next job.' Whatever the circumstances, wherever he might be, a former member of *Kelly*'s crew had only to appeal to Mountbatten to be sure — not of casual charity — but of serious consideration of his problems and efficacious aid in overcoming them. The archives of Broadlands bulge with thick files of letters testifying to Mountbatten's determination not to let down his men.

To labour such virtues risks making Mountbatten sound like an exceptionally high-powered social worker. So in a way he was, but though such a Captain would have been liked, loved even, respected perhaps, he would not for that alone have commanded the intense and enthusiastic support which Mountbatten enjoyed. 'We would have followed him to Hell if he had asked us,' said one member of *Kelly*'s crew. Some other, extra element was there, the element that gives leadership its potency and makes it mysterious to those who do not have the gift of exercising it. 'The presence of Mountbatten in our midst uplifted our hearts,' wrote Rupert Curtis, a Reserve officer who served under him in Combined Operations, 'and no one from the youngest rating could fail to realize that we were in the presence of a very gifted man and leader.'

'Now your Captain is dead. And we have all lost a very special friend. I at any rate have lost someone who was like a second father to me.' So spoke the Prince of Wales at the first *Kelly* reunion dinner since Mountbatten's death. Despite the shattering shock, said the Prince, 'he has, I think, left behind such a great example for all of us to follow. And I know this has been one of the things that I found about his death which has been enormously helpful, that, although one does miss him terribly, instead of thinking about it all the time, I found that I thought to myself of all the things that he did ... The marvellous things he thought about. The people he cared for. His intense thoughtfulness; again treating people as individuals. And his moral courage, which is a great example for us all to try and follow if we can ...' There can have been nobody present that night who would have challenged a word of what he said, for they all knew what *Kelly* had done and had been, they knew that her spirit lived on, and they knew that, be he alive or dead, that spirit was enshrined in her Captain, Louis Mountbatten.

## Notes on the letters

The letters reproduced in this book are facsimiles selected from over 900 written by Mountbatten to *Kelly* survivors, most of them to Rocky Wilkins, Honorary Secretary of the *Kelly* Reunion Association. Some passages of a personal nature and others irrelevant to the subject of this book have been deleted.

# Introduction

## Final Tribute

The unveiling by the Queen of the memorial statue of Earl Mountbatten of Burma which took place in London in November 1983 was the final momentous occasion in the history of one of Britain's most remarkable men.

Four years earlier, after Lord Mountbatten's shattering death at the hands of the IRA, whose members attached a bomb to his fishing boat at Mullaghmore in the Irish Republic where he was holidaying at his castle with several of the closest members of his family, the nation had mourned. The Mountbatten funeral, with colour and splendour but with deep solemnity, was meticulously planned, partly by the famous man himself, and it could only have been surpassed in ceremonial by a public farewell to a monarch. The circumstances of his death aroused world interest.

The unveiling of the statue by the Queen herself was certainly another glittering occasion. Apart from the kaleidoscope provided by the setting on Foreign Office Green, the gleaming uniforms and the bands, the ladies — with the exception of Mrs Margaret Thatcher, the British Prime Minister, who was smart in black — chose colour. It was a time for tribute and loving memories, not mourning, but the sadness remained, particularly in the Royal Family, of whom the late Louis Mountbatten was a loved and important member. The ceremony just off Horse Guards Parade provided the opportunity for a particular trio of ladies to pay tribute to a famous man and it is unlikely that anything like this can happen again.

Here was the Queen referring for the first time in public since the tragedy in Ireland to 'Uncle Dickie', as he was known in the Royal Family circle. 'We all speculate on what it is that makes for greatness in a man or woman,' said Her Majesty in her superbly written and impeccably delivered address. 'Why was it that the moment Lord Mountbatten came through the door he seemed to fill the room? It was first and foremost the vitality and force of his personality, combined with an astonishing range of abilities. He could be farsighted with enormous breadth of vision and yet he could also concentrate on the minutest detail of any problem — a perfectionist who always mastered his subject. Add to this unfailing courage, immense charm and a never flagging determination to get his

*The Queen unveils the statue of
Earl Mountbatten in Whitehall
with Prime Minister Margaret
Thatcher looking on.*

way, and you have a truly formidable character. Above all he was a natural leader who managed to convey to those who worked with him his sense of enthusiasm and dedication.'

The Queen went on to say there were many sides to this 'remarkable' man who had changed the course of history, referring to his command in South-East Asia in World War 2 and later as the last Viceroy of India. He had been a first-class professional Naval officer, equally at home with his sailors or Burma Star veterans, Hollywood film stars or world figures.

'But above all', added the Queen, 'Dickie delighted in being a family man and he was always ready to help any member of the family.'

Then Mountbatten's daughter Patricia, who after her father's death inherited the title of Countess Mountbatten of Burma, and Britain's first woman Prime Minister, Margaret Thatcher, added their tributes.

Lady Mountbatten caused a smile among the audience of 1,500 when she said of her father: 'I can't help thinking how much he would have enjoyed today', and everyone who had ever met Lord Mountbatten must have understood and agreed. Mrs Thatcher brought the minds of those present to that grim August Bank Holiday in 1979 when the Mountbatten family were victims of the IRA, whose deed was wanton and needless. The family were holidaying as they often did at Classibawn Castle, not a mile from the harbour in County Sligo. They had just sailed when the boat *Shadow V* was blown up by a bomb remotely controlled from the shore. In addition to Lord Mountbatten, his fourteen-year-old grandson, Nicholas Knatchbull, and a crew member, Paul Maxwell, who was fifteen, were also killed. The Dowager Lady Brabourne died next day from injuries. Also seriously injured were Lord Mountbatten's son-in-law and daughter, Lord and Lady Brabourne (now Countess Mountbatten) and Timothy, Nicholas' twin brother. The whole of Britain was aghast and angered. Mrs Thatcher made the only mention of the assassination. She said: 'Lord Mountbatten died at the hands of wicked men but his work lives on'. He was, the Prime Minister added, one of the great men of our time who had a unique place in twentieth century history.

Hardly any member of our large Royal Family was absent from the great array gathered to share the universally-held pride and affection for Uncle 'Dickie' Mountbatten. Prince Philip, whose life was so greatly influenced by his uncle, was, of course, one of those present. Philip, Lieutenant Philip Mountbatten, RN, when he was engaged to the Queen, has the looks, the mannerisms, the ability and not least the commonsense and straight-forward, no-nonsense virtues of his mentor. Also present was Prince Charles whose deep regard for the 'grandfatherly figure' in his family is well known. Prince Andrew, whose achievement as a Naval helicopter pilot in the Falklands War, would have been admired by Mountbatten; and Prince Edward, appearing for the first time publicly and indeed seen for the first time by members of the Royal Family in his Royal Marines uniform, were there, as was the Queen Mother who knew Lord Mountbatten for longer than any one of today's Royal Family.

After the Royals, including members of thirteen other reigning and ex-reigning foreign royal families, the statue was closely inspected by former British Prime Ministers Earl Macmillan of Stockton, Sir Harold Wilson,

*Mountbatten's younger Royal relatives watch the unveiling of his statue. From right to left; Princess Margaret, the Prince and Princess of Wales, Prince Andrew, Prince Edward and, far left, Princess Anne.*

Edward Heath, James Callaghan and Michael Foot — they had all had the closest associations with Louis Mountbatten both in his rise to head the Royal Navy and the Defence Staff and in his important roles in British civilian affairs.

Following the ambassadors and foreign dignitaries, the bemedalled Service chiefs representing every branch of Britain's Services and the representatives of such as the Gurkhas and Burma campaign veterans, there came a handful of men wearing Naval blazers and grey flannels, all with medals and a very special tie. These men, in their late sixties and seventies, had reason to appreciate, more than anyone, the imposing bronze statue by the Czech sculptor Franta Belsky.

The statue, with Mountbatten as if on the bridge of one of his ships, hatless, was holding binoculars, his eyes fixed on the Old Admiralty Building where his father presided and where son followed father. Belsky never met Lord Mountbatten. His nine foot tall statue, weighing nearly a ton, took almost two years to complete after Belsky had been chosen by a panel which included Countess Mountbatten. Working with the aid of photographs, Belsky portrayed Lord Mountbatten as an Admiral of the

*The statue of Earl Mountbatten of Burma, Horse Guards Parade, Whitehall.*

*Countess Mountbatten of Burma and Kelly survivors after laying wreaths at the Mountbatten statue on the 44th anniversary of Kelly's sinking at the Battle of Crete.*

Fleet in the mid-1950s when, after his onerous task as the last Viceroy of India, he had resumed his Naval career at his own request. If ever there comes a time when, perhaps in centuries ahead, there is cause to examine the interior of the statue, there will be found some interesting deposits. The sculptor Belsky places what he calls 'time capsules' in all his statues which, incidentally, include studies of the Queen, Prince Philip and Sir Winston Churchill. The Mountbatten statue contains a copy of the unveiling ceremony programme, four coins of the time, a history of the creation of the statue and some pages from *The Times* and *The Guardian* newspapers.

While Mountbatten is shown as an Admiral, those men in blazers, medals and the tie knew Mountbatten before he had achieved the highest rank. They remembered him first as the dashing four-ringed destroyer captain, Captain D with his own flotilla of eight destroyers, 'The Fighting Fifth'. The men looked approvingly at the statue and their old Captain would have been particularly delighted to have seen them there. Before they left Horse Guards to walk hatless in the drizzle across Whitehall to join the Royal families and the famous at a pre-lunch reception at the Banqueting House, one of them, ex-Able Seamen Rocky Wilkins, had presented to Countess Mountbatten a leather-bound *Book of Donors* containing the names of people who had between them contributed more than £100,000 to the concept and creation of the statue.

The men in blazers proudly wore the tie of the HMS *Kelly* Reunion Association. They survived the sinking of HMS *Kelly* (Captain Lord Louis Mountbatten) when the Flotilla Leader was attacked by Nazi aircraft during the Battle of Crete in 1941. Back in Alexandria in Egypt after rescue, Mountbatten told his fellow survivors to 'keep on' and eventually the Association was formed which is helping to immortalize *Kelly*. Since Lord Mountbatten's assassination the Prince of Wales has taken over the very active presidency. 'Uncle Dickie' would have been more than pleased.

Chapter 1

# The 'little house' in Kinnerton Street

This book would not have been written but for a talk I had with Lord Mountbatten some weeks before he met his death. I had met him on a few occasions since the wartime days when he had become Chief of Combined Operations and made an early visit to the West Coast of Scotland to see and accompany some of us exercising in Tank Landing Craft. We were ready for what seemed to be the far-off days when hopefully we would land troops on enemy-occupied beaches in Northern Europe — or so it appeared then. Had we known that one day, instead of assembling on Britain's south coast to load up for France, we would have orders to sail from England out into the lonely and fierce Atlantic and into the Mediterranean we would have thought, indeed, as we ultimately did think, that our masters at Admiralty, Mountbatten among them, must have been out of their minds.

Anyway, it was some 35 years later when I went at tea time to see Lord Mountbatten on a warm, sunny afternoon. A former colleague of mine who was running a periodical for the shipbuilding industry and the men who worked in it asked me to endeavour to see Lord Mountbatten for two reasons. One was to seek his views on nationalised shipbuilding, which was having a lean time because of labour problems, late delivery of vessels resulting in loss of money, sacrificed by penalty clauses, curtailment of orders and some limitations in management — a similar situation to that which was hitting much of British industry at that time. Secondly, the magazine was devoting space to features about famous British ships, merchant as well as warships, of the first half of the century. I had asked in a letter to Mountbatten if I might discuss with him HMS *Cavalier* in particular.

Mention of *Cavalier* was close to the heart of any destroyer man and Lord Mountbatten, in his earlier Naval days, was renowned as a brilliant and daring handler of destroyers, having been in command of HMS *Daring* and HMS *Wishart* in the 1930s before taking command of *Kelly* and becoming Captain D of the 5th Destroyer Flotilla. He wrote back to me promptly. There was no mention of the subject of shipbuilding at all but he said in his letter that he had been associated for some months in trying to help the HMS *Cavalier* Trust 'from the wings without becoming a trustee'.

*Cavalier* was the last available of the 1,000 or so destroyers built for the Royal Navy in over eighty years and Lord Mountbatten was particularly keen that the project to save her and put her on permanent show should be achieved successfully. 'I have ideas on how to do it . . . Therefore I would be happy to give what help I can in your article about the *Cavalier* though it must be remembered that my knowledge of her has only been acquired since she came up for sale!' So I was asked by Lord Mountbatten to get in touch with his private secretary, John Barratt, 'to see when I could meet you on an occasion when I am in London at my little house, 2 Kinnerton Street'.

Number 2 Kinnerton Street is one of three addresses Lord Mountbatten owned at the time and far more modest and different in location to the lovely Broadlands in Hampshire or Classiebawn Castle by the Atlantic in County Sligo. Leading off Knightsbridge, it is in a street of small shops and businesses and large numbers of flats in typical West End mews. In the curved street were one or two garages, a fine arts shop and two busy pubs. When I inquired of a friendly fruiterer he said 'Number 2, Lord Mountbatten's? Just across the road there.' Next door to Number 2 is the 'Turk's Head', a hostelry with a history, where the customer is reminded that the early Victorian house derives its name from the 'Turk's Head Coffee House' where in 1764 Dr Samuel Johnson, Sir Joshua Reynolds, Boswell and Burke founded their celebrated Literary Society. 'Today you are still welcome to savour the hospitality of this house in a traditional atmosphere akin to that in which Dickens, Macaulay, Trollope and their contemporary Victorian Literarists enjoyed the pleasures of good company and refreshment.'

As I rang the bell of Lord Mountbatten's 'little house' nine mounted guardsmen held up the traffic, for the Knightsbridge Barracks are close by, but although Lord Mountbatten was Colonel of the Life Guards the passing guards were merely exercising their horses and had nothing whatever to do with security. In fact security was not as much an everyday headline word in 1979 as it is today, but in retrospect it surprises me that, considering Lord Mountbatten was to be a victim of a carefully placed explosive on his boat on the West Coast of Ireland a few weeks later, there he was in his London home, totally unguarded and with only a tiny private household staff.

The door was opened by a manservant in black jacket and although I was calling there by appointment I might have been anyone with a pistol in my pocket. There was only one other of Mountbatten's staff in the house which was really two flats and used by him on private visits to London. At the foot of a short staircase sat John Barratt, the private secretary, at a small table with room for a typewriter, a telephone and little else. Barratt's conversation with me was interrupted by telephone calls. My eyes were constantly on a dusty plaster bust of Lord Mountbatten lying on its side on the floor of an open cupboard. While John Barratt and I talked two of his employer's visitors in turn said their goodbyes at the top of the stairs. The first, Lady Pamela Hicks, was seen down the stairs and to the doorway into the street by her father. The second was Miss Audrey Whiting of the *Sunday Mirror* who had been discussing the opening to the public of the famous Broadlands home. Audrey Whiting specialized in writing about Royalty and others close to Buckingham Palace and Lord Mountbatten, who didn't need to be told anything about the value of public and press relations, would be delighted at what the *Sunday Mirror* carried about Broadlands' attractions in the following Sunday edition. The large pieces about Broadlands at the time in newspapers and on television and radio were worth a great deal and it was not to be long before Broadlands loomed large in the stately homes visitors' league. Audrey Whiting and I must have been among the last journalists to have a personal talk with Lord Mountbatten before his murder. I have my tape recording of the conservation and it is now in the archives at Broadlands.

After greeting me Lord Mountbatten's first action was to examine closely the tie I was wearing. He pulled it closer to his eyes and said: 'Don't say a word!' He thought for hardly a second before he said 'An LCT, yes'. Then 'Don't tell me. Let me think . .' and added 'An LCT, Mark Four, am I correct?' He smiled almost triumphantly as I told him he was certainly correct. (LCT were the initials for Landing Craft Tank, a major vessel used in amphibious warfare in the Mediterranean and Normandy landings.) I said that indeed he himself possessed a similar tie because, in the earliest days of the Mediterranean Landing Craft Association, which I helped to found soon after World War 2 and was honorary secretary of for the first 21 years, I had a letter from Earl Mountbatten wishing us well. He was sent one of our first ties — we were proud to consider ourselves as one of his old boys. 'Of course,' Lord Mountbatten said. 'And I can tell you I have worn that tie you kindly sent me. It's one of a multitude I possess but I'm pleased to have it. But they were pigs to handle, those LCTs, I know!'

Lord Mountbatten was in uniform, with that huge display of medal ribbons. He said he had just returned from a Royal Naval Film Corporation lunch in HMS *President*, the Reserves' training ship on the Thames, where he had been with Prince Philip. I thought he looked tired and he excused himself for sucking a lozenge because he had a bothersome cough.

As I say, I had gone to see Lord Mountbatten to discuss the shipbuilding industry and HMS *Cavalier*. It was clear from the outset that he was disinclined to talk about shipbuilding and the poor state this industry found itself in in Britain. When it is clear that a person of Mountbatten's character does not wish to talk about a subject one simply makes no attempt to press it. I did venture to Lord Mountbatten that some words of encouragement or otherwise from him to those engaged in shipbuilding would be taken notice of and at once he said: 'I warn you right away I don't usually do what you are going to propose. I don't usually do back-seat driving. You've rarely seen me write anything of that sort, because it's not my line. I do ex-Service things. I look at the past.'

Then he added some words that I was to reflect upon for some time afterwards and more so when the appalling news came of Lord Mountbatten's murder. 'Funnily enough,' he said to me that afternoon at Kinnerton Street, 'having said this you may see a speech I am making at Strasbourg on the question of the nuclear arms race.* That is one thing I have got to do because I'm the only military member of the scientific Council of the Stockholm Peace Institute and I've got to make a speech there. Therefore I'm breaking my rules. It's the first time I've done it since I left being CDS [Chief of the Defence Staff].'

* See Appendix.

He returned briefly to the subject of shipbuilding which he virtually brushed aside. 'I can't possibly write and encourage everything that goes on. I shall be in my eightieth year next month and I'm really trying to keep out of things.' But as he put it he could probably kill two birds with one stone. 'I can give you an interview about the *Cavalier*,' he said, 'and you can start by saying that Earl Mountbatten of Burma was absolutely delighted to be able to help with this article not only because he is very keen on the *Cavalier* project but because by placing the article in *Shipbuilding News* he feels that this venture must be encouraged at this time and shipbuilding wants all the encouragement it can get.' He proceeded to reveal his deep interest in the HMS *Cavalier* project. Here is a splendid interviewee, I thought. He's decided to write the article himself!

He failed to pretend to me that he should not be taking the credit for *Cavalier's* preservation. He said he had absolutely refused to be a trustee or chairman or president of the project. He said his name would not be found anywhere in connection with the *Cavalier*. In fact, however, if it had not been for Lord Mountbatten the destroyer would have been scrapped years ago. In the background Mountbatten had been doing all he could to get people interested and to donate money to enable purchase of the vessel from the Admiralty. Had she been disposed of for scrap she would have been worth £60,000 or so, Lord Mountbatten explained. 'Therefore that was the price to us and we had to raise money to buy her. Mind you, in buying her we then had a solid asset so if we can't raise the money to put her on show we then can at least get our money back. It was, then, fairly easy to get the first lot of money and if not very easy at least people realized that they were not necessarily losing their money if the ship didn't eventually go on show — they'd probably get their money back. If the ship did go on show then their money was well spent. The *Cavalier* project, in my own opinion, is viable. The vessel was in apple pie order when we took her over. Absolutely marvellous to be on board.'

Then further money had to be spent on dredging a berth for the old destroyer and she had to be cleaned up and altered a bit so people could get round the ship easily. 'It's no good' Lord Mountbatten commented 'asking old ladies to go up and down steep ladders. You've got to provide more or less a bit of a staircase.'

When the famous and last destroyer, 27 years old in 1971 when she became the fastest ship in the Royal Navy in a full power trial, left Chatham and was towed into Southampton, Lord Mountbatten was among those on the bridge as she entered harbour. He asked me to get in touch (for more information) with the chairman of the HMS *Cavalier* Trust, Vice Admiral Sir Ian McIntosh, who in the war was one of our most distinguished submarine commanders, in famous vessels *H44*, *Sceptre* and *Alderney*.

At this last meeting with Lord Mountbatten, the former Captain D predictably eulogized about destroyers. More than any other he'd handled he had his beloved *Kelly* in mind and his words were like poetry to any Naval officer who had had the fortune to be the man in charge on the open bridge of a destroyer, especially at Full Ahead Together.

'Destroyers were by far the most glamorous of all the types of warship. It was the ambition of almost everybody to serve in destroyers. If they were, say, in submarines and came to do their big ship time and then went to destroyers or frigates they would be delighted. Able Seamen having done their big ship time always wanted to go to destroyers.

'The reason is the destroyer is the ideal company unit for a "family". On average a destroyer had 115 to 125 men when I had my first command, to double that with 250 officers and men on board the last destroyers. The destroyer had a small enough "family" for the Captain to know everybody by sight and by name. Also it was the most exciting way to serve, because whatever else happened destroyers were out in the fray the whole time. I suppose there were more people killed in destroyers pro rata than in any other form of naval warfare.'

Lord Mountbatten's mind was in the past and not the present as he concluded: 'Destroyers are very exciting. They are beautiful ships. They are also very nice to handle.'

It was an unforgettable privilege to be with Lord Mountbatten when he was reminiscing. How the Duke of Edinburgh and the Prince of Wales must have been fascinated by 'Uncle Dickie'. How lucky they were to have his fatherly interest. One didn't have to be in Lord Mountbatten's personal company to appreciate how the Royal father and son have been endowed with some of his style and mannerisms. Lord Mountbatten went on to say we ought to have preserved more of our warships. He mentioned HMS *Belfast,* now preserved in the Pool of London and attracting many thousands annually, but in the days when he went to sea we had battleships with 15-inch guns. Clearly but for the cost he would have been delighted if a battleship could have been preserved. He applauded the plan to get to the *Mary Rose* (since then one of Prince Charles' great interests). He talked of the opening to the public of Broadlands which, like HMS *Victory* and the National Motor Museum at Beaulieu, had the advantage of being in a great catchment area. He talked of television filming at Broadlands and spoke ecstatically of his fishkeeper who had been featured in the programme. 'He is a very nice man, very charming. If he charged overtime it would cost you £300 a week!'

The *Kelly* Reunion Association came up for discussion and I said I had not seen the honorary secretary, Rocky Wilkins, for some years. 'You must get in touch with him again' Mountbatten said. 'He'll be pleased and you must come to another reunion.'

'Jack! Jack!', Lord Mountbatten shouted down the stairs for his secretary John Barratt. 'Give Mr Pattinson Rocky's address.' That is how I was put in touch with Rocky Wilkins again. Shortly afterwards Rocky's former Captain was dead. I remembered that Rocky had for more than 35 years been in close touch with Lord Mountbatten mainly through *Kelly* reunion dinners. Rocky had in his home at Harlow in Essex a wealth of personal letters and a mass of photographs and other *Kelly* papers, which he loaned me for the preparation of this book.

Chaper 2

# Sid Mosses' diary

Earl Mountbatten left a mammoth collection of letters, papers and memorabilia in his archives at Broadlands where, in what he called his 'ship's passage', he had many *Kelly* items. Whenever he was asked when he was going to write his autobiography Mountbatten told Wilkins 'I will leave that to people like you'. In the December before his death he wrote to Rocky that he could well imagine the 'slight boredom' which comes on retirement. 'Have you thought of trying to put together the various reminiscences from members of the ship's company which you started into a manuscript which will give you some satisfaction and keep you occupied and if you can spare a copy for me I shall be most grateful.'

Sid Mosses joined *Kelly* in August 1939. He became a Leading Seaman and QM of the pom-pom crew and he left the Navy as a Chief Petty Officer. He spent many hours writing for his old Captain an article which he entitled 'The *Kelly* and I' and this account particularly delighted Lord Mountbatten because it was the *Kelly* story as seen by the lower deck. Most Servicemen recall the funny side of life at sea rather than the grim one. Mosses' personal epistle to his Captain, giving his unadulterated impressions from the time he joined *Kelly* until he went into the sea off Crete, was typical of some of the many revelations made to Mountbatten by his men two and three decades afterwards. Mountbatten enjoyed reading what they used to get up to, whether the tales were saucy, mischievous, sometimes startling or far-fetched.

Mosses was an Active Service rating aboard HMS *Bodicea* and just about to go on summer leave in July 1939, when 'the blow fell. Draft chit to RN Barracks'.

'Reported to the Drafting Office where the staff informed me I was due to go on a luxury cruise in the Med with the Great Lord Louis. Rumours were rife, buzzes were great. In fact one three-badge veteran told me His Lordship always picked his own crew, in fact he had seen him in the Drafting Office in conference with the Drafting Jaunty*. Apart from the

*See glossary for Naval slang.

normal goodies, he had a great leaning towards the skates. Stripey must have been right, we had the lot, comedians as well.

'Consulted my tailor, Mr Greenburgh, as to what I would require for the cruise. He in turn informed me that His Lordship never went anywhere without at least six strings of polo ponies, numerous Rolls-Royces, and anything that went with a man of his status, so I had to be prepared for anything.

'Went up to Hebburn with the Steaming Party and on turning to, met the Chief Gunner's Mate, Tusky Hales, just one of the many gentlemen I was to serve with. He introduced me to the Buffer and Coxwain, after which I met Lieutenant Commander Burnett* and the Navigator, Lieutenant Butler Bowden. I was to be QM, being the oldest, I was to get things organized. That night we made the first of what was to be many visits to the "Commercial". The natives made us very much at home. But to work. We went out and did speed and acceptance trials. She certainly was a beauty, why they even had a place where you could wash, and what is more, the water came out of taps, no more snivelling round the cook for a tickler tin of water to prime the iron deck pump, and all one mess washing in one bucket of water. After trials, returned to harbour, lower deck was cleared aft. I then had the honour of piping the still as the White Ensign was raised for the first time.

'There was a big party later on for all those who built her. We were not forgotten. Somehow or other white enamel buckets filled with various concoctions began to arrive on the messdeck and a good time was had by all. This certainly was the life. All too soon we bade a reluctant farewell to Hebburn. Little did we know what the future had in store for us.

'Down to Chatham and commissioning, received my new wardrobe. I was now ready to meet all the crowned heads of Europe. Alas it was not to be. Adolf had other ideas.

'The Captain was certainly some guy. He cleared lower deck, gave us a pep talk and explained the situation and how we were going to do in three days what would normally take three weeks. Some hopes! He must be quite good. We did it. Whilst doing the job we were in for another surprise. Not only did water come out of taps, but when anything had to be done the officers dug in with the ratings. Good for morale!

'We strutted round Chatham with our tiddly cap badges, HMS *Kelly*, visited all the local pubs, chatted the barmaids up, saluted the Captain as he passed in his chauffeur-driven Rolls with a silver signalman as the mascot. Don't know why we felt so happy, but we did.

'Goodbye Chatham, hello Portland. Paint ship overall from our lovely Med colour to the drab Fleet grey. Nobody excused bar the cooks. Remember seeing the Captain over the side with a crowd of lads painting away; Lieutenant Robin, the Gunnery Officer, on his knees in tears because they were painting all the gleaming steel work on his beloved guns. As our old friend Rob Wilton would say "Now the day war broke out", I was in the wardroom smoking free tailor-mades. The Captain was giving us a lecture on the Mountbatten Station Keeper when in walks the Yeoman with a signal — war has been declared. This was it. Leave was piped and everybody went ashore. Who knows, it might be the last

*Later Rear Admiral Burnett, *Kelly's* original First Lieutenant.

```
                                                    S. 1320h.
                                               (Established  October,  )

                  NAVAL   MESSAGE.

To:                                 FROM:

All concerned at Home and Abroad
         650 "A"                    ADMIRALTY

  ──────────────────────────────────────────────

                  MOST IMMEDIATE
                  ─ ─ ─ ─ ─ ─ ─ ─ ─

Commence Hostilities at once with GERMANY
                 1117/3


  W/T        P/L        1500        3/9/39
```

*The first dramatic signal received by* Kelly.

chance. Into the first hostelry outside the dockyard to top up, it was not long before the singing and dancing started. Boy Hunwicks started to play the piano, only snag was he only knew one tune, "The Teddy Bears' Picnic". Came closing time and a lorry driver offered us a lift into Weymouth, loaded up with some cases of beer and away. It was obvious something was going on for the natives were waving and cheering us as we passed. The character who wrote "In times of danger not before, God and the Navy we adore" certainly knew something.

'Went to sea the next day for anti-submarine exercises. I was on the wheel when a few crisp words of command came down the voice pipe. We had nearly been torpedoed. We were at war. The Captain certainly pressed the point home when it was all over. On thinking of the incident after all these years, it makes one wonder, for two ratings had seen the torpedoes approaching the ship and did not report them. They were to learn what war was all about as time went on. If the Captain and the bridge staff had not been on the ball I don't think I would be writing this today.

'A while later, we were "somewhere at sea". The weather was foul, the wheelhouse like an opium den, everything quiet, watch your steering and at the same time listen for any buzzes down the voice pipe. Be off watch very soon and into the hammock — it was not to be. My old mate Leading Signalman "Gert" Giddings poked his head in from the SDO with the news that the carrier *Courageous* had been torpedoed about forty miles from us. Full Speed Ahead, alter course and away. Head up the buzz pipe, I could not believe it, she had gone down. It seemed impossible a ship that size — we were learning.

'On being relieved on the wheel, went down to give a hand getting the survivors aboard. What a mess, got them on board and into the messdeck, laced them with rum and Ki, gave most of our kit away. One "rating", a short, tubby chap, obviously more shocked than the rest, started walking aft. We tried in vain to take him on to the messdeck, he mumbling and getting rather hostile. So we took him to the wardroom — how were we to know that it was *Courageous's* Commander (E).

'Having enjoyed the Indian summer in the south, we steamed north for

Scapa Flow (the matelots' heaven). Life was pretty grim. Northern patrols looking for the elusive pocket battleships. Cold, tired and hungry, four meals a day, two down and two up, plus the fact that we had no proper clothing for the job. Shortly after this, through the courtesy of Lady Mountbatten and Himself, we received good supplies of heavy weather gear. I believe one of the big hotels in London adopted us — was it the Savoy?

'Talking about clothes, we had an Ordinary Seaman and rumour had it that he was a Countess's son. He never dhobied like the rest and had a locker and case full of new gear, all his underwear was silk and on taking a shower he would throw the dirties into the corner of the bathroom; these were collected later by Brigham Young who in turn washed them and would parade round the messdeck in his finery amidst whistles and all kinds of remarks from the crowd. Let's face it, whoever heard of a pre-war matelot wearing silk underwear?

'Life in Scapa had its lighter moments for by now we were getting to know each other and the *Kelly* was becoming a happy and efficient ship. There was nowhere to go in Scapa but the canteen, so some of our most notable characters got organized: Leading Seaman Ginger Grubb and Bunker Boyd. Grubby was one of those matelots who was Petty Officer one day and an Ordinary Seaman the next, whilst Bunker could talk his way into heaven, plus being a good turn he played the accordion. They got organized with the crew of the flotilla tender *Daisy II*, who used to lay alongside of us, the routine being all tea urns and mess kettles were put on board *Daisy* before going ashore, topped up in the canteen and when things were quiet on return, would be smuggled aboard, after rounds we would have a good Sods Opera, Tusky Hales giving us such favourites as "Eskimo Nell" and "Gunga Din".

'Pusser's Ki, as the matelots call it, made from grated hard chocolate, boiled and thickened with custard powder, was no mystery to the sailor, was always appreciated by officers and men alike, so I was quite amused when I heard the following conversation down the buzz pipe one cold and bitter night:

'O.O.W. Lieutenant Sturdy: "I say Snotty, shall we have some Ki?"

'Midshipman Money: "Splendid idea Sir. I say Sir, where do they get this Ki?"

'Lieutenant Sturdy: "Don't really know, should imagine they keep it in steaming hot cauldrons in the galley. One simply calls down the voice pipe and it appears."

'The *City of Flint* incident* was not without its moments, everybody was praying that we would catch up with her and get a boarding party on her. Rehearsals were numerous, boarding ladders were rigged for'ard. I think we even had a bugler to sound the charge, but all to no avail. Although we did frighten the life out of one merchant ship's crew which was sneaking down the Norwegian Coast close inshore. We tore over at high speed and prepared to board and found it was the wrong ship. When the boarding parties fell out and returned gear, AB Percy Hansell brought the house down on the after messdeck when somehow or other he banged his rifle

*The *City of Flint* was a British merchant vessel aboard which the Germans had put a prize crew. *Kelly* tried to intercept her but failed and the ship suffered damage in a gale as she was making her way from the enemy coast at speed.

down with the safety catch off. The result — a loud explosion and a rack full of footwear with bullet holes in them!

'It was about this time that we were apprehended by a minute Norwegian TB destroyer who closed in on us with the for'ard gun manned and pointing at us. From where we stood we could see right through the barrel. It was not loaded. They had forgotten to close the breach. Many comments from the wits. The Captain asked the Norwegian Captain to give his best wishes to his cousin Crown Prince Olaf when he returned to port.

'I met the Crown Prince in June 1955 whilst serving in the carrier *Bulwark*. He inspected the ship's company on the flight deck. I had the honour to drive him round in a Land Rover. On completion he thanked me for the quickest inspection he had ever done and asked what ships I had served in during the war — a routine question — but as soon as I mentioned the *Kelly* he said: "You must have served with my Cousin, Lord Louis". I mentioned the incident with the TBD which he remembered.

'One day we were going along in the usual horrible weather when we went to a merchant ship which had been tinfished and was still afloat but upside down with the keel just awash. Think it was the *Aldington Court*. There was a heavy sea running as we raced down her side dropping depth charges to try and sink her. Had a terrible job on the wheel trying to steer a steady course. Thought we might finish up on top of her. Then the gunnery boys had a go — not sure if we sank her or not.

'Going along with a convoy one day in the normal, bad weather, steering was terrible. Without warning we started slewing round to port. Put the wheel hard to starboard but still she went on, finished up standing on the ship's side with the OOW, Mr Brownjohn, asking me what the hell I thought I was doing. If my memory serves me right twelve men were washed overboard from for'ard and eleven washed back inboard, aft, Nobby Clark being one of them. One did not return and it was a horrible sight to see him disappear astern. It was known as the BIG Roll, the starboard side of the iron deck was stripped, boats, guard rails, the lot. Never did find out how far we went over, rumours had it that the engine room staff had to swim for it when the sea came down the funnel!

'Back home again to Hebburn for repairs, where we received everything but the freedom of the city. We became members of all the clubs, pubs and the star attractions at the Power House dances. Very seldom slept on board as all hands were either courting or up-homers. I was going strong with the nursemaid from a pub.

'About this time Leading Seaman Alf Bareham and myself went to Cardington to do a Barrage Balloon Course. There were twenty matelots from various ships, had a great time when we went ashore for nobody had seen a Jolly Jack apart from on the movies. We were heroes. Completed the course and finished up in Pompey Barracks on the Balloon at the back of the wardroom. Visited the Drafting Commander every day to be returned to the ship. All I could get out of him was: "There's a war on". In the end I wrote to our Captain's secretary to see if he could do something. It took about 72 hours before the Drafting Commander sent for me and told me to pack my bag and get out as fast as I liked and never to darken his doors again. Never found out what was in the letter he got from *Kelly*, but it worked.

'Back to the "Home Town" again, reported to Lieutenant Commander Burnett who told me to join up with the ammunition dump guard at Jarrow Slacks, a nice comfy job, 24 hours about and living in a semi-detached on the quay; it was well used by neutral ships so we did very well for food and liquor. In fact quite a few of the ship's company used to spend weekends with us, plus the fact there was a very good pub just outside the gate and some very charming young damsels living nearby. But alas, all good things come to an end, so away to sea and war.

'North again. The job, escorting a neutral convoy on our own. We were going from ship to ship with the Captain giving them their orders. At the same time, to really let them know who we were the loudspeakers were playing our signature tune: " Has anybody here seen Kelly?". A German pilot had, and to let us know swooped down and tried to blow us sky high. He wasn't lucky. Last I saw of the Germans was in a rubber dinghy, thanks to the gunnery department. The weather was grim. You name it, we had it. I was peacefully asleep in my hammock when the whole world erupted. There was a terrific crash, the ship seemed about to turn over to starboard, the alarm bells sounded, all lights were out apart from the secondary lighting. We had been hit. It was all over in seconds for buzzes travel faster than light. Evidently on being hit a pre-arranged signal was sent out which read "I have been hit by a mine or torpedo"; back came the answer, "Not mine dear, me". It was from the 'Tribal' Class destroyer *Gurkha*. We had run into each other in the pitch dark with a snowstorm thrown in for good measure. We were left with a gaping hole just above the water line, about thirty feet long. On to Lerwick for temporary repairs, then on to Scapa to have plates welded on. We were in for another surprise. "Clear Lower Deck". The Captain asked us where we would like to go for repairs. Various suggestions were made, then came the stunner — London! Could not believe it, but London it was.

'We eventually arrived looking very war worn and sailed through the London docks system causing quite a stir to the large crowds of onlookers. We all felt about six feet tall, the sailors returning from the war. Tied up in the London Graving Dock.

'We could not do much as far as routine went so all kinds of training classes were started to keep us occupied during the day. I was passing for Leading Seaman at the time so we would take a whaler away in the evening with a volunteer boys' crew. In doing so we learned a few facts on survival, working on the old saying that "God helps those that help themselves". With great co-operation from the dockers we were able to acquire all kinds of food, sugar, tea, meat and even fresh fruit. As QMs we worked 24 about, used to stay in Greenwich with my mate Leading Seaman Alf Barham, whose brother-in-law had a big pub just outside the Blackwall Tunnel which was well patronized by the girls from Yardleys Perfumery.

'We acquired a new member to the crew, George, a lovable black mongrel from another destroyer in the dry dock. He in turn was up homers with Alf Barham, whose family thought the world of him; he used to go out with us and could sink a pint as good as any matelot.

'Came the time the refit was over and we were due to sail for Sheerness. Natives were given weekend leave and joined the ship at Sheerness. Monday morning came and time to depart, no sign of George. We had to go back without him. We were very worried. More so when we got back on board to be met by Lieutenant Commander Burnett. The first words from him were: "Where is George?" "Don't know", says Alf, "He went home with us but was not there this morning." We were told, "The Captain will not sail without him, the ship sails this evening, go back home and don't come back without George". All ended well. Alf and George both returned a few hours later. Forget if George was in the rattle or not.

'While we were in London things were going on. The Battle of Narvik took place, all hands were champing at the bit. Our turn was to come.

'North again and over to Namsos, a beautiful calm sea and then the trouble started. Over came the bombers. They were not so good at the time, still we all went and hid in the fog banks. We thought they could not see us, we were stood by the funnel taking the air when whoosh! followed by loud explosions, next thing we heard was that seventeen men had been killed in a destroyer ahead. They too had been taking the air. What we did not know was that D/F aerial on the foremast was showing above the fog. We were like ostriches. I was on the wheel as we went up the fjord although it didn't mean a thing to me, I couldn't see anything for the fog, the buzz was that we went up on the Asdic.

'Next day, one eye on the gyro [compass], one ear up the voice pipe, there was a big conflab going on with Captain and staff officers. Captain Vian in the *Afridi* was going in first and coming out first, whilst we were to go in last and come out last. Sudden change in plans, we are to change with the *Afridi*, first in first out. Talk of shore batteries and torpedo tubes covering the entrance of the fjord, quick discussion with Torps (Lieutenant Goodenough) and Guns, as to who is to do who if they tried to do us. All very reassuring as I listened to it. Up with the Battle Ensign and charge, wound down the cover on the steering window so as to see where we were going. What a sight when we turned the corner at the top of the fjord. The whole place was a mass of flames. Did the job and came out loaded with French Alpine Troops whose main armament seemed to be massive cheeses. Gave them a hand off with their gear and at the same time spirited a few cheeses away into the larder.

'Next step, head for home with the opposition party going flat out to stop us. We made it. Thought, if the *Afridi* had not changed places with us — well I wonder. Disembark the troops and down to Greenock. As all matelots know Greenock was a very hostile place, nobody loved us, least of all the police, so when leave was given I headed up to Glasgow to see my father who was on the *Monarch of Bermuda* which had taken part in the Norway evacuation with us — a glad reunion.

'*Kelly's* crew life was grand. We were going from one hostelry to another when AB Buster Brown was apprehended by the local constabulary for not having his "Not Under Command Lights" on, they started to put him in the hurry-up waggon, this was too much for us, the cry rang out "Up the 'Kellys', Keep On, Charge". By this time most of the Home Fleet had reinforced us, battle commenced, batons were drawn, it was hand-to-hand fighting. It finished up with the aforementioned police locked up in the hurry-up van whilst we all did a George 30 back to the liberty boat and safety. Forget what the outcome was for we sailed about noon for our next episode.

'Now to *Kelly's* torpedoing. We were trying to make contact with a force of German surface ships. We were going to make a name for ourselves at last. We had been closed up at action stations for some time. I was working the wheel with the coxswain. The sea was like a sheet of glass but a heavy black sky was reaching down to just above the horizon, which was quite clear. Had a visit from an enemy aircraft then a submarine contact, steamed in line abreast with the *Kandahar* and *Bulldog* dropping depth charges but no visible sign of the submarine. Night was closing in. In the distance the sky was being lit up by distant gun flashes. We were going flat out to join in the action. Next I knew we were told from the bridge that we would be returning to port as we were short of fuel and to break into two watches in about fifteen minutes time. We relaxed although feeling very disappointed. Asked the relief helmsman if he would go down and get some Ki. Leading Signalman Giddings came in the wheelhouse and we talked him into waiting for the Ki. Good job we did for the next thing I knew was a terrific explosion, a sheet of flame, and we started listing heavily.

'Reported to the bridge that the ship was not answering the wheel (seems stupid now), was told to come up top, found out then we were trapped, could not get up or down. Below was a raging inferno, the way out on to the point five decks was a shambles whilst the hatch on to the bridge was closed. I was going to be burned to death. Training and reason prevailed and after a few good knocks on the bridge hatch it was opened. Saved for the moment! Joined up with the general activities of ditching ammunition, etc, and was then kidnapped by the doctor down by the galley starboard side. Helped get the cook, or second cook out of the galley, couldn't tell who was who, they were in such a state. Remember poor old Brigham Young laying on the deck by the whaler moaning, tried to dress his head. He was too far gone. While this was going on a destroyer came bearing down on us with her fighting lights on, her fans making a hell of a noise. Thought it was a German, waited for her to blow us out of the water, nothing happened, it was the *Bulldog*.

'The Captain told us the ship was not sinking, things got really organized. Being a QM I found myself down the tiller flat on the emergency steering. What a job. We would pump the rudder hard to starboard and then to port, drive you round the bend. No sooner had you got it one way than it went the other, plus the fact we had had no sleep, no food for goodness knows how long and worst of all no drinking water. But our motto was "Keep On" and keep on we did. In the meantime we lived in a maze of E-boats running around the iron deck spoiling all the paintwork and non-stop visits from our friends in the German Air Force who were doing their best to stop us "Keeping On".

'Came up after a spell down the tiller flat to find the *Kandahar* putting her stern to our starboard quarter to take off the wounded. This was quite some seamanship as there was quite a sea running. Then we buried our shipmates with full honours. It was a very sad moment for me. I had lost so many friends, most of the Leading Signalmen had just been made up to Yeomen and had transferred to the Stoker POs' mess. They caught the brunt of it. But we made it into Hebburn, drank all the beer in the "Commercial", my B13 had come through, a grand farewell on Newcastle Station and down to RNB Chatham, then survivors' leave. We had come a long way.

'Been on leave about a week, received a telegram to report to RNB Chatham forthwith. Must be a mistake unless somebody has performed a miracle on the ship. Soon found out. Went over to Dunkirk as coxswain of a motor cutter, passed the time ferrying troops from the beach to the various ships, came back on the last in a trawler, landed at Ramsgate or Margate then caught a bus back to Chatham. Everything was chaos in barracks. Next thing we were formed up into mobile units stationed at Godinton Park not far from Ashford. I was on a 3.7 inch Naval gun mounted on an armour-plated lorry. After numerous invasion flags and exercises things eased off and we all returned to RNB. Made enquiries about the *Kelly* in the Drafting Office and was sent up to Immingham to join Lord Louis' staff, then based in the "County Hotel". Home again! Great to see so many old faces, the job, sentry on the first landing, 24 about, the top of the stairs was all sandbagged off with a machine-gun covering them. Soon fell into the routine and life was very good, "Clubs" keeping us well occupied with fencing. Being a small place everyone knew everyone else and many romances started. Often wondered how many unwed mums have said to their sons and daughters, "Your dad was on the *Kelly*". Life was pretty quiet, apart from air raids.

'Orders to move, said sad farewells to all our friends and down to Devonport, Captain D5's new headquarters, in the library of the Prince of Wales Hospital. Twenty-four about on the telephone exchange we shared with the Polish Maintenance Commander. Soon picked the job up, the main thing being as soon as number two indicator showed on the board, drop everything, it was Sir. Had quite a few air raids, as soon as they started we used to go into the hospital and give the nurses a hand to get the patients down to the air raid shelters and vice versa. Lived in the sailors' home just across the road so it was quite handy. Also had a good pub (the "Marlborough") plus the fact we were on the slate on blank weeks, it was to stand us in good stead later. Had one very sad memory of one of the *Kelly* boys from the start. He came up to see me. He was on a cruiser then but I remember going into Namsos, he was the wheelhouse messenger, a mere boy about five foot tall, looked like a young schoolboy one sees every day now. He was in a terrible mess, nerves gone, nobody had heard of trick cyclists those days. He had a week's leave but nowhere to go as he was an orphan. We fixed him up with us in the sailors' home. He left and just after this his ship was tinfished — poor lad, he is no more.

'Up to the home town once again, Hebburn. The ship was nearly ready once again, the new crew arrived, nearly all HOs (hostilities only ratings). This was something new. Clear lower deck and a pep talk by the Captain and then sort the jobs out. In the QM's staff we did quite well. We even had people who could steer. One of the main problems was to teach the Bosuns' Mates to pipe, used to take them every day down the tiller flat to practice, remember one day we had a good session and were going to a seven bell dinner, one new HO stayed behind, he was rather old for an HO and rumour had it that he was a bank manager who had volunteered. He became known as the Baron. When I told him it was time to eat he said "I'm blowed if I'm going to let any twopenny halfpenny whistle get the better of me".

'The time came to depart, but first degaussing trials, was sitting down the watchkeeper's mess with all the new crowd when the whole ship shuddered, everybody up top, we had had a collision with a merchant ship which was also degaussing. Bows all smashed, be in port for Xmas? Not so, the job was done and away for the working up and trials. Was on the wheel as we went through the breakwater and ship started to turn inside out, never seen so many lay down and die without a shot being fired! We were on our way to Scapa for the work up.

'I was on the eight to twelve when just before midnight the lookouts reported heavy gunfire ahead, head up the voice pipe again, conference with his Lordship and the staff. According to the Signals Officer none of our ships were doing gunnery practice in the area. It must be the enemy. The Captain was in a quandary. Here he was with an untrained crew, all seasick and wanting to die and the ship doing everything but turn over. In the best traditions of the Andrew, Sir decided we had to attack. Full Ahead, alarm bells ringing, into battle we went, somebody somewhere had failed to tell us that a cruiser was doing a night shoot. Hooray! Did our work up and headed south to Guz [Devonport]. Used to go out every night with the minelayers to Brest, lay the mines at the entrance and then have a "cab run" back shooting anything in sight.

'One night we had just been fitted up with a hen coop on the foremast, a thing called radar, we were on our way back from Brest when the radar reported an echo. We closed in, all guns trained on the bearing, open shutter [searchlight], open fire. It was a French fishing boat, down came the masts and sails and the crew running around waving to us. We circled in case it was a trap. They were Frenchman escaping to England, one of them was the Count de Mauduit whom we meet every now and then at our reunion dinner. Life was pretty grim. You spent the whole night laying mines and then had to come out through the German and French minefields. Never knew when you were going to get blown up. We used to get leave from four to six in the evening prior to our nightly jaunts. Used to head up for the "Free State" [sailors' home] in Devonport which opened at 16:00 and start tanking up and over to the "Marlborough" at five.

'Our chief gunner's mate, Tusky Hales, had a theory that the ship would turn over before she was sunk. We certainly used to go well over in bad weather and under helm. Thought the best place to be was on the upper and not closed in. Put in for a change and joined up with the pom-pom crew. Guz was a very lively place at night time, the opposition party coming over every night laying mines, no bombs as yet, until one night when I was on duty the sirens went, closed up. All hell cast loose, it was the first big raid on Guz. They wiped out most of the town.

'Everything is secret in war. When the Captain cleared lower deck and said that we were leaving and would not need Scapa scanties, we finished up in Malta. As we entered Grand Harbour we had a wonderful reception. No sooner tied up then away all boats. I was coxswain of the motor cutter, away we went with Guns aboard towards the harbour entrance. What a scene! The *Jersey* had blown up right across the harbour entrance. Went outside and started to pick up bodies and land them at the RN hospital. It's the first time I had seen matrons, sisters and nurses emotionally upset, all crying.

'Captain cleared lower deck and explained the situation. We would be going into six watches due to the constant air attacks. Went ashore that night with Cooky, Sam Stewart and Fanny Waldron. Good night out, slept on the lockers and was quite amazed to find out we had nearly been blown up a thousand times. Got into the routine, bombs by day and bombs by night. What used to annoy me was that as soon as the brief All Clear went at about midnight, the boat's crew had to go and pick up libertymen at the Custom House Steps. No sooner had you left than the signal would come through: "No boats to move in the harbour, mines laid". Too late — we were on our way. One night the opposition came back just as we were tying up. We all dived down the shelter and had a good wine and sing-song with a crowd of nuns, the main song being "Has anybody here seen Kelly?".

'Once Grand Harbour entrance had been cleared we had some relaxation at night-time by going out to intercept Italian convoys from Italy to North Africa. Had a good run one night when we blew hell out of Benghazi. The locals thought it was an air raid and put on a full-scale barrage. Left Malta eastwards; the invasion of Crete. Heard the *Gloucester* and *Fiji* had been sunk. My mate on the pom-pom, Rocky Wilkins, was very worried about his brother-in-law. Next night we ran into the opposition — invasion barges — sank them, then went on to bombard Maleme Airport as the German aircraft were landing. Did a good job. Next morning we were on our way back to Alexandria, all very tired and hungry. I was having my breakfast, a piece of bread, lard, salt and pepper, when over came one aircraft. He dropped a stick of bombs, missed us, we realized that he would make a sighting report to base. Not long to wait, over came the next lot, no hits on the *Kelly* or *Kashmir*. Would we make it? Did not have long to wait for just before 08:00 saw a load of aircraft on the port quarter. Things happened very fast, the ship twisting and turning, the noise of the guns, the smoke. Turning hard to starboard when I saw that the ship's side was folded up like a sardine tin, right up to the pom-pom. Over and over she went. Thought this is it, knocked the slip off the Carley Float and over we went still going at full speed. Remember seeing the funnel going into the sea, standing on the side of the ready-use ammunition locker and then water. We were trapped under the ship, saw a gleam of light, swam towards it, climbed through bollards, guardrails, you name it, bobbed up to the surface. Swam like hell to clear the propellers, everybody swimming around was smothered in oil fuel, one chap next to me asked what ship I was off: "Kelly". "I am off the *Kashmir*." Things had happened so fast did not know she was sunk. Seemed no hope now for the German aircraft were machine-gunning the survivors from the two ships. There *was* no hope, we would eventually drown, when up pops the *Kipling* and starts picking up survivors. It took a long time, for the bombers came in from every angle. I was with Petty Officer Buck Taylor when the *Kipling's* whaler passed. I knew the coxswain who was on the *Crescent* with me in '34. Shouted to him. He turned back and picked us up. We fought our way back to Alex and a heroes' welcome. To conclude I would like to say I have never been on a more happy or efficient ship, or sailed with a better Captain in my 22 years in the Navy.'

Earl Mountbatten received Mosses' '*Kelly* diary' almost exactly two years before his murder in Ireland. He replied to Mosses thanking him for his 'excellent reminiscences', particularly valuable because he had been in *Kelly* throughout her service. 'I was tremendously intrigued', Mountbatten wrote 'by the lower deck point of view of events which I had seen through the eyes of the Captain. In a way what struck me most was your happy memories of the good times you had which you never failed to recall and the fact that the hard and difficult times at sea are passed over in a nice light-hearted way.'

*Kelly's* former Captain went on in his letter to Mosses to make observations — and corrections. 'The story about the three-badge veteran who told you I always picked my own crew fascinated me. I have heard this astonishing legend before and it is, of course, absolutely untrue. I never picked my ship's company. Do you suppose I would have included so many bad hats, if I had!?

'I only made one remark when I visited the Drafting Office and that was to say that I did hope they would pick a Chief Cook who could really cook well, but I did not mind what he was like in other ways as I always believed that the contentment of a ship's company rested very largely on good food!

'You mentioned how surprised you were to find that domestic water supply was laid on to come out of taps. I am happy to say that this was an innovation which I pushed through personally, when I was in the Admiralty, for the new classes of destroyers.

'The Ordinary Seaman was not the son of a Countess but he was, in fact, the son of my chiropodist in London who was a very high-class, well-educated and wealthy man. I still go to his brother to have my corns dealt with when necessary.

'You refer to the famous Big Roll. This did not take place on returning from a convoy but took place when steaming back from Stadtlandet at the end of our *City of Flint* hunt. I left it rather late and I thought the Luftwaffe would be on our trail and so we went at 25 knots across a very tricky sea running in the North Sea. We managed to hit off at the wrong critical speed which meant to say that the movement of the following sea caught us in the same place continuously and finally we went right over to about sixty or seventy degrees.

'I do not think that more than a couple of men went overboard and certainly one got back and I did think the other one did too, but my memory may not be as good as yours.

'I enjoyed your account of our time in London Docks when you may remember we had the King and Queen on board for a film show one night.

'You are quite right to say that we went through the thick fog up Narvik Fjord on the Asdic (or Sonar as it now called). However, it let us down because at the critical moment the fog lifted and a cable's length ahead there was a rock sticking out which we hadn't got on the Sonar, so we had a lucky escape.

'I note that we owe the only Carley Float that the *Kelly* had in the water to you as you knocked the slip off. Thank you very much. I also never had a good description before of the actual hit that the dive bomber made on the *Kelly*. You say that the side blew up and folded right up to the pom-pom. I had thought actually that the hit was nearer the after superstructure and the twin 4.7-inch gun mounting, but it was obviously somewhere on the starboard side there.

There was a sad end to the Sid Mosses story. He was one the *Kelly* crew who were invited to Thames Television studios for the 'This is Your Life' programme about Earl Mountbatten. The programme and an extended version were shown immediately afterwards to all those taking part who wanted to see. As a party went on for all the people who had taken part in surprising Mountbatten, Mosses took the opportunity of asking some of the well-known men and women for their autographs. This was the last time any of Mosses' old colleagues saw him. It was not until some time afterwards that one of his friends — Mosses wasn't married and lived on his own — wrote to Rocky Wilkins stating that Sid had died and had been cremated. His medals (which he had worn on the night at the television studios) were also enclosed, to be kept by the *Kelly* Association. Wilkins was shocked at the news and on making further enquiries was told that Mosses was knocked down by a taxi as he was leaving the Thames Television studios. He was taken to hospital where he died.

In a letter to Wilkins Mountbatten said how very sorry he was to hear of the death of Sid Mosses. 'I remember him better than almost any member of the ship's company and had a great affection for him and can understand how much you will miss him.'

Chapter 3

# *Kelly's Career*

In those early war days stories of *Kelly's* exploits swept through the Navy, often garbled ones, that gave the destroyer the reputation of never being out of trouble; always out of one scrape and into another, always going back to the shipyard to be mended. People said she was famous only because her commander was the dashing Dickie Mountbatten and that she contributed little of value to Britain's defensive war at sea.

*Kelly* was unlucky and she was heroic. She had a more hectic life than was generally known even in other ships in the Navy where rumour was more plentiful than facts. She was in action from the beginning of her life which coincided with the start of the war against Germany. True, she spent periods in dockyard hands but when she was seaworthy and battleworthy the restless Mountbatten saw to it that she spent nine-tenths of her time at sea ceaselessly looking for and sometimes finding a formidable enemy with extremely capable ships and manned by highly trained crews. *Kelly*, laid down in August 1937, was built in almost exactly two years. She was JOB 615 until christened by Miss Antonia Kelly, daughter of the Commander-in-Chief Home Fleet, Admiral Sir John Kelly. 'May God guide her and guard her and keep all who sail in her.' She wasn't blessed with divine protection and in the end lost more than half her crew off Crete.

When Lord Louis received the Admiralty's general signal informing the Fleet at home and in the overseas stations that hostilities were to be 'commenced at once with Germany' Mountbatten over the loudspeaker system told his officers and men: 'When we leave harbour we shall be right in the face of the enemy who will be out to destroy us. We must find him and destroy him first.' *Kelly* was in the thick of it in the very morning after war started when she put to sea with HMS *Acheron* on an anti-submarine exercise. There was a 'ping' on the Asdic and the destroyers dropped their first depth charges in anger. Fuel oil appeared on the surface and a 'probable kill' was registered, but it was not confirmed. Two weeks afterwards *Kelly* received a signal that the aircraft carrier *Courageous*, which had been patrolling the Western Approaches with a destroyer escort, had received torpedoes from a U-boat and was sinking fast. When *Kelly* arrived on the scene *Courageous* had gone and a

Any further communication
should be addressed to—
The Secretary of the Admiralty,
London, S.W.1
quoting "M.F. 5568/37"

L.P.—No. 8

*Admiralty, S.W.1.*

6th May 1937.

7 — MAY 1937

Gentlemen,

    With reference to Admiralty letter M.F.12437/3
dated the 2nd April, I am commanded by My Lords
Commissioners of the Admiralty to inform you that the
second Flotilla Leader recently ordered from your firm
will be named H.M.S. KELLY, and to request that the
ship may be so referred to in all future correspondence.

    KELLY will be the class name of the Flotilla.

    I am, Gentlemen,

      Your obedient Servant,

*Kelly is christened, 6 May 1937.*

*The launching of HMS Kelly by
Miss Antonia Kelly.*

*Speed trials in 1939, just before the war.*

merchant ship was picking up survivors. Some wounded and others suffering from swallowing fuel oil were picked up by *Kelly's* motor cutter.

*Kelly* had encountered the war full-on as had dozens of destroyers protecting our convoys. German U-boats soon inflicted alarming havoc on our vital sea lanes. Shock came with the sinking of the battleship *Royal Oak* by U-boat 47 which had penetrated Scapa Flow. *Kelly* was on patrols in the North Sea and along Norway's coast. Mountbatten's sense of humour emerged when requested by a Norwegian patrol boat to pull away from territorial waters. He said to the Norwegian vessel's commander: 'Please give my compliments to my cousin, Crown Prince Olaf and tell him I hope he is keeping well'. *Kelly* suffered like many destroyers did from the weather itself — and her own speed. She lost boats, davits and guard rails and headed back for the Tyne for repairs. In three weeks she sailed again with the destroyer *Mohawk*. There had been a message that two tankers had been torpedoed or mined in the Channel outside the Tyne. As *Kelly* approached one of the tankers a loud explosion was heard under the keel which damaged *Kelly's* shafts, rudders and propellers. Two tugs had to take her back to the dockyard. Repairs completed, *Kelly* made for northern waters once more, this time on convoy escort duty. The weather was devilish. The 'Tribal' class destroyer *Gurkha* and *Kelly* were in collision and *Kelly* had to undergo temporary repairs at Lerwick in the Shetlands. Then, because the Tyne shipyards were full, she had to dock in the River Thames for a fortnight or so which delighted the London and Southern-based members of the crew and gave Mountbatten the chance of seeing his relatives and friends in the capital.

HMS Kelly on patrol, carrying out gunnery and torpedo exercises. She is approaching another destroyer in the 5th Destroyer Flotilla and is being 'attacked' by an RAF Swordfish.

Mountbatten on the bridge of Kelly with the Navigation Officer, Lieutenant Butler-Bowden.

There were other incidents, serious operations like Namsos in Norway which is mentioned later, and lighter, even pleasant and funny events aboard that linger longer in sailors' memories, but apart from *Kelly's* eventual loss at Crete the most dramatic episode in her first commission happened in the North Sea between 8 May and 13 May 1940 when *Kelly* sustained many casualties and nearly came to total disaster. The story highlights the determination of Mountbatten and his outstanding leadership and example in the face of tremendous odds.

*Kelly* was sent to Harwich with seven other destroyers to reinforce East Coast defences as the German threat to the Low Countries was mounting. As she was passing St Abbs Head the Commander-in-Chief Home Fleet sent orders for ships to intercept a German minelaying force of destroyers, motor torpedo boats and minelayers near Little Fisher Bank. *Kelly* and three other destroyers were already on their way and another force of five destroyers led by *Fury* was ordered out from Scapa Flow. *Fury* and her force were to engage an enemy force of six motor torpedo boats while the cruiser *Birmingham* and her group were to engage a larger force of three destroyers, a torpedo boat and four minelayers. At 19:40 our air reconnaissance reported the large enemy unit about seventy miles east-north-east of the expected position, but no speed was given unfortunately. It was assumed that the enemy was retiring at high speed and there was no chance of overtaking so the chase was abandoned. It was not until next morning that it was discovered that the enemy's speed was only about six

*Kelly after being torpedoed by the German E-boat E-40.*

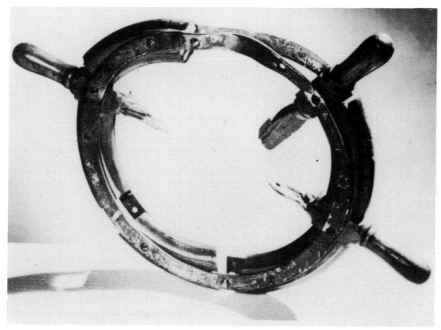

*The steering wheel of the German E-boat which crashed into Kelly. It was rescued by 'Scrounger' Scorer and is now in the Imperial War Museum.*

knots and that contact could have been made by about 23:00 that previous night. *Kelly* and *Kandahar*, who had already been detached to hunt a U-boat ahead, did not receive the air reconnaissance report until about 20:15 by which time the *Birmingham* was out of sight ahead. Both destroyers endeavoured to join *Birmingham* but visibility decreased and they never did. The destroyer *Bulldog*, which had lost touch with the *Fury* group, joined *Kelly* and *Kandahar* and 25 minutes before midnight sighted German motor torpedo boats.

Visibility was about four cables with banks of mist forming. In less than ten minutes a blurred object was sighted from the bridge of *Kelly*. This was an enemy MTB lying almost stopped. It put a torpedo into the side of the *Kelly*, blowing a forty-foot hole in her side from the waterline down to the keel. Flames rose internally and externally above the level of the *Kelly's* bridge and the foremost boiler room was blown open to the sea. The entire ship was enveloped in steam and black smoke from the explosion. *Bulldog* sighted *Kelly* well down by the bows and with a heavy list to starboard. At that time it was not established whether *Kelly* had been torpedoed by the MTB or a U-boat so depth charges were dropped by *Bulldog*. The fog became very thick but *Bulldog* succeeded in taking *Kelly* in tow and was heading for home within an hour of the explosion, having also conducted a U-boat hunt. *Kelly's* crew had thrown overboard topweight but she had an excessive bow trim and the starboard gunwale was awash; with this very cumbersome tow *Bulldog* was making only six knots.

Just after midnight on 10 May a German MTB emerged from the fog at high speed and accidentally rammed both destroyers. There was further damage to *Kelly* but the *Bulldog* was not seriously damaged. The MTB was thought to have foundered. Three hours after this *Kandahar* joined the two ships and later took off *Kelly's* wounded. While the ships were lying alongside the first German bombers arrived. They were repelled by gunfire and by an escort of Hudson aircraft that had just arrived. Later the same morning the *Fury* and the *Gallant* joined as escort and in the afternoon the cruisers *Manchester* and *Sheffield* also put in an appearance

**Above** *Returning to Hawthorn Leslie's shipyard on the Tyne after being torpedoed. Some people thought that she might have to be scrapped.*

**Right** *Kelly shored up in dry dock, showing the extent of her damage by torpedoing.*

and helped beat off repeated bombing attacks by the enemy. Twice on 10 May the *Kelly* became unmanageable and the tow had to be made longer and stronger. Next morning, with wind and sea rising *Kelly* yawed badly and the tow parted so it was decided to ask for the aid of tugs.

An Admiralty report said that at 14:00 *Kelly's* list had increased and it seemed that she might sink at any moment. Lord Louis decided to send out of the ship everybody not required to man the guns. The escorting destroyers had stopped and sent boats to transfer these men when the enemy made another and their heaviest bombing attack, but there were no hits. Six officers and twelve men were left aboard the *Kelly*. They were all volunteers. Towing was suspended because of the bad weather. *Kelly* was lying waterlogged and stationary when two submarines were reported in the vicinity. Mountbatten realised that *Kelly* was a sitting target and transferred his volueer party to *Bulldog*. Throughout the night the destroyers steamed round *Kelly*. Two rescue tugs arrived early next morning (12 May) and the volunteer party returned to *Kelly* while the tow was established again. The sea had remained calm during the night but by about eight in the morning had got up again and washed right over the starboard gunwale to the port side. There was a further bombing attack at noon but the skeleton volunteer crew, having to work the guns by hand because the electrical system was out of action, helped fight off the attack.

The badly damaged *Kelly* got back to the Tyne shipyard after 91 hours in tow or hove-to. It wasn't until early December that she was ready for sea

*The 5th Destroyer Flotilla on patrol, carrying out gunnery practice. HMS Kelly is leading her flotilla for the first time since her refit on the Tyne after torpedoing.*

again, by which time the 5th Flotilla had been transferred to Plymouth. *Kelly* performed escort duties in the Western Approaches and took part in minelaying operations off the French coast. In April she joined British Naval forces which, it was hoped, would intercept and bring into action the German battlecruisers *Scharnhorst* and *Gneisenau* that were expected to break out from Brest.

After a British Naval bombardment of Cherbourg, large shore batteries started firing back at our ships with the equivalent of six inch shells. The Captain of the battleship HMS *Revenge* considered his ships would not be severely damaged by such shells but the destroyers screening him might be, so he decided to make a signal to the destroyers saying that they should clear out of it and that *Revenge* would be all right on her own. The destroyers took no notice and the Captain of *Revenge* — a previous destroyer officer himself — said to his officers: 'There you are, you see what fine fellows destroyer officers are, standing by me even though I'd given them permission to get out of danger'. It wasn't until the ships had returned to harbour that they found the destroyers had never got the signal. The Captain of *Revenge* enjoyed telling the story and so did Mountbatten.

The Mediterranean Fleet was in urgent need of reinforcements and the 5th Flotilla — *Kelly, Kelvin, Kashmir, Kipling, Jackal* and *Jersey* — sailed from the United Kingdom on 12 April 1941 for Gibraltar and Malta where they arrived on 28 April. *Kelly's* next task involved her with Convoy 'Tiger', the passage of five merchantmen carrying tanks to Alexandria to replace losses suffered by the Army in the Western Desert. Five destroyers of the 5th Flotilla bombarded the port of Benghazi on the night of 10-11 May. The flotilla also had the Mediterranean Fleet's first experience of dive bombing by moonlight. Then there loomed the Battle of Crete. British and Allied troops withdrawn from Greece to Crete were to defend the island. A German airborne attack had been expected and because it was thought that this would be followed by a seaborne invasion a Naval force from Malta and Alexandria was sent to Crete to challenge this.

Chapter 4

# The Captain and his ratings

'He made me feel like an Admiral' said Ron Hall, who was an Ordinary Seaman in *Kelly* and later a successful businessman in the fish industry at Grimsby. Mountbatten regarded every man in his ship as important and he took the trouble to make them *feel* important. When Lord Louis could spare time away from the bridge or when the ship was in harbour, this was when he got to know his men thoroughly. He was fond of doing walkabouts. He surprised his crew by the hours he spent chatting to them in detail about their particular jobs in the ship, down in the engine room, in the communications offices, at the depth charges and torpedo stations, in the sick bay, in the galley, everywhere. Rocky Wilkins saw more of his Captain aboard *Kelly* than he saw of any other Captain he served with. As an anti-aircraft gunnery rating his task was to look after the pom-pom, maintain it, keep it clean and efficient and finally to fire it.

'I was fully aware that it was my responsibility to see that the gun was perfect. When I came face to face with the Captain I was working on the gun and he was doing one of his private walkabouts on his own. He climbed on to the gun platform and introduced himself. 'Wilkins is your name? Right, tell me something about your gun, explain it to me.' I thought to myself this was something new, what does he want to know about his own gun? I started by saying it was a four barrelled pom-pom, said what sort of shell the gun fired and the rate of fire. Then he got on to the tracer shells. How many tracers we were using. I thought to myself how very unusual it was for a Captain to come and discuss the technicalities of a gun with an Able Seaman. It was something he should take up with the gunner's mate or the gunnery officer. But he clearly knew all about it and he wanted to make sure I did. He turned round and said: "I like to discuss these sorts of things with the people who are actually going to fire the gun". I still thought I was on a very unusual ship where the Captain also seeks his information from all the people directly involved and not just those passing orders to do the job.

'This was going to be a good ship. I'm going to get my information straight from the Captain as well as those directly above me. His whole life was wrapped around his ship and his men, officers as well as we on the lower deck. Nothing seemed to be done at all on that ship unless the lower

*Rocky Wilkins with his pom-poms
on board the* Queen Elizabeth *the
year after* Kelly's *sinking.*

deck knew about it. Obviously for security reasons he could not tell us
certain things but if we put to sea and we were going on an engagement or
expected action then he would tell us exactly where we were going, what
the ship hoped to do and what we were expected to do. We were not like
most ships where the lower deck was kept in the dark about it. It was far
better when we knew what we were up to. It eased people's minds and we
could prepare ourselves better for action. There was nothing worse than
going into action when those on the bridge knew what was likely to
happen and you and others below didn't know at all.

'He was just as interested in the cooks as he was in his men in the engine
room and every department of the ship. There was a legend that he
handpicked his crew and he always denied this. Jokingly he used to say: "If
I had been able to choose people I wouldn't have picked the skates I have!"

He was a handsome man, always smart, very impressive. When he spoke to you he looked you straight in the eye as much as to say: "I'm going to ask you a question and I want the truth".

'If you had personal trouble he would take you into his confidence and see that you were helped in some way. Not that he gave you leave — he didn't believe in sending a person home unless he considered it entirely necessary. If personal problems could be coped with by somebody calling at home on his behalf and then reporting back it was much easier. He couldn't afford to have a man off the ship but at the same time he couldn't afford to have one man worried. If he did tell a man he would take up his case he knew he would get someone to go and look into it. When I read about his father, Prince Louis of Battenberg, I realized they were exactly the same, both were out for the welfare of their men more than anything else. He had this habit of asking everybody about their own personal lives. He believed that if a man had problems at home it affected his life aboard the ship and he worried about that. He thought that if a man had a happy homelife he would be all right aboard ship. He would sometimes telephone Lady Louis and she would get someone in the town to go around and see what could be done.

'We never forgot Lady Mountbatten's thoughts for us and her kindness. She herself would send comforts to the ship, particularly clothing. We had gaudy sweaters sometimes with big initial letters on them — it is nothing to see them these days but to see them worn aboard a destroyer forty years ago was really something. The Mountbattens had so many friends around the world, especially in America, that many comforts came aboard. As well as clothing there was a lot of fruit, from gallon tins of canned apples from Canada to oranges from various countries. They would be shared among the flotilla so it was a privilege for other ships to be with the *Kelly*.'

*Kelly's* crew were given all encouragement to enjoy shore leave whenever it was possible. Mountbatten was a fan of the cinema. He gave one of his senior officers the duty of looking after the ship's cinema and the films. When he could not get the films to show on board, he liked to go ashore to a local cinema. He liked to discuss films with his men. Sometimes when the ship arrived back in harbour he would suggest to one or two of his officers a visit to the local picture house when they were tired and would far rather have turned in for the night. He liked to gather a few men around him on the upper deck and discuss a particular film they had all seen.

About twenty men with HMS *Kelly* capbands were in a queue for a cinema in Plymouth one night. The Captain spotted them from his Austin 7 car and he beckoned to his men: 'What's on tonight?' It was a Valerie Hobson film and he went to the cinema to see it as well. On this occasion he was accompanied by his chief steward, Micallef. The end of the show coincided with a bombing raid and there were casualties in Union Street, one of the city's main thoroughfares. The little car stopped and Mountbatten took part in a ferry service taking casualties to hospital. Next day he did not discuss the air raid, which was a substantial one, but he did gather the ratings around him to talk about the film and Valerie Hobson's acting.

On another occasion when the ship was alongside at Plymouth for a few days and one of the watches had 48 hours' leave, he got the commanding officer of the barracks to send to the ship a party in overalls to do some painting. Only a skeleton crew was aboard *Kelly*. Where had the rest of the men who were not on 48 hours' leave gone, the barracks party asked. 'Half have gone on leave. Most of the other half have gone ashore for the day. Off to a pub on Dartmoor to play darts with the Old Man,' it was explained. While part of the barracks party painted the ship others helped to take aboard a small piano which had been sent by a wellwisher — *Kelly* men said the 'buzz' was that it was a present from Mountbatten's sister, the Queen of Sweden. It was specially made to fit into the *Kelly* and anyone who could play the piano played it. There were sing-songs around the piano both in harbour and when life was quiet sometimes at sea.

Lord Louis always took the services on Sundays. Fridays was the day for a talk. Nearly every Friday he would go to the fo'c's'le, stand on a capstan, and muster as many of the crew as possible standing and sitting around him as well as on top of the guns. 'Can you all hear me?' he shouted. Then he would fire away with a pep talk, discuss how the war was going, reminisce about events that had happened on board or about some personality in the ship. He tried to finish off his Friday chat show with a joke.

The only time he went to the messdecks was when he did Captain's rounds once a week. He gave all the crew's quarters a thorough going-over. He wanted to believe there wasn't a cleaner ship in the flotilla. It was his habit to take a brisk walk backwards and forwards on the quarterdeck between the depth charges and the galley, often chatting with a rating walking in step with him, or he would sit on an upper deck locker listening to singing.

It was to have been Christmas day moored in the Faroes and one of the Captain's friend's, someone in motion pictures, sent money for the ship. There was £5 for each mess, quite a lot of money in those days, but the turkey, Christmas puddings and fruit had to wait while the ship was sent on submarine patrol. Back in harbour, when Christmas Day was celebrated in style, the youngest member of the ship's company donned the Captain's uniform, an old Navy custom. A very short lad with trousers turned up and the Captain's hat over his ears, he paraded round with Lord Louis following him, taking greetings to the messdecks. In Scapa Flow there was a visit from Frances Day, one of the leading show personalities of the time. She boarded *Kelly* for lunch with the officers and gave an impromptu performance on the messdeck to the accompaniment of a harmonium played by the chief stoker.

Lord Louis appreciated a man with determination. When libertymen went ashore for a night at Rosyth one Able Seaman returned next morning but there was a heavy mist with visibility down to about nil. The rating couldn't see his ship and when he went for information he was told by a shoreside Chief Petty Officer that *Kelly* had left for Chatham. The man went to the Railway Transport office and said he had missed his ship so they sent him on a train for Chatham. In fact the ship had not left the Forth. She was still in the fog. The Able Seaman arrived at Chatham but obviously could not find *Kelly*. He was told she had gone to Greenock on the Clyde. The rating got a warrant for Greenock and travelled there, but in the meantime *Kelly* was on the way to Chatham! The poor chap eventually got to his ship after about a week of travelling, thoroughly exhausted, and had to tell his story to the Captain. 'Here's this man,' Lord

Louis said, 'with all the intelligence under the sun. He arrives at the jetty in plenty of time to join the ship. He can't see us because of the fog. He doesn't go to the proper authorities while we are still here. He asks some watchkeeper who's heard a 'buzz' that we've gone to Chatham and when he gets to Chatham we are, of course, not there. We've gone somewhere else and the poor chap's been travelling searching for us all this time.' Although this rating had been given travel warrants he was due to pay back the train fares to Admiralty. 'But I will be fair to him', said *Kelly's* captain. 'At least he did try to get back to his ship, he has arrived and I will pay his fare.' The lesson for all the crew, said the Captain, was: 'If you get stranded and we have left go to the right authorities and enquire!'

But Mountbatten was a strict Captain and nobody got away with serious crime. Punishment fitted the offence. An Able Seaman who was regarded as a stroppy character hit a Petty Officer, a serious crime in the Navy. The Captain said in normal circumstances he would deal with him in the only way the AB understood 'on the fo'c's'le with fisticuffs, but I'm not allowed to do that because I'm the Captain'. The man got six months in a Naval prison.

On a very hot day in Malta, just before the *Kelly* sailed for Crete, it was arranged that the First Lieutenant (Lord Hugh Beresford, who lost his life in Crete) should take a party ashore on a 'nature run' and to look at historic buildings and ruins. As soon as the walk started the ratings started to peel off in ones and twos. The first batch of 'deserters' dived into the first bar, the 'Golden Anchor', near one of the dockyard gates. They watched the sailors carrying on marching up the hill. The same thing happened further on and when the party arrived at the Catacombs the First Lieutenant had 'lost' all but four who were all CW (commission worthy) candidates, potential officer material. The others later in the day drifted back to the ship. The Captain said to Lord Hugh: 'You should know better, Number One, than to take ratings ashore. You must have known you would lose them before you got to Kingsway!'

Lord Hugh Beresford was one of only two First Lieutenants to serve in *Kelly*. Like his predecessor, Philip Burnett, he was one of the most popular men in the ship. First Lieutenants as much as Captains can have great influence on the making of a 'happy ship' and these two officers were greatly respected and liked by the lower deck as well as the wardroom.

Beresford, having got away from *Kelly* when she sank at Crete, was supervising rescue efforts from *Kipling* when he was killed in an unfortunate accident. Survivors still talk about him. Like Mountbatten, Beresford had a Naval pedigree. His great uncle, Lord Charles Beresford, was a former Commander-in-Chief Mediterranean. When Lord Hugh Beresford was appointed to *Kelly* Mountbatten called his officers together and told them: 'Hugh Beresford is a member of the Oxford Group and I've told him that the officers can look after themselves. If he tries to convert you, you *are* to look after yourselves in this respect, but I told him if he tried to convert any of the sailors he was out!'

With two Lords in the ship (Mountbatten and Beresford) the wardroom enjoyed composing jocose messages purporting to come from their superiors back in Admiralty ('Their Lordships view with growing concern . . .') and Mountbatten enjoyed many a scintillating witticism aimed at himself.

Chapter 5

# Butler for the Queen

The Captain's galley in HMS *Kelly* was a problem both for Lord Louis and for the rating who was going to do his cooking in harbour and at sea. As a destroyer Captain, and more so because he was Captain D of the 5th Destroyer Flotilla, Mountbatten had his own spacious day quarters in addition to his sea cabin. As Lord Louis was a member of the Royal Family, and had a large number of distinguished men and women among his friends who were potential visitors, it was obvious that some thought had to be given to the Captain's quarters, his table and the 'kitchen'. One of the first tasks for *Kelly* after commissioning was to have been a visit to Belgium with Britain's new King and Queen. It was important for *Kelly's* Captain that attention should be paid to the galley and its equipment. Therefore, while the ship was building he sent his Maltese Petty Officer Steward, Guiseppe Micallef, who had just been appointed to *Kelly*, to the shipyard. 'Joe' Micallef was a friend of Lord Mountbatten. They had met in the Navy two years before when the ships in which they were serving were based in Malta.

When the Petty Officer went to Hebburn on Tyne and was shown the separate Captain's galley by the ship constructors who were fitting out the destroyer, he immediately said: 'I can't possibly cook dinner for a Captain's party on a stove which has so small a top'. The stove had only two hot plates and Joe wanted at least four. He reported back to Mountbatten who was still at Admiralty and at once *Kelly* officers already at Hebburn heard from their Captain. He wrote and asked whether he could please have a bigger stove fitted, a stove adequate for the kind of entertaining any ordinary destroyer Captain might have to do. No doubt Lord Mountbatten followed up this request personally at Admiralty and in due course he — and PO Micallef — were provided with a stove and hot plates that would produce a dinner for twenty people and not a mere handful. With the stove Micallef was provided with a bigger hot cupboard so that, having prepared the food, the cook could keep it hot. It was, as it turned out a galley fit for a king!

Joe Micallef was one of the few ratings who served in HMS *Kelly* throughout the ship's life. He knew his Captain before, during and after the war. He was one of many Maltese who joined the Royal Navy between the two Great Wars, and until Malta was given her independence, almost evey major Naval vessel from destroyers to capital ships had Maltese stewards and cooks who were excellent ship's servants and as loyal as any other Naval rating.

Micallef first met his future Captain in Malta in 1937 when he was serving in the flotilla leader HMS *Keppel* and Lord Louis was Captain of the destroyer HMS *Wishart*. War was far from Maltese minds and the role of the many warships in the Mediterranean Fleet based on Malta consisted of exercises and visits to foreign ports. There was in peacetime much showing the flag and hospitality, and good ships' servants were an asset.

I met Joe in 1982 in the open air restaurant in Victoria Square in the centre of Malta's capital, Valletta. Here, when Malta's Grand Harbour and Sliema Creek were full of Royal Navy ships that kept the great dockyard fully employed, was a busy meeting place for Naval men based in Malta and their families. The day we had coffee and brandy together Malta was a far different place, Grand Harbour was practically without a vessel of any sort. Sliema Creek, where destroyers used to secure, was occupied by two or three grimy merchant vessels at the massive buoys and a large number of small private craft and ferries. The Navy, the Army and the Royal Air Force had long since left Malta and though the dockyard was still working on a number of merchant ships, hardly any of them British, employment there had sadly declined.

Micallef, a bent figure nearing eighty, recalled the days before World War 2 when one of the big events was the Mediterranean Fleet regatta. Forty-five years previously, Joe was very keen on boat pulling and was unbeatable among the ratings. Mountbatten took an interest in Joe because he was one of his ship's oarsmen in the regatta. Lord Louis too was a keen and able oarsman who used to row in the officers' whaler race and he displayed his own strength and prowess in the open sculls event, the race of ships' dinghies pulled by one oarsman. About eight boats took part in the race and Lord Louis was outstanding in this, Joe recalled.

Two years before the war, Micallef was posted to the Red Sea station and Lord Louis called him back to join *Kelly* three months before the ship commissioned in 1939. As Captain D's Petty Officer Steward, Joe was in all the actions in which *Kelly* fought and was lucky to come out of the Battle of Crete alive. Another Maltese shipmate of his, Leading Steward Dominic Camenzuli, who was the CO's valet, was one of the 121 crew members who perished. 'As the *Kelly* disappeared before our eyes and the German Stukas machine-gunned the survivors in the water, Lord Louis showed us the stuff he was made of by making us sing. We sang as we struggled to survive but out hearts were broken at the loss of so many of our shipmates', Joe said. When *Kelly's* crew was alerted that a batch of German Stukas were about to attack, Lord Mountbatten's valet was on his way up to the bridge to take the Captain a cup of cocoa. As the valet came down, Joe heard a huge blast and it seemed to him *Kelly* took no more than two minutes before she turned over and started going down. 'All I remember is that I came to a rope wire and I kept pulling and pulling until I got to the surface. I remember having some wounds in my back from German aircraft fire. They were strafing us. That is about all I can remember. I was taken to a hospital ship, HMS *Maine*. I don't remember anything until 12 June, almost three weeks later. In fact, as far as my wife knew, I was lost. Later she had another telegram saying I was safe but dangerously wounded. I was totally burned up and lost a knee cap, caused by shell splinters from explosions in *Kelly* as she was sinking. Anyway, I survived. I was eleven months in hospital before I was returned to Malta. We came back in a convoy which lost two or three ships. When I had recovered and after I had been discharged from the Navy as no longer fit for service I had another job as a supervisor in what we called the Victory Kitchens. Maltese people used to have a ticket to enable them to get food. I had served in the Navy on active service for almost fifteen years up to the time I was discharged. Then, after recovering, I spent twenty years in the Royal Air Force as a civilian employee.'

Being so close to *Kelly's* Captain, Joe Micallef has a lot of confidences and memories of Lord Mountbatten and of visits to *Kelly* by people that had to be wartime secrets. When *Kelly* was commissioning there was great urgency to get the ships ready for the war which was coming. Instead of 'working up' for six weeks the crew achieved this in three days. They were putting ammunition and torpedoes aboard all the time, working day and night. Mountbatten himself and the other officers were down below working, even helping to paint the ship's side.

Once while hunting a U-boat the Captain, smelling victory, told him: 'Micallef, prepare an extra plate. We are expecting a guest for dinner.' The U-boat was sunk but the German commander was picked up by another destroyer and the sinking by *Kelly* was not confirmed. Joe suspected that Lord Louis was disappointed in being deprived of entertaining his German rival.

More important guests to dine in *Kelly* were the King and Queen (now the Queen Mother), and the Duke and Duchess of Kent, who went to *Kelly* when she was in dock in the Port of London. That same day Joe had a telegram from Malta saying his house had been bombed. The telegram interested the Queen who said how pleased she was that his family were safe. Micallef had many reasons to appreciate Mountbatten's own interest in his family back in Malta, and his consideration and generosity. While *Kelly* was undergoing major repairs after being torpedoed his Captain sent Joe to Malta on short leave when Mrs Micallef was expecting a baby. 'It was not the Captain's fault that the baby did not arrive during my short stay in Malta but on my return I witnessed the rebirth of the *Kelly.* The ship, looking as good as new, was a sort of compensation for my other disappointment.'

*Kelly* went to Cherbourg soon after war started to embark the Duke and Duchess of Windsor. 'And their dogs!', Joe added. 'The dogs were vegetarians but not the VIPs! Joe particularly remembers the Duke's fondness for whisky!

Joe says his Captain rarely if ever ate in his cabin at sea. In all kinds of weather and war conditions he prepared sustenance for the Old Man to consume on the bridge. Mountbatten's tastes were simple. One frequent meal on the bridge was a favourite among submariners — tinned sardines consumed with the aid of a fork straight from the tin, with bread and butter and tea or cocoa, sometimes ginger ale. 'No intoxicating drink — but perhaps very occasionally he might have a glass of port, or even cocoa laced with sherry.'

After *Kelly's* loss Joe Micallef's close friendship with Lord Louis was to continue right up to the assassination in Ireland. Micallef was pleasantly surprised when Lord and Lady Mountbatten made a point of seeing him on their way to India when Lord Mountbatten was going out to be Viceroy. Then, when the task of giving India independence was completed and Lord Louis returned to both the Navy and the Mediterranean, he soon sought out his former steward, this time for service as a civilian in the Mountabatten household in Malta. When Lord Mountbatten resumed his Naval career in command of cruisers, and again when he became Commander-in-Chief Mediterranean, it was automatic that Mountbatten should 'borrow' his former steward from his duties as officers' mess manager for the Royal Air Force personnel based at Malta's Luqa Airport. Micallef had a busy time, for the Mountbattens did a great deal of entertaining both privately and for visiting Service chiefs from Europe and other continents. When Mountbatten was away from Malta Micallef would return to work for the RAF.

Micallef regards as the highest compliment paid to him by Mountbatten the occasion when his former Captain recommended him to the Queen (then Princess Elizabeth) and the Duke of Edinburgh as their butler when Prince Philip was stationed in Malta in 1950 and 1951. Prince Philip served in HMS *Magpie* and Princess Elizabeth spent much time on the island. The Royal household during their time in Malta included, in addition to the Princess's lady-in-waiting and other staff brought from England, a Maltese housekeeper, Maltese girls employed as waitresses and an RN Petty Officer   Micallef pleased Britains's future Queen and her husband. To Joe it was 'like working with a happy family of your own. They were all extremely nice. Sometimes we had the Mountbattens' two daughters staying with Princess Elizabeth and their cousin Philip. Princess Margaret came out. She was the life and soul of the party. It was wonderful to be of service to them. The Princess Elizabeth was easy to please. We had hardly any complaints. It is well known she likes only a little food. If she was having a dinner party, I would present the proposed menu with the chef after we had discussed what the Princess would like.' The Queen and Prince Philip did not forget Micallef, who had a Christmas card from the Palace every year. When the Queen and Prince Philip had their 25th

*Old friends meet again in Malta –
Mountbatten with his former Chief
Steward, Micallef.*

*Mountbatten has a reunion with two of his former shipmates on a visit to Malta. On his right is Joe Micallef and on his left Salvo Baldacchino who is behind the bar in his own house on the island, which is yet another* Kelly *'museum'.*

wedding anniversary thanksgiving at Westminster Abbey, Micallef and his wife were invited by the Queen to go to London to join in the celebrations. 'On the evening of the service at the Abbey we were entertained at Buckingham Palace with the Royal staff, some of whom I knew when they used to come to Malta with the Princess and her husband. When we went to London we had with us the Maltese lady who was housekeeper at the Villa Guardamangia when the Queen stayed. The Queen paid for everything, for our flight, and our stay at the Cumberland Hotel.'

When Lord Mountbatten ended his Mediterranean Naval duties and became First Sea Lord, he maintained contact with Micallef. He invited Micallef to meet him when he was in Malta and they met at *Kelly* dinners in London.

The last time Mountbatten visited Malta, shortly before his death, he as usual made a date with Micallef and another Maltese who served on *Kelly's* first commission, Salvo Baldacchino, who became a successful business-man. On this last occasion Mountbatten went to the Baldacchinos' attractive villa at St Andrews, where he was delighted to be entertained in the villa's *Kelly* corner with a bar, many mementoes of the destroyer and a portrait of himself.

Although *Kelly* had only a brief asssociation with the George Cross island, Louis Mountbatten himself and many of the crew who had been in the Navy in peacetime had longer associations with the island. In the War

Museum which has been created there *Kelly* has a corner of its own. Like Mountbatten, many *Kelly* survivors revisited Malta for many years after the war, to stay on holiday with old shipmates and former friends. Mountbatten himself went to Malta in 1976 and visited the *Kelly* Corner of the museum at St Elmo where he presented one of his Captain's white uniform suits worn in *Kelly* before her departure for Crete. Among many *Kelly* souvenirs are the last picture of the whole *Kelly*'s crew taken just before she sailed for Crete and there is even a pair of shoe-trees used by Lord Louis. How the museum got these is not at all clear and he himself expressed surprise at this exhibit. He said 'The shoe-trees are certainly the type I still use although they may be an odd thing to put in a museum.' Malta reserved this special place for *Kelly* as a tribute to Mountbatten, who loved the island and its people. His presence in Malta brought famous people including Royalty and he was C-in-C Mediterranean on his way to the top.

Mountbatten himself took the salute when the British flag was hauled down in Malta and the island became independent. The *Kelly* Reunion Association had at their dinner the honorary secretary of the museum, Philip Vella, who has been mostly responsible for the collection of a splendid array of exhibits illustrating Malta's immense role as a fortress in World War 2. Malta's defences are centuries old and Fort St Elmo where the War Museum is located is celebrated because of the defence against the invading Turks in the Great Siege of 1565, one of the most important episodes in the history of Malta. In the fort itself six Maltese soldiers died in defence of their homeland on the very first day of the war and in July 1941 their comrades stopped a daring attempt by the Italian Navy to get into the harbours of the island.

The museum exhibition shows what Malta's civilian population endured between 1940 and 1943 and the dreadful conditions under which the islanders lived in the densely populated part of the island during the almost daily bombing. The museum emphasizes Malta's association with the Royal Navy and Merchant Navies in which so many Maltese served with distinction and died with honour. One of the prime exhibits is a Gloster Gladiator single-seater biplane fighter, one of the finest aerobatic machines before the Hurricane and Spitfire. In June 1940 the fighter force available on the island consisted of just four of these Gloster Gladiator biplanes, three of which were destroyed in battle. 'Faith', the so-badly damaged survivor, was presented to Malta in 1943 and by 1974 it had been refurbished to take its place in the museum.

Chapter 6

# *The King meets a burglar*

It was as well that *Kelly's* galley was fitted to cope with large and important dinner parties. Apart from distinguished visitors, politicians like Winston Churchill and other ministers, senior Service officers and film and stage people, there was the Royal Family.

While based in the south of England *Kelly* was at sea much of the time, mostly at night, patrolling the Channel and its approaches, escorting minelayers and such like, and hunting U-boats and E-boats, Mountbatten hoping to encounter the enemy. When she returned to harbour in the morning, there was plenty of work cleaning the vessel, which was often in bad shape after a rough night, and making her ready for a dusk departure again. There was little time for shore leave, just a few hours occasionally for each watch.

One noon while tidying up went on there was a 'buzz' that King George and Queen Elizabeth were arriving on board for a brief visit. Not with the ship in this state, the crew thought. The rumour was confirmed when Lord Louis got on to the loudspeakers and said that, indeed, the King was paying a call. 'Clean ship' went on feverishly and then everyone got into rig of the day. The King, Queen and the Princesses Elizabeth and Margaret and their dogs were received at the gangway by the Captain. The officers and crew were lined up and the Royal party stopped to chat with various ratings. It was unfortunate, all the ratings thought, that the King picked on one of *Kelly's* 'comedians'. Every ship had a 'Lofty' and the King stopped to meet *Kelly's* 'Lofty', from somewhere in London's East End. The conversation, which many overheard, went like this:

The King: 'How long have you been in the Navy?'
Lofty: 'Six months sir.'
The King: 'Only six months; do you think you will like the Navy?'
Lofty: 'Well it's not a question of like the Navy, sir. It's a question of will I get used to the Navy?'
'I see' said the King. 'What was your job in civilian life?'
'Oh! I was a burglar, sir.'
The King might have been taken aback but didn't show it.
'A burglar. Were you a good burglar?', he asked 'Lofty'.

'Not very good sir. Not very good. I spent more time in prison than I did out, sir.

The King walked on down the line while Mountbatten stepped back and said to 'Lofty': 'I didn't know you were a burglar.'

The reply:

'Well, it's something I don't broadcast, sir.'

★   ★   ★

*King George VI's first visit to HMS Kelly in 1940, the occasion on which one of the crew told His Majesty that in 'civvy street' his occupation was burglary!*

Another visit to *Kelly* by Mountbatten's Royal relatives was when the *Kelly* went into the London Graving Dock at Blackwall for repairs after she was damaged in the collision with the 'Tribal' Class destroyer HMS *Gurkha*. Old ex-dockers still admire the way Mountbatten handled his ship into the narrow dock without assistance. Word soon got around dockland of *Kelly's* surprise arrival and women and children joined workers at the main gate to see the King and Queen arrive with other members of the Royal Family.

Of all the *Kelly* crew Harry Lord had cause to remember the visit best. He was detailed to tidy up the torpedo pistol store, situated in the wardroom flat directly under the officers' companion ladder. He was busy coating the deck with red-lead when the torpedo gunner told him to put the light out at once as 'important people' were about to descend to the wardroom. His superior then lowered the hatch over Lord but said he would let the hatch cover rest on the butterfly clips on the combing because of the strong smell and fumes from the red-lead in the store where Lord was working.

'This gave me a six-inch gap enabling me to see who our visitors were, and I stood on the rungs of the ladder and looked up. First came King George and Lord Louis, Lady Edwina, the Duchess of Kent and others. I heard the Queen say that 'one needed to wear trousers to negotiate these warship ladders'. I also noticed that Royal legs were no different to other women's!

'After the wardroom door was closed behind the visitors I attempted to push open the hatch but it was armoured and I found it too heavy. After an hour or so I started to feel dizzy owing to the red-lead fumes from the deck I had painted. I then heard the wardroom door open so I shouted for assistance. King George knelt on one knee and, with his face a few inches from mine, asked if I needed help. I explained my predicament and a passing Maltese steward helped the King to lift the hatch. I quickly thanked His Majesty, who disappeared into the bathroom, and took myself to the upper deck for a breather. I decided to keep "mum" on this one and so apparently did HM as I heard nothing more.'

When *Kelly* got into France on 13 September 1939 to embark the Duke and Duchess of Windsor there was one member of the ship's company who caused great commotion. Mountbatten's errand was to bring his cousin, who was also his best man when he married Edwina, and the former Mrs Simpson back to England from their home in France. The ship's company were smartly fallen in, including the ship's dog George. George, like the rest of the crew, had not had a run ashore for a fortnight. At Cherbourg the Duke and Duchess stepped aboard and their chauffeur followed with four corgis on a lead. They were at once spotted by George. 'You never saw such a scatter in all your life when George went for them', one of the crew said. 'George had to be confined to barracks for the journey back to England.'

Mountbatten had for some reason warned his officers not to be swayed by the charm of his best friend, the Duke. 'Don't fall under his spell', he said. The Windsors went down to the wardroom and the officers found them delightful company, interesting to converse with. One of *Kelly's* officers had a King Edward VIII shilling which he brought out. The Duke was pleasantly surprised. 'Oh! I've got lots of those. Would you like one?' He had them in his trousers pocket and insisted on giving a coin to every officer.

In daylight *Kelly* left the French coast and crossed to Portsmouth at high speed. Apart from a diversion when there was a suspected enemy submarine scare there were no untoward incidents. The Duke of Windsor spent part of the journey on the bridge with Mountbatten and while the Captain's steward attended to the Duke's request for his favourite beverage on the way back to the country from which he had not long since abdicated the throne, the jovial Harry Lord had his own encounter to relate for *Kelly's* chronicles. He rarely missed a trick and was sound on detail. *Kelly* had arrived in Cherbourg during the First Dog Watch; Lord was depth charge sentry and, it being watch and watch about, meant his next turn as sentry was the First Watch, 20:00 hours to 24:00 hours. As he was below he had missed 'all the fuss' at Cherbourg. Soon after closing up during the ship's dash back to Portsmouth he was surprised, he said, to hear female laughter in the middle of the English Channel aboard a destroyer. 'Quickly flinging my fag over the stern I turned round to see the Duchess of Windsor with another lady groping their way round the after superstructure accompanied by one of our officers. As the ship was doing nearly forty knots with the stern down with the roar of our wash it was difficult to hear what the lady asked me. I quickly explained about the depth charges and my duties. I did hear the Duchess say "Aren't we going fast". The Channel was quite calm but they did not linger long and as they retreated round the port side, which was to windward, the Duchess nearly lost her headscarf. I managed to grab it as it was whisked from her head. As I handed it to her I was conscious of a strong perfume which seemed to linger on the quarterdeck for days. It was only a "brief encounter" but I will always remember the Duchess's smile and "thank you" as I handed her scarf back.' Years afterwards Lord was still saying 'I can sense that perfume to this day'.

As *Kelly* reached Portsmouth, Randolph Churchill, Winston's son, caused some amusement. He had been with *Kelly* to act as ADC to the Duke of Windsor. He was in Cavalry uniform and was about to go ashore with his spurs upside down. Lord Louis had noticed the error but decided not to tell Randolph as he thought it would be rather fun to see what happened, but the Duke spotted it before the party was put ashore and exclaimed: 'Randolph has his spurs the wrong way!' He saved young Chuchill further embarrassment because there was quite a retinue of brass hats and officals awaiting the Duke and Duchess. The preparations annoyed the Duke. It was dark when *Kelly* came up to the jetty and as she was going alongside great floodlights were switched on and there were guards and bands to greet the Windsors. The Duke was very angry indeed. He said, 'This is all quite wrong. It's not what I've come back for.' The Windsors were supposed to be returning to England secretly and ceremonial was not anticipated at all. Furthermore, the guard had been kept waiting on the quayside for a long time because *Kelly* on her hush-hush mission did not and was not intended to signal her expected time of arrival. As it was the Duke of Windsor was invited to go and dine ashore by the C-in-C. He declined and said he was going to stay on board and dine with Dickie. It didn't go down too well ashore. The sailors stayed up to give him a send-off when he went but they had rather a long wait. . .

Chapter 7

# 'Case dismissed'

The former HMS *Kelly* rating who was given the honour of handing over the *Book of Donors* at the unveiling of the Mountbatten Memorial, Rocky Wilkins, had an unexpected encounter early in 1940 with his Captain, Lord Louis Mountbatten.

Wilkins had been in *Kelly* only a few months when the destroyer went into Devonport Naval Dockyard for minor repairs and the crew were all given short leave, watch and watch about. It was nice to be going home in those days but the 200-odd mile train journey through the night was an ordeal in itself. The blacked-out trains packed with Servicemen and civilians invariably started from the West Country full up yet seemed to stop at every station and tiny halt to pick up mail and more people. They were compressed into corridors and guards' vans to spend what always seemed to be an interminable night getting what sleep was possible with heads on kitbags and other luggage and being constantly disturbed by the feet of the train's occupants groping their way through smoke-filled carriages and corridors and by clonking and shunting whenever the train was stopped.

When the worn-out Wilkins, a Cockney, arrived in London he found that his young wife had been bombed out during the previous night. Their place had been destroyed and she was homeless. He helped her and the relatives with whom she lived to rake among the rubble to salvage what objects they could. It left Rocky looking grimy and almost asleep on his feet but he was particularly concerned about his sailor's uniform, which was decidedly shabby, torn and dirty.

He was worried about his wife and worried about returning to his ship next day, as well as facing another ghastly train journey to be back on time. He thought about his Captain. Lord Louis' philosophy was a mixture of strictness and kindness. He didn't believe in sending his men home unless it was entirely necessary but there was nothing he would not endeavour to do if he could help one of them.

Rocky Wilkins had left *Kelly* on 48 hours' leave and had just missed by a few hours the kind of German bombing attack valiant Londoners were now getting used to. He decided that he just could not leave his young wife with no home. Like so many women she had a wartime job which started before dawn every day. Wilkins decided his best bet was to go to the Admiralty and seek advice; at least they could contact his ship. Eventually he arrived at a place named Rex House in London's Haymarket where the Admiralty had one of its many departments near Whitehall. He arrived there in the early hours of the morning, with his wife. He was hardly conscious of his ripped uniform and was covered in dust; Ann Wilkins was in much the same state.

At the door of the Admiralty's premises he brushed past a Rear-Admiral who stopped him and said 'Why don't you salute an officer when you see one?' The half-dazed Able Seaman promptly muttered that he had not recognised the very senior officer, apologized, and put him in the picture about why he was there.

The Rear-Admiral quickly appreciated the situation and soon the unhappy Wilkinses were shown to an office to be questioned by a young Sub-Lieutenant. Wilkins explained that his home had just been bombed and he'd like to contact his ship, tell them what had happened and if possible get extension of leave. When he said his ship was HMS *Kelly* the young officer said: 'Well, your Captain happens to be in the building at present'. 'You mean my Captain, Lord Louis Mountbatten, is here?', asked the surprised Wilkins. 'Yes' said the Sub-Lieutenant. 'Do you wish to see him?' Wilkins said 'No, but if you would let him know that I am here, and tell him what's happened, I am sure he will understand'.

The officer jotted down some particulars and left Rocky and Ann in his office. He returned and asked Wilkins if he had his ship's station card with him. Taking the card, he returned again and asked if they had had breakfast and would they like to wash and clean up.

On return Wilkins was told: 'Your Captain will see you now'. The two Wilkins' were shown to another office and the uniformed Lord Louis stood up from his desk, looked his visitors up and down and asked 'What have you been up to?'

'We got bombed out last night . . . All I want if I can is an extension of leave. I have to get the wife fixed up somewhere and go back to the ship.'

'Right', Lord Louis stated immediately. 'That's not a problem. First of all I'll give you an extension of leave. I'll give you another 48 hours. Will that be sufficient?'.

*Kelly's* Captain picked up the telephone to get through to the ship at Plymouth and Rocky was relieved to hear arrangements being made for a further 48 hours' compassionate leave. Then Lord Mountbatten said: 'We've got to get you somewhere to stay'. He asked whether there were any members of her family Mrs Wilkins could move in with. She emphasized that her home had been completely lost. Lord Mountbatten then said his main concern was, were they all right for money? He added: 'We've simply got to get you fixed up with somewhere to stay. Will an hotel do you? Would you like to stay in an hotel?' Mrs Wilkins said she had to go back to work the following morning and for this her home had been convenient and she didn't feel like going to work from an hotel. She added that she might be able to stay with some other relatives in another part of London and the thankful Rocky told his Captain that, now he had got extra leave, he would get his wife fixed up with accommodation, salvage what was possible from the old place and things would be all right. 'Right', said Lord Louis. 'You go away and do what you need to do and report back to your ship and I will see you when you come aboard.'

After he had found new accommodation for his wife, Wilkins got back to HMS *Kelly*, and on time, but there was an unpleasant surprise for him. The first person he met was the First Lieutenant and Wilkins was promptly told he was adrift, 48 hours adrift. When he explained that he had returned to find his wife bombed out, that he had seen the Captain in London and that he had been granted 48 hours' extra leave, the officer said he knew nothing about it. Wilkins was in 'Captain's Report', which meant that he had to appear with defaulters before his Captain.

When it was 'Off Caps!' before the Captain, Lord Mountbatten first enquired what the charge was then looked sternly at Wilkins and asked, 'Were you adrift?'. Wilkins explained the situation and Lord Mountbatten needed no reminding that it was he who had arranged the extension of leave. The Captain said: 'Number One, did you get my telephone message saying I had met Able Seaman Wilkins in London and that I granted that extension? Did you get that message?'.

The First Lieutenant had not received such a message. The Captain asked who had been officer of the watch and demanded that the young officer be brought at once. The OOW got a blasting! Not only had he

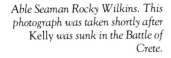

*Able Seaman Rocky Wilkins. This photograph was taken shortly after* Kelly *was sunk in the Battle of Crete.*

disobeyed orders by not passing on his Captain's orders about Wilkins' extension, but the young officer, asked why he hadn't passed it on, said he did not believe it had been the Captian on the telephone. He had thought it was one of the sailors having a joke. Lord Mountbatten, confounded, repeated what the unfortunate young officer had said: 'One of the sailors having a joke! And you really beieved that?'

'Yes, sir.'

'Right!' The Captain proceeded to admonish the junior officer in no uncertain manner. 'For your beneift it was I who was talking to you and if I sounded a bloody jokester remember my voice in future! Case dismissed.'

This was Rocky Wilkins' first major contact with Lord Mountbatten. The entire crew, officers and men, had soon come to realize that Lord Louis was not only a great Naval officer, a brilliant man, but was also someone they learned they could trust as well as being a man who was as strict as any senior officer in the Navy, who stood no nonsense and was quick to stamp on any misdemeanour, inefficiency or shortcoming. He expected, demanded and received extreme loyalty. And he bore no malice. That young officer who made a mistake made his Captain furious and got a severe rocket but that was the end of it.

Mountbatten's concern for the ship's company and the large Flotilla staff he carried in *Kelly* was legendary and constantly demonstrated. He wanted to know all about his men and asked questions about their home life and outside interests. He wandered round his ship and talked to them all. He knew their names, their tasks aboard ship, and much about their private lives. Rocky was asked how his wife was faring in London after being bombed out. She was all right, Rocky told him. The wife had moved in with her mother now. A nice little place. But they hoped to have their own place soon. Ann Wilkins was continuing her war work, she was working for the railway. 'Oh do tell me about it', the Captain would say, 'I'm very interested.' He listened as Rocky told him she drove a horse and cart for the railway and went down to the fishmarket daily with her mate, another woman. They loaded up and delivered fish to shops in London. 'That's the sort of work they are doing,' Rocky said. It was either that or being sent to the Midlands or the North on munitions and Ann Wilkins didn't want to do that. They were quite happy to be working around London, blitzes or no blitzes

Those who served with Mountbatten during the relatively short life of HMS *Kelly* from the time she was launched and then commissioned on the Tyne certainly got to know him personally, every one of them, from his Flotilla staff officers to the youngest rating. The ship's survivors did not realize that they had only started what was to be a long and unique friendship with their Captain. After *Kelly* sank off Crete with more than half her crew lost, the survivors had a sad farewell when they were landed at Alexandria in Egypt following the dreadful experience of having seen the ship go down, then being peppered by German aircraft gunfire. When Mountbatten addressed them in Alexandria and the survivors split up to continue their service in other ships and RN establishments, or to be invalided out of the Navy in consequence of sufferings in *Kelly's* sinking, they did not realize that they would ultimately meet their Captain again after the war had finished and become his friends.

After his own harrowing experiences in the Mediterranean, Lord Louis Mountbatten had gone on to greater things: as Chief of Combined Operations, helping to plan the great assault on Hitler's Europe; as last Viceroy of India; and then back to the Navy he loved, sailing in his cruiser squadron; as Commander-in-Chief, Mediterranean; and then as First Sea Lord and chief of all the nation's fighting Services, before he retired to other important civilian tasks. 'Britain's great odd-job man', he was once called.

Although her war service was brief, albeit eventful, Mountbatten loved *Kelly* as he had loved no other ship. To those other survivors also the *Kelly* experience was mesmeric. Their affection for their ship increased as time went on. There can hardly be a man who served in destroyers in the Royal Navy who had not an insatiable affection for this greyhound of a warship.

Of *Kelly*, Mountbatten wrote these words, quoted beneath a painting of the ship which he specially commissioned so that a framed print could be given to every remaining *Kelly* survivor on his eightieth birthday. 'To me she was quite unlike any other ship I served in . . . I knew and loved her from the time of her birth when her keel was laid until the keel was the last thing visible as she sank beneath the waves.' Throughout the history of the Royal Navy there hasn't been a Captain's epithet to surpass those words.

*Mountbatten the younger! Just fifty years old, he relaxes with former shipmates at the first* Kelly *reunion dinner.*

*Mountbatten with fellow survivors at the reunion dinner in 1951. On his left is Rocky Wilkins and on his right is Jim Cook. Standing, left to right, are Tom Newstead, Fred Lucas, Paddy Milton, Freddy Waldron, Tug Wilson and Vernon Shaw.*

As a result, having fulfilled his other tasks and after *Kelly* officers and men had been widely scattered, Lord Mountbatten could not conceal his delight when he was told, five years after the war had finished, that his old shipmates, largely through the inspiration of Rocky Wilkins, had decided to form the HMS *Kelly* Reunion Association.

★   ★   ★

There are hundreds of reunion associations throughout Britain and overseas wherein men and women regularly meet to recall their war years and remember those who did not return. The *Kelly* men, both those who survived other sea warfare after their ship was lost off Crete and later returned to civilian life, and those regular Servicemen who retired, believe their association is unique — and they were encouraged in this by Lord Mountbatten himself. The *Kelly* Association, in spite of their most grievous loss when their old Captain was murdered, carry on holding reunions that have become famous, and have been enjoyed by many privileged people who never served in *Kelly* but who became associated with her in one way or another.

It was in 1950, nearly ten years after *Kelly* went down, that Rocky Wilkins and a few lower deck shipmates who had kept in touch for the remainder of the war, and had occasional get-togethers immediately afterwards, formed their association. Of course, they invited their old

*Lord Mountbatten welcomes his former shipmates at one of the early* Kelly *dinners.*

Captain to be President. By this time, Lord Mountbatten had gone to take up the new appointments that made him famous in countries far beyond Britain and its Empire. It is interesting to contemplate how, when the war started in 1939 and *Kelly* had just been completed at Hebburn on the Tyne, Louis Mountbatten must have considered his future in the war. Ambitious as he undoubtedly was, he cannot have foreseen that he was destined to play a far greater role than purely Royal Navy duties would have provided. When war came he was already vastly experienced in the Royal Navy in war and peace. He had followed his father into the Navy and was a cadet in 1913 before World War 1 started. When boys of his age were still at school, he served in a number of warships during three years of that war. He was well known throughout the Navy, first as the boy Prince Louis, whose father had risen to be head of the Navy, and then as the Royal sailor whose reputation for spectacular ship handling and mercurial leadership had become increasingly talked about among other officers and men who were making the Navy their full-time career. In 1939 there were a great many distinguished officers in the fleet who were many years his senior, however.

The rise of Hitler and his Nazi party had become an urgent threat to Britain and it was clear that our Navy was inadequate to meet a second

Great War. Already there had been an increase in shipbuilding and recruiting and these were speeded up even more feverishly once war had been declared. Rapid promotion was available and even young men who joined the Royal Navy at the outset as officers in the Royal Naval Volunteer Reserve rose to the rank of Commander and even Captain. Had he remained in the Navy and at sea throughout the war, it is by no means certain that even in five years Mountbatten would have become Admiral of the Fleet and a Naval Commander-in-Chief. Had he thought that he would be limited to less than two years as an active sea-going officer in command, Louis Mountbatten would have been dismayed. Though long before his death he had declared himself a man of peace who realized the terrors of atomic warfare, he was a man of action when it came to the defence of his own country. By virtue of his natural talent and his store of Naval strategy, his prospects in the Royal Navy were second to none. Nevertheless, rapid promotion was possible through success in action against the enemy at sea as well as brilliance in ideas in planning.

Like all other Naval officers in command of warships, he must have been thrilled as well as solemnly relieved when, on 3 September 1939, he received aboard the *Kelly* the crisp but dramatic signal by wireless telegraphy from the Admiralty addressed to 'All concerned at home and abroad'. 'MOST IMMEDIATE Commence hostilities at once with Germany.' *Kelly* was in much hazardous action in her short life. For his own bravery and skill in handling his ship against intolerable odds, Mountbatten was awarded the Distinguished Service Order and mentioned in despatches. But Mountbatten was not, for the time being, to be one of the triumphant and celebrated sea dogs like Cunningham of the Mediterranean, Captain Vian of the *Cossack* who daringly raided the *Altmark* and released her prisoners, or Commodore Harwood, whose cruisers caused the German pocket battleship *Graf Spee* grievous damage and ultimate scuttling off the River Plate in one of the first actions to provide beleaguered Britain with good news and a brief breathing space for national joy. Other destroyer Captains and submarine commanders operating in the Atlantic and other sea theatres who were contemporaries of Mountbatten had the chances for spectacular success at sea that were denied to the captain of *Kelly*. However, great opportunities were swiftly to come the way of Mountbatten.

After Crete, where the British lost three cruisers and six destroyers (including *Kelly*) but evacuated 18,500 out of 32,000 soldiers. Lord Mountbatten commanded the aircraft carrier HMS *Illustrious*. This was for but a short spell before he was elevated to the post of Chief of Combined Operations, an imaginative decision by Winston Churchill who, even at that early stage of the deepening and widening conflict, had his eye on the day when Britain and her allies would be landing back on enemy territory, particularly the Europe that had been overrun by Hitler's huge forces. Mountbatten went on to his greatest military task as Supreme Allied Commander in South-East Asia where our fighting forces, sometimes referred to as the 'forgotten army', were in great difficulties trying to stem the onslaught of the Japanese. After he had caused the turning of the tide in his own difficult theatre — he became Earl Mountbatten of Burma, a title he chose and cherished — and the Japanese had succumbed to President Truman's atom bombs on Hiroshima and Nagasaki, Mountbatten was persuaded by the King, George VI, and Britain's new Prime

Minister, Clement Atlee, to return to the Far East as Viceroy of India to preside over the onerous duty of giving that sub-continent its independence.

So, when the *Kelly* reunion dinners started in 1951, those traceable HMS *Kelly* survivors who were involved with the North Sea drama with E-boats and those rescued from the sea off Suda Bay, Crete, were to become reunited with a man who had achieved remarkable fame. To them, however, he was still 'the Captain' and Lord Louis was to become involved with his former destroyer officers and men even more than he had in wartime. By then Mountbatten had commanded millions of men of many nations and he was always glad to meet as many of them as he could. Not only in Britain but in many parts of the British Commonwealth, Mountbatten was associated with twenty reunion associations including the great Burma Star gathering in London but, till the end of his days, Mountbatten's heart was closest to the *Kelly* and the men who sailed with him.

When Rocky Wilkins and company started the *Kelly* Association, they had only a skeleton list of names. As time went on, Lord Mountbatten became the Association's best recruiter. Wherever he went at home and overseas, men would introduce themselves as ex-*Kelly* men. From Australia to North America, they approached him and introduced themselves as ex-*Kelly*, those who served in *Kelly's* first commission and second, final commission. Mountbatten hastened to inform Rocky Wilkins about these meetings and if the claimants were upheld — some claims were not always authentic — they became members of the *Kelly* Reunion Association. Rig of the day: blazers, *Kelly* tie, a specially-made and bona fide *Kelly* badge and war medals.

In running the *Kelly* Association Rocky had more than 800 letters from his old Captain, whose enthusiasm helped to make *Kelly* dinners famous. Over the years there was a wide range of guests in addition to former shipmates of high and modest rank. They were family affairs as well. Mountbatten was proud to take his own family and relatives, including Prince Philip and the Prince of Wales, and famous people from many walks of life including show business. Rocky and his fellow crew members took their wives, children and grandchildren.

Mountbatten was deeply interested in the wellbeing and health of his *Kelly* men. His letters throw considerable light on his generosity and care for the men he regarded as his friends, men whose lot in life was on a vastly different plane to his own. Mountbatten was never other than an exceedingly busy person with an astonishing variety of interests, but he spared time to keep in touch by personal letters and often telephone calls to the men who served with him, especially if they became ill or fell into straitened circumstances.

# Chapter 8

# *Story for the film stars*

The idea of the reunions of *Kelly* survivors had nothing to do with Mountbatten or any of his officers. The *Kelly* Reunion Association was created by men who served on the lower deck and the mainspring was Rocky Wilkins. He and a handful of shipmates who survived *Kelly's* sinking got together almost a decade afterwards and decided on a reunion.

Their former Captain was by this time at the Admiralty as Fourth Sea Lord in 1951 when, three days after receiving a letter from Wilkins, he wrote back from his home in Wilton Crescent, Belgravia. 'I am delighted to hear that there is to be a reunion of the survivors of the *Kelly*, and I should very much like to attend it. I think, however, it is only fair to warn you that I expect to be relieved at Admiralty fairly early in the New Year, and after that I hope to be able to arrange some leave abroad before taking up the Mediterranean command; so it may be a bit tricky to fit in this reunion. However, if you will let me know before you have settled on a date, you may be sure I will do my best to arrange to be there'.

In the ten years since *Kelly* was sunk Wilkins had seen Lord Mountbatten only once. In the years to follow, and particularly the twenty years right up to his death, *Kelly's* Captain was to strike a close friendship with Rocky Wilkins in particular and many of the ratings who served under him in *Kelly*. Apart from at reunions and other occasions concerning *Kelly*, Mountbatten was regularly in touch with Wilkins, by telephone and by letter, from his home in London, from Broadlands, from the Admiralty, sometimes from Royal residences where he frequently stayed. One of the last letters Rocky received from Lord Louis referred to the anniversary birthday surprise Rocky's family had given him. 'I see you have at last been caught, like I was, by your own family . . .' Mountbatten was referring to the surprise sprung on himself when his daughters, some of the Royal Family, and former *Kelly* officers and shipmates were involved in the television programme 'This is Your Life'.

Mountbatten wrote to Rocky: 'No Able Seaman in the history of the Royal Navy has done so much to perpetuate the history of his own ship with the ship's company and, indeed, with the media than you have. Your original conversation with the late Able Seaman Godfrey Winn started the ball rolling. He was a wonderful author and a great friend of our family and he obviously helped you get the *Kelly* Reunion Association underway. Since then it has gone from strength to strength and you have had the most remarkable set of VIPs attending your dinners and they seem to get better and better.'

Rocky Wilkins acknowledges the fact that the *Kelly* Association would not have become perhaps the most outstanding of all ships' annual reunions without the encouragement, the drive, the influence and string-pulling by Lord Mountbatten. Lord Louis, as all his *Kelly* lower deck shipmates called him, regarded the *Kelly* get-together as something special and personal. Mountbatten made suggestions about the *Kelly* Association but no plans were made by him without seeking concurrence of Wilkins and his shipmates.

Rocky Wilkins, well-built and stocky, was born in Clerkenwell, London, in the year Louis Mountbatten became a Midshipman in the Navy. Like Mountbatten's father, who became Admiral of the Fleet and First Sea Lord, Wilkins' father had been in the Royal Navy, a Chief Petty Officer killed in a cruiser sunk in the North Sea in World War 1. Rocky's mother was a hard-working woman and sixty years ago she was Pearly Queen of Finsbury. At weekends she dressed in the full regalia of the pearlies and with little Rocky also in pearlies she collected money for the funds of various hospitals. 'So really Lord Louis and I had something in common. We were both "Royalty". He was the son of a prince and I am the son of a queen, even though she was a pearly queen.'

Rocky left school at fourteen and was first in uniform in the Army. The only thing to do in those days was to join the Army, he says. He had an elder brother who was a Regimental Sergeant Major in the Royal Scots stationed in Edinburgh, which is why he chose the Army and the regiment. But he didn't like being the only Cockney among the Scots when the battalion moved to Aldershot, so young Rocky 'went over the wall', as he describes it, and joined the Navy the next day. He was a deserter. In the first days on parade in navy blue Rocky felt he must have appeared more disciplined than the other recruits. He was good at arms drill and when he was asked where he had learnt it all, particularly his obvious familiarity with firearms, he said, 'with the Territorials' and no more questions were asked. He remembers telling Mountbatten much later on in life that he was an old soldier as well as an old sailor and the Admiral just raised an eyebrow (diplomatically doubtless, he didn't want to know) and that was that.

Rocky served before World War 2. He started in destroyers and the first time he saw *Kelly* was at Namsos when he was working with a shore party having lost his trawler *Aston Villa*. Mountbatten brought *Kelly* alongside a pier in the blazing Norwegian port and evacuated British and French troops. 'That's what I call a ship', Rocky said to one of his shipmates, 'but in a ship like that you'd have to be tough.' Back in the Naval barracks at Chatham he went to a sale of dead men's effects. It was the custom for ratings to hand back what was bought so there could be further bids, destined to raise money for next of kin. Rocky needed a ditty box to replace the one he'd lost in Norway and eventually it was knocked down to him for a £1. Opening the box he saw that it had belonged to a stoker who had been killed in *Kelly's* action against a German E-boat and he thought it best to return the ditty box to the man's widow. When he returned to his mess in the barracks a Chief Petty Officer asked him what he had bought and Wilkins showed the box. The chief said, 'That's strange lad. You've just got a draft to *Kelly*'.

One of the draft on the way to Hebburn on a wet and cold November morning, a young man from Wales going to his first ship, said his mother had written to him saying how pleased she was that her boy was being drafted to *Kelly* and did he know that the Captain was the King's cousin, so she didn't think they'd go to sea much!

As soon as the gear belonging to the new members of the crew had been put aboard the destroyer, still in dry dock, they were told to muster on the quay. Their new Captain wished to speak to them. Lower deck was cleared and Lord Louis stood on a box and gathered around him his new ratings, half of whom had not been to sea before, but many of whom had not only been to sea but were survivors from ships already lost by the Navy. Captain Lord Mountbatten left them in no doubt about what he expected from them. He wanted a happy ship, he also wanted an efficient ship and while the whole ship's company worked hard storing and painting *Kelly* there was soon established a fine relationsip between older Regular Service ratings and War Service only ratings, the experienced men teaching the newcomers the vitally important fighting roles they were to undertake.

Mountbatten's men soon learned that he had the interests of every man jack of them at heart. He talked to them individually about their roles in the Navy and their careers in civvy street, about their families, their leisure interests, their duties in the ship, their action stations and the weapons they would handle. He got to know everybody in his ship and encouraged his officers to do the same. In the wardroom was kept a book of names and columns for ticks and crosses. The officers were invited to put names to faces and faces to names and those officers who knew their men best and came out on top every week were rewarded with a drink on the Captain. This was one of the reasons why every man who served in *Kelly* considered Mountbatten was the best Captain in the Navy. Mountbatten's philosophy was that it was better to talk with and get to know men on the daily rounds than merely see them when they appeared at Captain's defaulters. Naturally, Mountbatten had the deepest concern and interest also for the officers who served with him in *Kelly*. He lost some of them in action. Those who lived remained in touch with him. Some of them became distinguished Naval officers and, although scarcely any served with Mountbatten again, they did see him again at reunions. Mountbatten saw to that. He never ceased to locate officers as well as ratings, wherever they had gone in the world, and he got Rocky to add them to his list of survivors to be invited to reunions in London.

As honorary secretary of the *Kelly* Association, Wilkins was in a privileged position to become a special friend of Mountbatten. Through his old Captain he met a large number of people in high places, including the Duke of Edinburgh, the Prince of Wales, high ranking Naval officers, captains of warships and shore establishments, film stars and show-business men and women, and businessmen who were invited by Rocky through Mountbatten to attend *Kelly* dinners.

One Sunday morning in 1970 Rocky Wilkins was telephoned at home by John Barratt, Lord Louis' private secretary, who said Mountbatten would be in touch in a couple of days about a trip overseas. Lord Louis had been awarded the Humanitarian Award of Variety International and it was to be presented in Puerto Rico in three months' time. When Mountbatten spoke to Wilkins by telephone he said the organizers of the dinner had asked for someone to tell the story of the *Kelly*. It had been suggested at first that a film actor might fulfil this task but it was decided to have a survivor from the destroyer and Mountbatten had suggested Wilkins. Could he go to Puerto Rico? Rocky accepted right away but, when he was told the trip would be for one or two weeks, said he did not think he could get time off from his work as a Post Office engineer. To this Lord Mountbatten said 'Rubbish, you can get time off. You've done so before.' There was no need for Mountbatten to intervene on Rocky's behalf. Rocky told his bosses at the Post Office and they gave the trip their blessing.

Rocky went to glamourland to mix with Hollywood stars at banquets and generally live it up. He flew with John Barratt and Mountbatten's valet to Miami where they joined Mountbatten who was coming from the Bahamas en route to Puerto Rico. 'It was at this stage when I was getting a bit concerned about expenses', Rocky said. 'Just one night at the hotel had almost cleared me out of pocket money and I asked John Barratt "what about expenses." He relpied "Don't worry, you'll be taken care of when you get to the other end." But it was at Puerto Rico where I really got worried. All the showbiz big wigs, the stars and the Press were waiting for Lord Louis and I could gradually see him disappearing into the mist and I felt completely lost.'

However, Mountbatten stopped the procession of people surrounding him and shouted 'There he is! Come on Rocky, we don't want to lose you at this stage.' Before they moved on it was arranged for Rocky to be looked after by a Mr George Hoover of the Variety Club of America, who drove him to the 'Americano' Hotel in San Juan where Rocky was not only given a sumptuous apartment but a valet as well. 'There I was, I had brought only two suits with me, a dinner suit and a lightweight and some casual gear — and I was given my own valet!'

That first evening in Puerto Rico Rocky strayed. He wandered down to the hotel foyer and watched all those rich Americans dressed up to the nines going into a banquet. 'I wondered what was going on and went off to one of the local bars where I sat quitely for the evening drinking. Next morning there was a call from Lord Louis. Where was I the night before? I said I knew nothing about it. He pointed out that during his speech he mentioned me and a searchlight went around to an empty space! I was missing! After that he made sure I was never out of his sight for a moment. This whole atmosphere went on for a week.'

It was the eve of the final day of the festivities, the day of the presentation to Mountbatten when Rocky had to do his piece. He hadn't prepared anything to say. Then there was a rehearsal and a scriptwriter handed Rocky typewritten sheets of what he was expected to recite. To say Rocky wasn't happy about it is an understatement. It just wasn't on to tell such a story about the *Kelly*, about things that didn't actually happen. It was too much illuminated, too glorified for Rocky who went to Lord Louis and said 'I can't possibly say this. It is a load of rubbish!' Mountbatten read the script and agreed with Rocky, whom he told to go away and quietly write down his own story, in his own way telling what happened on the day the *Kelly* went down.

There was only one anecdote Lord Louis did not want Rocky to relate. He didn't want Rocky to 'steal' the story about the stoker who came to the surface as *Kelly* was sinking and referred to his Captain as 'scum'. It is a story which became famous at *Kelly* reunion dinners. Lord Louis was in the sea with another officer when Stoker Garner, who had managed to extricate himself from the ship, shot to the surface and, looking directly at Mountbatten, exclaimed 'Isn't it funny how the scum rises to the top!' Of course Garner always insisted that he was referring to the debris and the fuel oil from the bilges that came to the surface as the ship sank. He certainly forever denied that he was referring to his Captain. But the Captain, whose face was clogged with oil, always said Garner knew 'bloody well' who he was looking at when he said it. It was a favourite Lord Louis story and although Garner stuck to his version it remained one Mountbatten enjoyed telling to his crew and guests for 35 years. If anybody laughed more than Garner it was the Captain himself who liked the tale because, he said, it demonstrated that a man, be it an officer or rating, could nearly always have a sense of humour even in the throes of adversity.

Rocky's own speech, typed for him by a hotel secretary, was listened to appreciatively by a thousand guests. Rocky Wilkins was not the sort to be overawed by the Hollywood atmosphere, the famous screen faces, Maureen O'Hara, Cary Grant, Sinatra and the rest who had flown from Los Angeles, the bright lights, the band, the military pomp or the massive number of micrphones. Describing one part of the survivors' experiences in the sea off Crete he said the German bombers were gone for a few minutes and it was very quiet ... Rocky had his audience absolutely still too and with timing that couldn't have been bettered by the film stars who were listening he went on to relate how out of the quiet came singing. It was Captain Lord Louis starting to strike up one of Britain's spirited wartime songs, 'Roll out the barrel'. The Captain was holding on to a young seaman who was severely wounded and his song was picked up, by the other survivors, many a considerable distance away, most of them almost choking with oil, but still singing as loudly as they could, inspired by their Captain's efforts to keep up morale.

Rocky had many congratulations from among those who heard him. One of the nicest tributes was from Cary Grant with whom Rocky flew in the actor's private aircraft back to Miami. Grant told Rocky it was a marvellous story, marvellously told. 'I felt I was actually living the part myself, living in the water', said Cary Grant. 'I could feel and actually realize what you people were going through ... it was not something out of a film. It was real.'

The Variety Club of Great Britain got Rocky to do a repeat performance at a dinner at the Dorchester Hotel. Sir John Mills, who played the part of Able Seaman 'Shorty' Blake in Coward's film *In which we serve* (based on HMS *Kelly*'s career), sat next to Rocky. John Mills, an honorary member of the *Kelly* Association, also praised Rocky's moving account. He had heard Rocky in Puerto Rico and said: 'Splendid, and you haven't changed a word'.

There was a third occasion on which Rocky Wilkins was called upon to make his speech. This was at an impressive gathering at the Guildhall in the City of London when the White Ensign Association held its silver anniversary banquet. Rocky was asked to speak by the chairman, Sir

Donald Gosling, who is also an active supporter of the *Kelly* Association and was a great friend of Lord Mountbatten. When Mountbatten was First Sea Lord in 1957, he and Sir Charles Lambe, then Second Sea Lord and Chief of Naval Personnel, were concerned for the future of several thousands of officers and men who were 'axed' by defence cuts after hostilities in Korea ended. Through Mountbatten's inspiration, financial expertise of men in the City of London became available to assist ex-Naval men seeking civilian careers. The White Ensign Association was founded in 1958 with offers of help from banks, institutions, companies and individuals including Stock Exchange members. With headquarters in HMS *Belfast* in the Pool of London, the association has expanded its activities to give wide-ranging advice and assistance while men are still on active service as well as resettlement of personnel up to around 55 years old who come out of the Navy at the rate of about 400 officers and 5,000 ratings a year. Prospective employers realize that a great deal of technical and managerial talent, from flag officers to highly-skilled ratings involved in the use of sophisticated equipment in the modern Navy, is regularly becoming available. The Admiralty gives company representatives the opportunity to spend time at sea in RN ships to get first-hand knowledge of the potential.

The silver anniversary banquet, attended by a distinguished gathering of 750, was to have been attended by Lord Mountbatten had he lived. As it was Rocky was the only *Kelly* survivor present. The Royal Marines drummers rolled before a Naval party piped the still and Wilkins was called upon to speak in honour of Mountbatten and the *Kelly* victims to an audience of Royalty, lords, ladies officers and famous faces. The Prince of Wales, who had been invited as well as Lord Mountbatten to go to the Guildhall, was there, and he and Rocky discussed the *Kelly*. Since Lord Mountbatten's death it had been in the minds of Rocky and his colleagues how appropriate, and what an honour, it would be for the *Kelly* Association if His Royal Highness would consent to become its next President. Rocky appreciated the fact that the Prince, although he had been at sea and in command and was indeed very much a Royal Navy officer, had not seen war service himself. He wondered how he would feel about being asked to take over an association of old sailors, ex-destroyer men. That would be a nice way to put it, thought Wilkins.

His Royal Highness said how much he would like to have served in *Kelly* when his 'uncle' was in command. The Prince inquired about the Kelly Association's future; would they carry on? Then Wilkins took the opportunity of asking the Prince of Wales: 'Would you take over, sir?' 'Take over as your President?' asked the Prince. Rocky said 'Yes' and the Prince replied 'Yes, I would very much like to do so'. The ex-*Kelly* men considered this a tremendous honour. It could hardly happen to any other ship's reunion association, created by the lower deck, never sponsored, to whose dinners the officers were invited guests. So the Prince became President of what the *Kelly* men think of as a unique association. Lord Mountbatten's elder daughter Patricia, the Countess Mountbatten of Burma, became Patron and Rear Admiral Philip Burnett, the much-loved surviving first First Lieutenant of *Kelly,* carried on as Vice-President.

23rd November 1951

My dear Wilkins,

Thank you for your letter of 19th November. I am delighted to hear that there is to be a Reunion of the survivors of the KELLY, and I should very much like to attend it.

I think, however, it is only fair to warn you that I expect to be relieved at the Admiralty fairly early in the New Year, and after that I hope to be able to arrange some leave abroad before taking up the Mediterranean command; so it may be a bit tricky to fit in this Reunion.

However, if you will let me know ~~the moment~~ before you have settled on a date, you may be sure I will do my best to arrange to be there. In fact, I would suggest that you ring up my Assistant Private Secretary, Mr. Brice, at the above number, and discuss it with him to see what can be arranged.

Yours sincerely

Mountbatten of Burma

---

30th April, 1952.

Dear Wilkins,

I feel I must write a line to thank you and the Members of your Committee very much indeed for having organised that wonderful Re-union of the KELLY survivors and having asked me to the party.

It could not have been better run or a greater success, and I have rarely enjoyed an evening so much.

I am almost most grateful for the photograph of the KELLY group, which will be one of my most treasured possessions.

Please do not forget to let my Private Secretary have a note for how much I owe for my share of the dinner, and in any case of course I want to pay for the telegram and any out of the way expenses.

I hope you will be successful in forming a more or less permanent organisation for the future.

Yours sincerely,

Mountbatten of Burma

---

30th November, 1953.

Dear Wilkins,

I would be glad if at the next KELLY Reunion you would inform the assembled company that on the 22nd October, 1953, H.M.S. SURPRISE passed Gavdos Island where the KELLY and KASHMIR were sunk on 23rd May, 1941. I was on board with my wife and I had the ship stopped and a guard of Royal Marines paraded who fired three volleys and then the buglers sounded the Last Post and Reveille.

This is the first opportunity I have had of paying honour in person to the KELLY and the KASHMIR and to the ship-mates whom we lost. I thought that the survivors would like to know that.

I came across another "old KELLY" onboard the GLORY. He is Petty Officer (A.H.1.) S.G. Nichol and I suggest that you write to him on board the GLORY and send him particulars so that he can join the Association. I told him I would get in touch with you or Bottoms.

Yours sincerely

Mountbatten of Burma

---

28th May, 1954.

My dear Wilkins,

Thank you for your letter of the 23rd May enclosing the excellent photographs taken at the KELLY Reunion held last month.

I do not yet know when I will be relieved in this job since my two years as British C-in-C are up but my two years as NATO C-in-C will not be up until the 15th March next year.

On the whole I think you could book a tentative date about the same time next year or perhaps better still in May or June. I suggest you book a room and let me know what dates you propose and I will have to let you know whether that will be convenient as soon as I know what my future movements are. I certainly want to attend the next reunion if at all possible.

The Editor of "Illustrated", who used to be on my staff in C.O.H.Q. and in S.E.A.C. has been out with a photographer to get some pictures of destroyers etc., out here largely in conjunction with publicising the KELLY serial in "Illustrated".

I thank the Committee for their congratulations on the successful visit of the Queen to the Mediterranean Fleet in Malta. The visit certainly was a great success.

Yours sincerely

Mountbatten of Burma

Chapter 9

# *Talks at the drawing board*

It was said that Mountbatten hand-picked his officers but this was not so. If he had preferences he might have been persistent in making it known to those responsible for appointments, even attempting a bit of string-pulling, but it very much depended on what officers were available. With war threatening long before *Kelly* and other ships of the 5th Destroyer Flotilla were anywhere near completion there was huge demand on manpower resources, not least for officers and senior ratings trained for destroyers. Naturally, like every other Naval person given the command of a flotilla of destroyers — a fine appointment for someone not yet forty years old — he did whatever he could to make sure he got first-class staff officers and the right commanding officers for the 5th Flotilla.

Having been 'born' into the Navy and in uniform since he was a thirteen year-old cadet, a Midshipman half way through World War 1, during which he had battle experience, then regular promotions between the wars, Mountbatten served alongside a large number of officers and in many ships and shore establishments. He knew personally many officers and their qualities. They might not actually have set eyes on him, but there was hardly a Naval officer who had not heard of Lord Mountbatten.

Having heard of his impending appointment to be Captain D of the 5th Destroyer Flotilla while he was working in the Naval Air Division at the Admiralty, Lord Louis at once set about doing his 'homework' concerning the officers who were to be his companions, confidants and friends. It was not difficult in the Royal Navy to make enquiries about an officer. Mountbatten's information about officers was by no means confined to those who were trying to serve with him. He spent his whole life getting to know people and trying to remember their names. He was always wanting *really* to get to know anybody he had ever met. He knew many when the war started. At the end of his Naval service he probably knew personally more officers than did any other flag officer. If Mountbatten had not already met a man it was easy to find someone who had. It was Mountbatten's habit to invite an officer destined for service in his ships for a meal and a chat so he could weigh him up.

Mountbatten's reputation was sufficiently known in Naval circles for officers to regard the 'summons' to a meeting with varying degrees of awe. Some have confessed they were apprehensive, even 'terrified'. Nevertheless it was clear that, without exception (so far as one can gather), officers were delighted at the prospect of joining Lord Louis. An appointment to serve with him was likely to be of distinct advantage to a young officer's future. Mountbatten was extremely loyal to those who served him well and took a continued interest in their Service advancement. Later in life, when he was in a position to do so, he helped their promotion whenever possible and was proud to be associated with their subsequent successes. In certain cases he helped them to secure civilian posts when the time came for retirement — often early retirement.

One of the earliest appointments in *Kelly* was that of the original First Lieutenant and a Flotilla staff officer, now Rear Admiral Philip Burnett. He stood by *Kelly* while the vessel was building and served in her first commission. Philip Burnett became aware of Mountbatten when Lord Louis was a signals school instructor on a course which Burnett attended in 1930. Burnett, then a Sub-Lieutenant, eight years younger, had heard Mountbatten described as something of a playboy. However, in those days the Commander-in-Chief Home Fleet organized about half a dozen winter lectures available to all officers, not just young ones, and Mountbatten was chosen to give a lecture on relativity. Philip Burnett said: 'I did not go to this lecture but it impressed me that a chap I'd really only heard of as a playboy should be giving one of the C-in-C's lectures, on relativity. I wouldn't like to do that now! That was when I realized he wasn't just a playboy.'

They met in 1938 when Mountbatten invited him to Adsdean, the large home the Mountbattens had rented twenty miles from Portsmouth with a lot of servants and facilities for entertaining and handy for Mountbatten going backwards and forwards to Portsmouth Naval base. When Burnett arrived in late afternoon Mountbatten started a conversation about destroyers while he was changing after golf. Mountbatten had plans of the ship and told Burnett how the new design of *Kelly* was influenced by a meeting with a top designer, Mr A. P. Cole, who had got to know Mountbatten in a bizarre way. When one of Mountbatten's previous destroyers had been docked in Malta, he had asked the dockyard to do some small job to improve the facilities of his cabin. Cole had been critical of him getting work done for his own convenience, and Mountbatten came to hear of this. The long and the short of it was that Cole had been invited aboard for a discussion, and had been satisfied that there had been nothing irregular requested by Mountbatten. On the contrary, Cole was friendly, Mountbatten — who enjoyed people with an enquiring mind — also liked him, and a friendship developed.

When, not long later, Lord Louis was in the Naval Air Division at the Admiralty, Cole was head designer in the destroyer section of Naval construction and in the evening Mountbatten used to go down and give his ideas on design. Albert Percy Cole is remembered well by the wife of an old colleague of mine, Mrs Peggie Taylor, who was Cole's secretary for a time when he was at the Admiralty. Mountbatten and Cole had great respect for one another and they greeted each other with: 'Good evening Mr Cole,' 'Good evening Lord Louis' whenever Mountbatten arrived for a chat about *Kelly* in the designer's office. Cole, who was English of course, went to a German university and spoke fluent German.

The 'J' and 'K' classes of destroyer, to which *Kelly* belonged, were quite different from what had gone before as a result of the Cole-Mountbatten discussions. These involved the frame of the ship, the guns, the bridge, and the outline. The new vessels had one funnel instead of two because Mountbatten stressed the importance of a low sillhouette for a destroyer, particularly at night and more so before they all got radar. Cole, the Naval architect, acknowledged the help and backing of Mountbatten the practical man.

These were the sort of things Lord Louis was telling Philip Burnett while he changed from golf. One can imagine the scene, golf shoes in one hand, plans of *Kelly* in the other. 'Lord Louis was still in the Air Division and, in fact, this meeting was probably before I was actually appointed, and was with a view to deciding if I was going to be appointed,' said Admiral Burnett. 'But, poor man, he had no choice because I was the only A/S [Anti submarine] officer available and an A/S officer was always First Lieutenant of the Flotilla Leader at that time. I don't think they could have found anybody else if he'd said "No, he's not suitable".'

Mountbatten knew that he was soon due to finish his stint at the Admiralty and having impressed his ideas on Cole as to how a destroyer should be designed following his taste of destroyer life in *Daring* and *Wishart*, he wanted to be a Captain D rather than go to a battleship or something similar. No doubt he had suggested in appropriate quarters that he might be a suitable candidate for *Kelly*.

Burnett went to *Kelly's* launching before he was actually appointed. In January 1939 he joined the chief engineer officer, Lieutenant Commander Mike Evans, and two Warrant Officers already at Hebburn, other officers joining as the year went on. Mountbatten went to Hebburn regularly and privately to see how construction was going and to 'encourage' the builders and the Admiralty contract staff. 'He knew more about the ship than I did', Burnett said. 'Each time he came up he alerted me to some new problem of which I had been totally unaware.' He was a technical man certainly but mainly a very practical man seeking to get things right in such a sensible way, much better than most Naval Captains would have done. Among minor problems he resolved were those of getting his seat on the bridge made so that it would be comfortable and the need for an adequate-sized stove in the galley!

Mountbatten even appeared to care more about paintwork than others. Before *Kelly* commissioned he let it be known that after commissioning and a short work-up they were to take the King and Queen on a State visit to Belgium. The shipyard having been told about this, Lord Louis said with a twinkle in his eye: 'Don't be surprised if they take a great deal more care over their painting then they otherwise might'. It worked. It helped a good deal in the way the shipyard's painters finished the wardroom as well as the Captain's quarters. They 'painted them beautifully'. As it was the war prevented the Royal visit to Belgium.

Dickie Mountbatten became a great admirer of the builders Hawthorn Leslie, especially Managing Director Robin Rowell and his managers who were, he thought, a very good team. He was constantly saying to his officers: 'The way they run this shipyard is the way a ship ought to be run'. It was a compliment indeed and the management's friendship with Mountbatten lasted many years, attending *Kelly* dinners and meeting Mountbatten when he went to Hebburn after the war to pay tribute at the graves of men lost in the North Sea. Mountbatten was struck with the frankness and honesty of Hawthorn Leslie. His faith in the shipbuilders was exemplified in one incident during the first sea trials. Run entirely by the dockyard, these had to be abandoned because in rough weather too much water was being shipped through some fans due to a technical hitch caused by forgetful dockyard mateys. The shipyard manager confessed to the Managing Director that there had been a bloomer and said 'I'm very sorry' — and that was the end of it. Mountbatten, who happened to be with the Managing Director, said this was the right form of relationship.

This rapport was emphasized when the *Kelly* was back in dockyard hands once again after the North Sea torpedoing. There were many officers and shipbuilding officials aboard when she was towed and secured outside a cruiser which was refitting. Reluctantly, Lord Mountbatten and Lieutenant-Commander Burnett agreed to the suggestion that the half dozen officers and dozen sailors who made up the towing party, by then exhausted, should go ashore and salvage men (not Hawthorn Leslie employees) would look after the ship. Next day a lot of officers' and sailors' gear had been stolen and gone from the wardroom was a silver cigarette box Hawthorn Leslie had presented to *Kelly* when she commissioned. It had been inscribed 'From Hawthorn Leslie, ship-builders, to HMS *Kelly*'. The story of the theft got about and, when the repair work had been completed, the day before *Kelly* was to sail again the dockyard manager arrived on board for a farewell drink. He had a brown paper parcel containing an identical cigarette box but the inscription now included 'shipbuilders *and repairers*'! It was extremely unusual for a ship to go back to the same yard three times especially in such a short time, and Mountbatten appreciated the leg-pull.

Admiral Burnett gave full credit to Mountbatten for saving *Kelly* when she was so appallingly damaged in the North Sea. The reason the destroyer did not sink was that in the summer of 1939 Lord Louis had gone to America to do a US damage control course. Damage control was a phrase just beginning to be heard in the Royal Navy. Most officers hardly knew what damage control meant. Mountbatten knew that with loss of buoyancy there was danger of the ship capsizing and his first reaction was: 'Throw everything topweight overboard'. Torpedoes, ready-use ammunition and boats, things on and above the upper deck, even crew members were transferred to get rid of topweight to avoid capsizing. They were also transferred because they weren't any use on board; there was no heating, no cooking facilities and they might just as well be in another ship rather than in danger on board *Kelly*. There was nothing they could do and they had to be fed. 'Damage control was something I think only one in fifty destroyer Captains were familiar with,' said Admiral Burnett. 'Any other destroyer damaged in that way would most certainly have capsized but like so many other technical subjects Mountbatten had a thorough knowledge of it.'

Burnett was one of those officers who confessed to being 'daunted' at the prospect of joining Mountbatten. He felt he was never able to be on equal terms with Mountbatten as he was with most other men. But the Captain had great regard for his First Lieutenant and they got on well. To Mountbatten it was always 'Egg' Burnett, not Philip. He was always known in the Navy as 'Egg' since his cadet days at, Dartmouth when he had eczema on one ear; this was painted with acid which made the skin turn yellow. 'I can imagine it when Mountbatten asked who was going to be his A/S man and they said "Egg" Burnett!'

When *Kelly* was in London docks for repair Mountbatten invited Burnett to dinner and on to a private theatre club to see the newly-written play 'The Jersey Lily'. (Lily Langtry was the beautiful daughter of the Dean of Jersey who caused a sensation among her friends when she became the first society women to go on to the stage, and whose admirers included King Edward VII and Prince Louis of Battenberg, Mountbatten's father.) In the taxi from the docks to the West End, Lord Louis told Burnett the story about his father running away from home to ask Queen Victoria if he might join the Royal Navy, and how his father became First Sea Lord. Mountbatten recalled that his father had been thrown out of the Navy's top post because of his German ancestry when he had spent his life trying to be British, how it had affected his two sons and of his own determination to vindicate his father's honour by becoming First Sea Lord. This, thought Burnett, was the driving force of Mountbatten's life much more than his own personal ambitions.

Before *Kelly* went to the Mediterranean Philip Burnett became anti-submarine training commander at HMS *Osprey* at Dunoon, and he and Mountbatten met again in that part of Scotland when Lord Louis became Chief of Combined Operations and went to visit landing craft training there. They were lunching together when the German battlecruisers *Scharnhorst* and *Gneisenau* boldly went up the Channel in 1942. In later years, Mountbatten invited his old First Lieutenant to be present when he received the Freedom of the City of London, and then they met by chance in a restaurant in London just after the announcement that Mountbatten had been appointed Viceroy of India. Burnett had just become engaged to his future wife and they were naturally celebrating. The Mountbatten family, including Lady Mountbatten and their two daughters, was at the other end of the restaurant. Dickie wasn't the man to fail to recognize an old shipmate and he left his table to greet the then Captain Burnett. 'I had heard of the appointment to India and said I didn't know whether to congratulate him or not', Burnett remarked. 'From his comment it seemed clear to me that I shouldn't have done. He hated the idea. He said: "What can you do when the King tells you to do it? But I got him to promise that as soon as I have finished I will return to the Navy".' Lord Mountbatten had also been cautious about the idea of going to South-East Asia as Supreme Allied Commander in the first place because he feared it might divorce him from the Navy to such an extent that he might not get another job, and Burnett knew very well Mountbatten's real ambition.

While Mountbatten had his successes in the East, Burnett had a distinguished war in Western Approaches Escort Groups and afterwards became Chief of Staff to the Commander-in-Chief, Portsmouth. He is as strong a supporter of the *Kelly* Reunion Association as was Mountbatten and is the Vice-President.

When Captain Edward Dunsterville was recommended to be 5th Destroyer Flotilla Signals Officer he was at Signals School at Portsmouth, where Mountbatten went to interview him. It was the start of a friendship which lasted for the rest of Lord Mountbatten's life. Dunsterville joined *Kelly* in June 1939 and survived the sinking after being Signals Officer of the Flotilla for the whole of the two commissions. He served with Mountbatten for a greater length of time than any other *Kelly* officer, and later met up with Mountbatten again when he was Chief Naval Signals Officer for South-East Asia. Then, when Mountbatten went to the Admiralty, Captain Dunsterville was Director of Signals. Before he joined Mountbatten, Dunsterville met a friend of his future Captain who told him: 'He'll drive you mad for six days a week. Then on Sunday he'll do something so nice that you don't mind being driven mad for the next six days and that is the way life goes on.'

There was one firm rule for officers in *Kelly*: they must never argue with Mountbatten on the bridge. 'We always had to argue with him in his cabin which was a very good rule indeed. If he wanted something done you did it straight away. If you got the chance you went down to his cabin and said "I disagree with you entirely". It was absolutely grand. He would always listen and say "We have done that and this and we will do that", once he had made up his mind. He was very much amenable to argument. It was a wonderful trait of his. He never stood just on his dignity.'

As the Flotilla Signals Officer, Dunsterville was very much like a Flag Lieutenant as well, the man who was keeping an eye on his Captain, looking after much of his arrangements. Mountbatten could be quite secretive at times about what he was trying to do and sometimes planned things without his officers knowing quite why. Frequently, of course, he had to do this for security reasons, but there were other occasions when his officers would know the immediate objective but were never quite certain what Mountbatten's end objective was. Whereas all Service messages, important or otherwise, came through the Signals Officer, Mountbatten was quite capable of thinking and planning his own personal arrangements without revealing them.

While the ship was in Blackwall in the Thames, being repaired after the collision with another destroyer, Dunsterville was duty officer one day when Admiralty Supplies rang up to say there were some stores for *Kelly* which they were sending north. Where did *Kelly* want them sent? Dunsterville said to Scapa as the ship was going there. He told Lord Louis when he arrived on board that evening and Mountbatten said: 'Oh Christ!' 'I'd got it completely wrong', says Dunsterville. 'You ought to have had them sent to Rosyth', his Captain complained. 'Why to Rosyth?', Dunsterville asked. 'Because I've invited the Duke of Kent and somebody else on board for dinner and I was going to make taking on those stores my excuse for going into Rosyth.'
'He was not going to tell me that he'd invited the Duke of Kent on board for dinner in Rosyth!' says Dunsterville. 'And this kind of thing happened more than once.'

Captain Dunsterville was on the bridge with Mountbatten at critical moments — when *Kelly* was torpedoed in the North Sea, in *Javelin* when that destroyer was badly damaged by German destroyers in the Channel (and Dunsterville was wounded) and again in *Kelly* when she saw her last action off Crete. 'We were hit in my cabin on the upper deck. I saw my golf clubs going up and we just started to capsize straight away. A most extraordinary feeling. I held on to the compass. I think I had my feet on the

shoulders of Mountbatten.' Dunsterville did not discover for more than forty years that in the water Rocky Wilkins was hanging on to his back. Rocky said to Dunsterville: 'I've never dared to admit that I saw you going past with a lifebelt. I hadn't got mine on, you had your lifebelt and you took me up.' Until he got to HMS *Kipling*, Dunsterville did not know where Lord Mountbatten was and for all he knew the Captain might have been lost. As soon as they got on board *Kipling* everybody was trying to find out about Mountbatten' fate. Suddenly, there he was, already on board. But neither he nor Dunsterville could see. They had oil in their eyes which was very uncomfortable for the rest of the morning. It didn't help matters when *Kipling* hit *Kelly*'s hulk and in so doing punctured her own auxiliary oil tank just on the water level which created a slick of oil about fifty yards wide. On the way back to Alexandria the Stukas had no trouble at all following the ship with her heavy load of survivors. Captain Dunsterville remembered that, in all, *Kipling* was attacked 108 times. Everybody was completely bomb happy after the first twenty, shouting at the German pilots comments such as 'Gosh you missed!' and 'Cor, you're no use!' There were about 600 people all told aboard *Kipling* and it would have been grim had she been sunk.

Lord Mountbatten's secretary had been killed so Dunsterville went with him to stay with Admiral Sir Andrew Cunningham, the Commander-in-Chief Mediterranean, acting as Flag Lieutenant and helping his Captain to get his affairs in order. Everybody was pretty exhausted and Dunsterville slept for three days; it was about two months before he felt all right again. Eventually Dunsterville went to the East Indies as Fleet Signals Officer stationed in Colombo (Ceylon, now Sri Lanka) with Lord Mountbatten at Kandi SEAC headquarters. Dunsterville was as much on Mountbatten's staff as he was on the East Indies staff of Admiral Arthur John Power, seeing his former Captain frequently.

Mountbatten was a great man in an important job, but he was very lonely. His wife, Edwina, was on the South-East Asia Command station but she was frequently away doing her St John and Red Cross work. Dunsterville and another former *Kelly* officer, Alastair Robin, also by then at Colombo, went to Kandy at Mountbatten's invitation for dinner and stayed the night. Mountbatten wanted to have these two old shipmates so that he could privately 'sound off' and say exactly what he thought about his senior staff Generals and Air Marshals, knowing he was speaking his mind to a private and trusted audience. 'I understood that very much,' said Captain Dunsterville. 'You know you come home at night and tell your wife exactly how you feel about things. A marvellous thing to be able to do. Edwina was nearly always away and he never had the chance to let off steam to her as she was very busy with her own work. She was a marvellous person. He absolutely adored her.'

Dunsterville was again associated with Mountbatten when the latter was C-in-C Mediterranean, for he joined him as Assistant Chief of Staff.

**COMMANDER-IN-CHIEF,
MEDITERRANEAN STATION.**

2nd July 1954

Dear Wilkins,

Thank you for your letter of 23rd June.
I have made a note of the date of the 1955 Re-union
as being on the 21st May and will do my very best to
be present.

I am glad that you presented a replica of
the KELLY's crest to the Chief Petty Officers' Mess
of H.M.S. PRESIDENT.

It is very satisfactory that we have got
130 members. I do not know how many are left who would
be available to join. The original ship's company
consisted of 260 of whom some 20 were killed in May 1940
and I imagine that about 200 new members joined on re-
commissioning at the end of 1940 of whom about 130 were
killed in May 1941. A rough calculation would therefore
be that there were 460 people who served in the KELLY of
whom at least 150 were killed leaving perhaps 210.
Allowing for 10 of those having died since it looks as
though there are not more than 70 left who would be
eligible to join.

yours sincerely,

Mountbatten of Burma

---

**FIRST SEA LORD,
ADMIRALTY,
LONDON, S.W.1.**

9th December, 1955.

Dear Wilkins,

I think I should report to your
Committee that my wife and I visited
on the 30th November, 1955, the graves
of the 27 men who were killed in May, 1940,
on board KELLY at ~~Hawthorn Leslie.~~ Hebburn

This grave has also a memorial stone
for all those who lost their lives at
Crete.

We were accompanied by Sir Robin Rowell,
Managing Director of Hawthorn Leslie, two
able seamen of the old KELLY Ship's Company
(Mr. Cash and Mr. Ellis); and two relatives
(Mrs Parker and Mrs McIntyre). The principal
foremen who worked in the construction and
repair of the KELLY were also present.
Afterwards I went and visited the T.S, KELLY
Sea Cadet Corps at Hebburn.

I enclose a series of photographs
which were taken on that occasion which
you might like to keep.

I enclose a letter I received from
Miss Louise Wilson, fiancee of Ordnance
Artificer Squance, which explains itself,
also a copy of my reply.

Perhaps you might care to send a
word to her expressing appreciation for
the way she has attended the grave at
Hebburn.

yours sincerely,

Mountbatten of Burma

---

9th December, 1954.

My dear Wilkins,

I thought that you should know that
we had a small but very successful KELLY
Re-Union at Admiralty House on the 2nd
December at which 8 survivors and their
families were present.

2 others serving in the fleet could
not be present as their ships were not in
harbour.

A group photograph was taken and in
the back row reading from left to right
you will note, Chief Steward Baldacchino who
was the Wardroom messman, Petty Officer
Steward Micallef, who was my steward and was
invalided after the Battle of Crete and is
now the catering officer at the R.A.F. Mess,
Luqa, Chief Petty Officer Wells now in the
FORTH who used to be the postman, Chief
Petty Officer Roe, who is now in the
CHARITY Petty Officer Steward Vella the late
pantry hand, the youngster at the end is the
son of Wells. In the next row are relations
of the survivors and in the front row,
Captain Dunsterville, Mrs. Dunsterville
myself, my wife, my younger daughter, Pamela,
and Captain Burnett and in front is
Micallef's young boy holding the KELLY shield
which was presented to Captain Burnett at
the last Re-Union.

yours sincerely

Mountbatten of Burma

P.S.

I also enclose a carbon copy of a letter
written to Cdr. Ferguson giving news of
another survivor ~~called~~ Foster whom I have
asked to get in touch with you or Bottoms.

Yeoman of Signals

---

**FIRST SEA LORD,
ADMIRALTY,
LONDON, S.W.1.**

12th June 1957.

Dear Wilkins,

On going through my papers the other day
I came across the enclosed photostat copy of
the signature of Admiral of the Fleet Sir John
Kelly, after whom our ship was named, which
was presented to the ship by King George VI
with an inscription in his own handwriting.
The original was framed and hung in a place
of honour in the Wardroom and, of course, went
down with the ship, but I cannot help feeling
that this photostat copy of such a unique
trophy should now rest with the Kelly Reunion.

yours sincerely

Mountbatten of Burma

Chapter 10

# *Escape in HMS* Javelin

Mountbatten was lucky to get away with his life during his time at sea in the early days of the war. He and some of his staff officers had a hair-raising escape in a Channel battle with German destroyers which was a little known story. While *Kelly* was having her extensive repairs made at Hebburn, Captain D took over the destroyer *Javelin* as leader of his 5th Flotilla. They had been doing sweeps on several occasions towards France with the possibility of meeting the enemy. On the night he met up with the German destroyers, Mountbatten had five ships and there was a similar number of Germans. At that time the Germans had flashless cordite whereas the British had full flash cordite, which was a distinct disadvantage. *Javelin* opened fire but at a very early stage she was hit by two torpedoes, one striking forward and the second striking aft. The results were very different from those experienced aboard *Kelly* when she was torpedoed in the North Sea, since all the unfortunate crew in *Javelin* forward and aft were trapped in those sections and sunk.

Captain Alastair Robin, who at the time was *Kelly*'s and the Flotilla's gunnery officer and had transferred to *Javelin* with Mountbatten, put it like this: 'We were left in the middle bit of *Javelin*. One of my memories is that breakfast was still sizzling on the hob. All we could do was to sit down and have bacon and egg and await somebody to come and pick up the bits.' The rest of the battle had continued somewhere else. *Javelin*, with no bows or stern, looked more like a tug than a handsome new destroyer when she was towed back to Plymouth. In addition to the men who lost their lives when the two ends of the vessel were torpedoed and sunk, there were injuries in the middle section of the ship including wounds sustained by the Flotilla Signals Officer, Lieutenant Dunsterville.

Alastair Robin's association with Mountbatten began before the war, in Malta when he was the gunnery officer with another famous destroyer Captain, then Commander Warburton-Lee, who was a Flotilla Divisional Commander when Mountbatten was a Sub-Divisional Commander in the same Division. Robin was in *Decoy* and Mountbatten CO of *Daring*. Both men were keen polo players — as were most officers in the Division — and Captain Robin said: 'I had tremendous admiration for a man who was prepared to spend time teaching a starter in the polo pits, a concrete pit

*HMS* Javelin *after having been torpedoed fore and aft.*

with a wooden pony, where a learner was shown how to hit and how not to hit.' Life was extremely pleasant for a young Lieutenant like Robin in those pre-war days in the Mediterranean when he was able to drive a car and play polo on his pay alone. Wealthy officers like Mountbatten owned their own ponies but others were available for hire by less fortunate officers.

So they were not strangers when Mountbatten invited the then Lieutenant Robin to lunch at Broadlands to chat him up with a view to his appointment as gunnery officer of his new Flotilla. Robin was clearly much sought after. Only a week later he had an invitation from Warburton-Lee who would have liked him to have been his Flotilla gunnery officer. (Warburton-Lee and his ship HMS *Hardy* were in the battle of Narvik, where Warburton-Lee was killed.)

Discussing Crete in later years, where his gunners behaved heroically and manned their anti-aircraft guns until the ship went down, Robin said those on the bridge were more fortunate than the others, being above any structure and fairly well away from the bomb. 'We were really simply swept out of the bridge. My own recollection of getting to Alexandria was having no possessions at all and having to go out and first of all buy a suitcase and a suit of clothes. Then I came back to the United Kingdom in *Otranto* via the Cape, in extreme luxury compared with what one had been doing before, stopping to have tremendous receptions in Durban and East London and then way out into the Atlantic to avoid submarines and so on. After a few months at home in Edinburgh I was off to Norfolk, Virginia, to join *Illustrious*. Lord Louis, though he was appointed to be Captain of *Illustrious*, didn't actually put to sea in her but among other things he went to Pearl Harbor and gave lectures to United States naval officers. Before he was able to take *Illustrious* to sea he was appointed Chief of Combined Operations.'

In *Illustrious* Robin, now promoted to Captain, went to Madagascar for the Allied landings there. For his part in the battle for Crete he was awarded the DSC. Lord Louis would, of course, have recommended him for the award but it was most pleasant for Robin to receive a letter from Mountbatten sending his congratulations and saying that his attention had been brought to the award by King George who had read of it in the newspapers and had noticed the name of the ship *Kelly*. 'It was a very kind thought of Mountbatten to write in that vein.'

Mountbatten's public appearances were tremendously well prepared, said Captain Robin. As well as having a good sense of timing Lord Louis was very conscious of the need to prepare every statement extremely carefully. Indeed, a great deal of some staff officers' time was taken up with assisting him in checking the histories of individuals the Captain was going to meet. While Mountbatten encouraged his officers as well as his ratings to enjoy themselves in their spare time, his own idea of how to enjoy spare time did not necessarily coincide with the ideas of others. His passion for the cinema was such that even when the ship had returned from an all-night patrol, and his officers were looking forward to a 'kip', Mountbatten would be keen on going to the nearest 'flick' ashore. This was the last thing most of the wardroom wanted to do, having had very little sleep at night!

One of Mountbatten's favourite films was the fantastic send-up of Hitler and Mussolini by his old friend Charlie Chaplin. It was obtained with great difficulty pre-release when the King and Queen and the two Princesses visited *Kelly* in dock in London, so that they could be entertained to their first viewing — a novel Royal premiere.

'Mountbatten was a great admirer of Chaplin (who had made a comedy featuring the Mountbattens when they were in Hollywood during their honeymoon),' Robin said. 'How he obtained the print of *The Great Dictator* I do not know, but it was a great success despite the limitations of *Kelly*'s wardroom. Lieutenant Dunsterville remembers that, as "OC Films" he had to make some ingenious improvizations in order to screen the film: the projector had to be mounted in the pantry and the film reflected off a mirror through the pantry hatch on to the screen! But it worked splendidly and the King and Queen were delighted.'

Captain Robin has several anecdotes concerning Mountbatten. When he was Assistant Fleet Wireless Officer in Malta there was a fancy dress dance in Valetta, the capital, and against all regulations 'Dickie' appeared as a Leading Telegraphist in modern-day uniform. This was absolutely taboo. It was not permissible to parade like that in Naval uniform unless the uniform was old fashioned, say one hundred years old. There was a gasp of surprise seeing Dickie arriving dressed as he was, but the high-spirited Mountbatten got away with it.

Long before it was standard practice to have zip fasteners, Mountbatten had some fitted to his trousers and demonstrated that they were perfectly safe. Everybody was intrigued to see this alternative to fly buttons, as it was literally the first time they had ever seen zip fasteners used in this way. It was typical of Mountbatten. He liked gadgets and liked to be the first to introduce them to his officers and here he was, the first in the Mediterranean at any rate, catching on to a new idea in men's dresswear.

Although there was some criticism that the Navy was without air support in their task in endeavouring to prevent German landings on

Crete — it was virtually a battle between ships of the Navy and the German Air Force — there was no carping about the lack of aircraft by Mountbatten, said Captain Robin. Lord Louis deeply recognized the hard work done by what resources the RAF had in Malta and what they achieved under impossible circumstances. *Kelly* had been in Malta while the island was being bombed to blazes and he was loud in his praise for the heroism of the few fighter pilots based there. There had been an occasion previously, when *Kelly* had been bombed in the English Channel by the Royal Air Force, and then Mountbatten did criticize them. There had been complete absence of liaison between the Navy and the RAF concerning recognition, and while the Navy had been able to recognize the aircraft the RAF appeared to be unable to recognize their own ships. German destroyers had two funnels whereas *Kelly* and her sister ships had one, and it was felt by Mountbatten to be really bad that bombs should be dropped on the 5th Destroyer Flotilla.

As a gunnery officer, Alastair Robin was in a different 'trade' from Mountbatten, who was a signals specialist. Much as Mountbatten did know about guns and gunnery, Alastair Robin felt that possibly he could 'pull the wool over his eyes' more readily than could the Signals Officer, Lieutenant Dunsterville. 'But', said Captain Robin, 'Mountbatten had done a lot of gunnery in his own ships. The standard of gunnery in *Daring* and *Wishart* had been extremely high, so high that Mountbatten had taken Flotilla prizes. One certainly felt sympathy with 'Dusty' Dunsterville who was forever under the eye of the ex-Fleet Wireless Officer!'

Captain Robin considered it should be recorded how Lord Mountbatten displayed a continued interest in the fortunes of his officers when they left the Navy. Captain Robin had a number of important appointments in the Navy after *Kelly*, in *Illustrious* and the East Indies Command and he was finally in command for two years of the cruiser *Bermuda*. 'One always felt one wouldn't be out of order at all to write to him. The personal relationship he established with everybody was such that if you had a crisis it was quite in order that you could put extra weight on him, such as a bit of help with the next job. One felt that one was being helped tremendously in appointments such as the Captain of the Fisheries Protection Fleet which I am sure I wouldn't have got without his help when he was, I think, First Sea Lord, and the same when I got command of HMS *Bermuda*.

'It ought to be said how very supportive "Dickie" was with jobs in the Navy and outside. The last supportive action for me was in getting me a splendid job as secretary at the Westminster Medical School. I'd had a year unemployed after I retired from the Royal Navy. I tried to get a decent job in Scotland. I couldn't get anything I wanted there. I did a year with Lloyd's Register of Shipping then this one as secretary of the Westminster Medical School came up. There were a lot of applications. One had to put in referees and I wrote Lord Mountbatten saying I hoped it would be all right to use him as a referee. As usual he wanted a bit of a breakdown on what would be useful for him to say.'

Captain Robin's wife was impressed by the example of 'homework' Mountbatten carried out for a speech at the first *Kelly* Reunion that she and her husband attended. Mountbatten invited the pair of them for a drink at his Wilton Crescent house. Mountbatten said to Mrs Robin: 'Are you interested in jade?' She said she would love to look at jade and he showed her cabinets of green and pink jade saying: 'I just want to get a few anecdotes from your husband because I haven't prepared my speech for tonight.' Fifteen minutes later the Robins drove with Mountbatten to the *Kelly* Dinner where he made his usual excellent, humorous, off-the-cuff speech using the information he had gleaned from Captain Robin. Mrs Robin also recalled a ceremony at Westminster Hospital many years before when a library was opened in memory of Lady Mountbatten because she had done her VAD training there. Mountbatten was there but he was ill and he stumbled and gave what was thought to be for him a noticeably bad speech.

ADMIRAL OF THE FLEET THE EARL MOUNTBATTEN OF BURMA.
K.G., P.C., G.C.B., G.C.S.I., G.C.I.E., G.C.V.O., D.S.O.

FIRST SEA LORD,
ADMIRALTY,
LONDON, S.W.1.

14th May, 1958

My dear Wilkins,

Thank you for your letter of the 9th May, with the details of the guests. I am glad that you will have the Captains of JAVELIN, JUPITER, KIMBERLEY and KASHMIR, but am sorry that KIPLING has fallen out through sickness.

There was some confusion about speeches which I thought I would clear up personally.

When I come to the Re-Unions I shall always be glad to make a speech, if desired. What I felt was that I would prefer not to come every year. My reason for this is that I am asked to a dozen or more Re-Unions every year of the various Armies, Corps, Divisions, Air Groups, etc., quite apart from naval re-unions, and although the KELLY Re-Union has a very different place in my heart, I feel it is best, on the whole, to come about every second or third year, rather than every year.

This year I shall be quite prepared to make a further short speech about the present position of the Navy, provided there are no press reporters taking down what I am saying.

Yours sincerely

Mountbatten of Burma

FIRST SEA LORD,
ADMIRALTY,
LONDON, S.W.1.

19th May, 1958

My dear Wilkins,

I am writing to congratulate the Chairman and yourself very much indeed on the most successful dinner and dance which has yet been staged by the KELLY Reunion Association. All the guests to whom I spoke were delighted with the evening and very impressed.

Please let me know well ahead the various dates which you would suggest for next year's reunion in Hebburn.

Since there was some confusion about the routine for the sitting and standing for toasts on H.M. Ships I enclose three copies of a separate chit on the subject for future reference.

Yours sincerely

Mountbatten of Burma

CHIEF OF THE DEFENCE STAFF
⬛⬛⬛⬛⬛⬛⬛⬛⬛⬛⬛⬛⬛⬛⬛⬛⬛⬛⬛⬛
⬛⬛⬛⬛⬛⬛⬛⬛⬛⬛⬛⬛⬛⬛⬛⬛⬛⬛⬛⬛
⬛⬛⬛⬛⬛⬛⬛⬛⬛⬛⬛⬛⬛⬛⬛⬛⬛⬛

at Government House, Bulawayo,

6th October 1960

Dear Wilkins,

At a Garden Party in Nairobi
among 4,000 people Lieutenant Commander
Kirkus was introduced to me.     His face
was familiar and I asked where we had met
before and he said he had served in the
KELLY, but he obviously was not an
officer at the time.

He had never heard of the Kelly
Reunion Association and I told him
I would give you his name so that you
could rope him in, if in fact he was
in the KELLY.

I enclose a card from the
private secretary to the Governor of
Kenya with Kirkus's address.

yours sincerely

Mountbatten of Burma

---

19th June 1961

't the last KELLY Reunion Dinner I had a word with Cook,
the Chairman, and Wilkins, the Secretary, about the attendance
of officers.

They pointed out that in some years they get a very full
attendance, perhaps more than really necessary, and other
years they get hardly anybody.

I myself have said that in principle I would attend every
other year, that is to say, in the odd-numbered years, but
there are 10 other surviving officers and I would like to
suggest that of those 10 we should always try and have not
less than 2 or more than 5 to attend a dinner.

I have spoken to Turnbull, who was at the last dinner,
and who goes very faithfully most years, and he has kindly
said that he would not mind acting as a sort of clearing house
for the officers for the KELLY Reunion Dinners.

The whole object would be to retain the great pleasure of
the Reunions without making them a duty in any sense of the w
but clearly the Ship's Company would value an opportunity of
seeing each of their former officers at least once in every fe
years, which I feel would not be asking too much if we are to
keep the Reunion Dinners alive.

To save you from writing unnecessary letters may I sugge
that you reply to this letter direct to Turnbull, and let him
know whether you are in agreement with my proposals.

If you are not in agreement, then please write direct to
with your suggestions.

Commander M. Evans, Royal Navy,

---

ADMIRAL OF THE FLEET THE EARL MOUNTBATTEN OF BURMA,
K.G. P.C. G.C.B. G.C.S.I. G.C.I.E. G.C.V.O. D.S.O.

CHIEF OF THE DEFENCE STAFF

MINISTRY OF DEFENCE

LONDON S.W.1

TELEPHONE  WHITEHALL 7000

15th November 1961

Dear Wilkins,

I have never worried over the inaccuracies on the
printed heading of our notepaper, since it certainly was
not worth the expense of getting it re-printed, but I
would like to draw your attention to the fact that on
the News Letters, which are typed fresh each month, it
is wrong to put "R.N.(Ret'd)" after the name of Admiral
Burnett.  Once an Admiral, always an Admiral, and in
the Royal Navy we do not recognize any others, so that
this is the one rank where R.N. is superfluous!

In my own case, the letters "A.F." may be used by
an Admiral of the Fleet with his signature, like a
Field Marshal uses "F.M."   It is never put in type
or print after an officer's name.   My full, but un-
necessarily long, description appears at the head of
this notepaper, but I would suggest that the right an acceptable
way to describe me in future would be:-

        "Admiral of the Fleet
         The Earl Mountbatten of Burma"

        yours sincerely

        Mountbatten of Burma

---

CHIEF OF THE DEFENCE STAFF

MINISTRY OF DEFENCE

STOREYS GATE, LONDON S.W.I

TELEPHONE  WHITEHALL 7000

20th February 1962

Dear Wilkins,

It will be a real help to me if
you could send me the various accounts
you have so far received of the action
in May 1940, as this would help refresh
my own memory when I try and write my
own account, and when I get it I will
send it to you to forward to Mr. Ibison,
meanwhile I return his letter to you.

        yours sincerely

        Mountbatten of Burma

Chapter 11

# Regard for Petty Officers

Mountbatten had immense respect for Naval Petty Officers and Chief Petty Officers. When his men arrived at the Hebburn shipyard from Chatham barracks to join for the second commission he, as usual, cleared lower deck to address the newcomers and afterwards assembled the Chiefs and POs to say he would regard them as commissioned officers because in a destroyer they had the responsibilities of officers.

A particularly proud man to join *Kelly* was Petty Officer Edward West, a man with many years' service already, who returned to England in August 1940 after serving in China and the Far East. After a higher gunnery course at Whale Island he went back to his depot, Chatham, where every day the notice boards were eagerly scanned by men who were due for a ship. The day came when his name was down for drafting to *Kelly*. The name *Kelly* had no special significance to West at the time as he had been away from the United Kingdom for so long, but he soon learned of her exploits and the name of her Captain. Although some of the original ship's company who had been through the North Sea drama had recommissioned, they formed a small percentage of the new crew, three quarters of whom had not been to sea before. Regular servicemen like West were therefore confronted with a huge task and a number of different instruction duties. The one aim was to make *Kelly* an efficient fighting unit again, and as soon as possible.

Apart from his action station at an AA gun, West's main duty was Petty Officer of the messdecks, an onerous job at the outset when most of the crew had not seen a messdeck in their lives. At first his unpopularity got him down. It all started when he warned the seamen, stokers and signalmen that it was not the thing to leave their hammocks slung after the hands had been called for the day's duties. He made it clear that the owner of any hammock left up would in future 'be taken aft'. The following morning after both watches had been fallen in he took the names of sixteen men who had disregarded the warning and their punishment was five days 'slack hammock drill'. The irony was that West himself had to turn out one hour before the rest of the hands to muster the offenders when they brought their hammocks to be inspected. Such was the price of discipline he felt.

With a 'green' ship's company, the destroyer set out for Scapa Flow. The same night gun flashes on the horizon led to Action Stations being called and there was consternation because, unprepared as they were, the new ratings were about to have their baptism of fire. The men had had initial training ashore but there had been no time for drilling at *Kelly*'s guns fire control or damage repair. All the 'old hands' worked feverishly, doing in minutes what would normally have taken days of drill to do, telling each man his particular duty should the ship engage the enemy. West said afterwards that enthusiasm carried the day and he was positive the ship's company would have carried out their duties in the best tradition of the Navy had it been necessary. Happily gunfire was not called for. It was units of their own Fleet causing the gun flashes as they carried out exercises of which *Kelly* was unaware.

PO West provided *Kelly*'s youngsters with their first sight of fire when he blazed away with a quadruple set of Oerlikens at one of our own aircraft which had strayed over Scapa and which had to drop its recognition flares as the pilot sheered off in a hurry. There was another diversion when turkey and plum pudding were delayed on Christmas Day while the ship dropped patterns of depth charges chasing a suspected U-boat.

Hard work and persuasion by the experienced hands eventually licked the 'beginners' into shape and the fighting qualities of HMS *Kelly* ran fairly smoothly, but West still had responsibility for the unenviable and routine task of ensuring the cleanliness and proper running of the messdecks. Peacetime regulars in the Navy could look after themselves in this respect but it was not so with average HO (hostilities only) seamen, considered West. He used to remember the first sea-going ship he went to in 1926, the coal-burning battleship *Emperor of India*. After his training in the 'stone frigate' HMS *Ganges*, the famous boys' training base at Shotley on the East Coast, the mess deck was 'strange as well as frightening'. Years afterwards, writing his memories for Lord Mountbatten, West said 'Imagine, therefore, what it was like for the men I suddenly found under my care'.

In 1940, unlike the superb messing facilities of the 1980s where there is a wide-ranging choice of meals that the crew have professionally prepared for them, most of the crew had to be taught the rudiments of cooking, or at least the preparation of food in the trays and pans for cooking. In destroyers each mess was responsible for preparing food for its own meals. They then took the food to the galley where a ship's cook saw that it went into the oven and was properly done. Each man in every mess was detailed to prepare the food and scrub out the mess over a period of 24 hours. 'Some of the dishes thus produced I leave to your imagination', West wrote.

The worst part of West's job was when *Kelly* returned to harbour. Invariably the messdecks got flooded after a spell at sea and after constant watches — at times they were at Action Stations all night — the men would return to their quarters and flop down where they could. West always insisted on the drying and cleaning of the messdecks, all wet clothing hung up and messdecks thoroughly ventilated before his men relaxed. Eventually his charges realized that what he made them do was for their own good, so he did not mind his own 'temporary unpopularity'.

West's account of life down below in *Kelly*, a detailed narrative amounting to some thousands of words, was acclaimed by Lord

Mountbatten who scrutinized it before it went into his collected papers at Broadlands. Mountbatten found West's recollections 'human and moving' and said 'It gives me quite an insight into what the lower deck felt about it all'.

West had a memory for happenings on the lighter side that made Mountbatten chuckle. *Kelly* put into Dartmouth to embark a detachment of Commandos for 24 hours' sea training. The Commandos were well-equipped and well-clothed, including superb leather jerkins. After *Kelly* disembarked the soldiers and left harbour to return to Plymouth, West raised his eyebrows. He said he couldn't understand how such a number of the crew appeared in leather jerkins!

On Saturdays 'His Lordship', as West called him, did Captain's rounds. He inspected the ship from stem to stern, a routine in every ship in the RN, war or no war. After all his bullying and cajoling West was proud of the results achieved and 'without boasting thought *Kelly* had the cleanest and brightest messdeck in the entire flotilla, as it should have been because the leader should set an example'. This particular morning he spurred on the cooks of messes and sweepers into making the after seamen's mess vie with the forward one and the stokers' with the signalmen's. 'Everything was sparkling, neat and shipshape and I waited to stand the rounds on the after seamen's messdeck. Looking at one of the mess shelves I saw something was out of place and told the cook of the mess to rectify it. In doing so he upset a large tin of dried peas, which rolled to every corner of the mess. At the same time I heared the Quartermaster piping the Captain on his rounds. We went on our hands and knees frantically chasing peas and only succeeded in making it worse.'

'I leave it to your imagination', West told Lord Mountbatten all those years later, 'what I told the cook of the mess when I had him on the mat afterwards'. West's face was red at the time but Mountbatten appreciated the hilarious situation.

Another awkward moment the Petty Officer got away with happened while out on patrol in the Channel one night. He was on the bridge when he saw Mountbatten's cap just inside the Captain's sea cabin. West picked it up and put it on. West said his head was average size, nevertheless the Captain's cap dropped right over his ears and eyes. West was walking to his gun, hands stretched out before him, mimicking a sleep-walker, saying 'The blackout is blacker than usual', when he walked right into Lord Louis!

Pin-ups have come on a long way since 1940. But there were some rare, and for those days daring, collections in destroyers. 'Going down through the centre of the PO's mess was the gun support of No 2 gun. Plastered all round was the best collection of pin-ups it was ever my privilege to see. One weekend afternoon when we were lying in the dockyard at Portsmouth, the Captain came over the fo'c's'le brow with Lady Mountbatten. He must have informed her ladyship that the POs of the *Kelly* were keen students of art because he lifted her up to gaze through the porthole at our pictures.'

A typically magnanimous gesture by *Kelly*'s Captain concerned leave-breaking. 'Woe betide the man who came aboard adrift. Leave-breaking was taboo.' But West recalled the case of the rating who arrived back in London docks two or three hours late because of a damaged ankle. Mountbatten himself took up the incident in comments he made on Petty

Officer West's recollections. 'I remember the story particularly well', Lord Mountbatten wrote in June 1973. 'It was a stoker who sprained his ankle on leaving his home at Hebburn. With great pluck he carried on and with the help of shipmates he found at Newcastle Station and in London actually limped back ... I cleared lower deck and told the ship's company that next time he would get full leave with both watches, though of course our sailing for the Mediterranean prevented me from carrying out my promise.' West commented: 'The skipper was always like that, scrupulously fair, full of encouragement, but down on offenders like a ton of bricks when they really deserved it. Many and varied are the tales that are told about him but to me he was a Captain under whom it was an honour and privilege to serve. There wasn't a single man in the whole of the *Kelly* ship's company who would not have followed him to hell and back if the need had arisen.'

On the way out to Malta West took the opportunity of telling his men what they could expect 'in the way of shore leave'. Any sailor who had done a commission before the war knew that the forms of relaxation were many. No visit to Malta would be complete without a visit to 'The Gut', the narrow and notorious street in Valletta which in peaceful pre-war days was full of dance halls, cafés and bars. The owners of various nationalities vied with one another, he told them, to entice the sailors into their establishments. 'Come in Jack. All your ship's company inside. They both drunk.'

When West and his shipmates got ashore, however, it was a vastly different Malta from the place he had known in 1930. 'Gone were all the bright lights, the laughter. "The Gut" was deserted, most of its cafes and bars were closed. Even the sunlit streets, once so gay and thronged with people, had taken on that sombre look which only catstrophe can give. Catastrophe had indeed struck the island. The Luftwaffe were working themselves up to a frenzy to knock out this little island which was the remaining bastion between the eastern and western Mediterranean.'

In the short time *Kelly* was based at Malta, the bombs continued to pour down day and night. It seemed, West said, that all the hate and spite of the Germans was being concentrated on tiny, gallant Malta. He railed at the 'toad Mussolini', the Italian dictator, who asked to send his own bombers in, thinking they were on to an easy thing, and he referred to 'Pip, Squeak and Wilfred' the three obsolete Gladiator biplanes which, apart from the AA guns, were Malta's only defence against the Luftwaffe until reinforcements of Spitfires were flown in. (Here Mountbatten, who vetted every line of his ratings' offerings, corrected PO West. 'The three fighter planes which defended Malta: I always thought they were called Faith, Hope and Charity'.)

Mountbatten made no comment on the following passage in West's saga. He was as proud as any Naval officer of the destroyer he commanded, both in its efficiency and appearance, so we can assume the story is accurate or that Mountbatten enjoyed it whether it was mythical or not. 'We were at sea one day when we passed very close to HMS *Warspite* (Admiral Cunningham's flagship). I am afraid we did not stick to any conventional uniform aboard *Kelly*. In fact to see us you would have thought us the worst looking lot of cut-throats you had ever seen. I heard afterwards that they had it piped aboard *Warspite*, "The destroyer now passing us is Captain Lord Louis Mountbatten and his gang of pirates".'

Petty Officer West's mention of the Oerlikon gun brought some appreciative remarks from his Captain. The 20 mm Oerlikon was adopted by the Royal Navy in 1938 as its standard light anti-aircraft weapon on all ships. Shortly afterwards the US Navy made the same decision and the Oerlikon was also extensively used by Germany and Japan. Mountbatten stated: 'It is interesting to note that West was manning the port Oerlikon and [Leading Seaman] Crisp the starboard one because recently our navigator, Captain Butler-Bowden, wrote and said that the Oerlikon guns which I had requested didn't arrive in time to be fitted. I was certain his memory was at fault and now this confirms that we did have Oerlikons . . . I am gratified by his [West's] remark, "It is in my opinion, as well as that of any other man who had used one, that they were the finest close-range weapon we had". I say this because it took me several months to persuade the Admiralty to take the Oerlikon and I only finally got it through by seeing the new First Sea Lord, Sir Roger Backhouse, about this personally.'

CHIEF OF THE DEFENCE STAFF
MINISTRY OF DEFENCE
STOREY'S GATE, LONDON S.W.I
TELEPHONE WHITEHALL 7000

8th May 1962

My dear Wilkins,

I am writing to send my
very best wishes for the Annual
Dinner of the H.M.S. Kelly
Reunion Association on Saturday,
and I am sure it will be the
greatest success ever.

I shall be thinking of you
while I am in Athens where I am
to attend the wedding of two of
my cousins.

By curious coincidence
the date is the 49th anniversary
of my joining the Royal Navy as
a small naval cadet on 8th May
1913.

Yours sincerely,

Mountbatten of Burma

---

CHIEF OF THE DEFENCE STAFF
MINISTRY OF DEFENCE
STOREY'S GATE, LONDON S.W.I
TELEPHONE WHITEHALL 7000

8th July 1963

My dear Wilkins,

I feel I must tell you a word
about ( a U.S. writer ). I am told he
is a very high class author and he
asked my concurrence to write a story
of my life. He is the fifteenth
author to have made this request and I
am determined not to be personally
associated with any biography written
during my lifetime.

I personally have refused him all
co-operation, but naturally I cannot
prevent him from seeing those who
served with me. If we cannot stop this
book then it is better that he should
get the truth than write something half-bak

I therefore write to say that I have
no objection to any help you would like to
give him on your own responsibility provide
it is quite clear that this book will not
be authorised by me or helped personally
by me in any way.

Yours sincerely

Mountbatten of Burma

---

CHIEF OF THE DEFENCE STAFF
MINISTRY OF DEFENCE
STOREY'S GATE, LONDON. S.W.I
TELEPHONE WHITEHALL 7000

at King Edward VII Hospital.

2nd March 1964

Dear Wilkins,

I am writing to thank you and
the other members of the KELLY
Re-union who signed that really
delightful card which has gone down
very well with my nurses.

Yours sincerely,

Mountbatten of Burma

---

MINISTRY OF DEFENCE

MAIN BUILDING, WHITEHALL, LONDON, S.W

TELEPHONE WHITEHALL 7022

7th July 1964

Dear Wilkins,

I was so glad to hear that the visit to Hebburn-
on-Tyne went well. The proposal to place a book
recording the names of those who died aboard KELLY
in St. Cuthbert's Church sounds a good idea.

I am asking the Navy Department Casualty Section
to send direct to you the official list of those who
were killed or died from wounds in the action with
E Boats in the North Sea in May 1940 and also a list
of those who were lost when the ship was sunk in the
Battle of Crete in May 1941 or died subsequently of
wounds.

Yours sincerely

Mountbatten of Burma

Chapter 12

# Norway: Gallant destroyers

As Lord Mountbatten approached his eightieth birthday he planned a tribute to his *Kelly* survivors in the form of a print of one of the best and latest pictures of *Kelly*. The marine artist Mark Myers was commissioned to paint *Kelly* turning to go into Namsos town to rescue beleaguered British and French troops during the disastrous campaign in Norway in 1940. Mountbatten had to take *Kelly* at considerable speed up the fiord. It was a bold piece of seamanship to lead a Flotilla at 26 knots along such a narrow fjord to help extricate nearly 5,500 of our troops there, an adventurous and tricky role of which Mountbatten was proud. Namsos was exposed to air attack and Admiral John H. D. Cunningham (later Sir John Cunningham, C-in-C Mediterranean and First Sea Lord), who had sailed from Scapa with the cruisers *Devonshire*, *York* and *Montcalm* (French), the *Kelly* and other destroyers and three French transports, was anxious to complete the rescue in one night. It was considered ashore in Namsos that this was inconceivable in the few hours of darkness and Cunningham decided to use some of his warships to augment the transports. The British General Carton de Wiart said that during that last endless day the Navy sent him a message that they could evacuate the whole of his force that night. 'I thought it was impossible but learned a few hours later that the Navy do not know the word.'

Myers' Namsos painting, an inspiring work showing *Kelly* making a fast and graceful turn to starboard at 22:00 hours 1 May 1940, with the red blaze of Namsos in the background, entailed visits to Namsos by the Cornish artist to get the light and even the ship's angle absolutely right, and Mountbatten carefully supervised and approved every stage of the work. When he saw the final sketches he declared to Myers: 'That's it. You've caught it exactly.' The prints, signed by Mountbatten, were to have been presented by him to the *Kelly* Association members at their 1980 reunion but this was prevented by his murder. Mountbatten's daughter Patricia gave permission for each print to bear his facsimile signature. She said: 'My father was deeply involved with this project from the start and indeed chose the subject himself. To ensure authenticity he made his private records available to the artist. He was delighted with the results.' Framed prints were eventually handed to the *Kelly* survivors, officers and men, by the Prince of Wales. A limited number of prints were also sold to raise funds for the Mountbatten Memorial Trust.

Having been active in the Norway campaign in other ways, it had been Mountbatten's wish to return to Namsos to see the little town for himself. As it was, it was not until after his death that a *Kelly* Association party of eight, led by Lord Mountbatten's friend and Flotilla Signals Officer Captain Edward Dunsterville (who had been in *Kelly* when she went up the fjord) and organized by C. R. (Tug) Wilson, went to Norway to be fêted by the town's civic leaders. They sailed from the Tyne to Oslo in September 1981, went overnight by train to Trondheim and Steinkjer and on to Namsos by coach. At a civic gathering fully covered by Norwegian television Captain Dunsterville presented the town with a copy of the Namsos painting for permanent display in the town hall and he and two of the party, Harry Lord and John Morrice, who were also in *Kelly* when she entered Namsos, related accounts of their experiences. Some of the older townsfolk recalled that the Germans destroyed the town and would not allow rebuilding by its inhabitants, many of whom had to live in rough conditions in the surrounding rugged countryside, sleeping in barns and caves in the hills. The *Kelly* party feasted on salmon caught in the fjord by the Mayor, who led a convoy of cars to the summit of the highest hill featured in Myers' painting so the party could have a bird's eye view of the fjord their ship had to negotiate before turning to head for the town which was ablaze from the German bombing. Captain Dunsterville also laid a wreath on Namsos war memorial.

The Norwegians are mindful of the part the Royal Navy played in the early part of the war when it tried in vain to stop the German occupation of their country. *Kelly* played an important and successful rôle but there were other British destroyers whose famous actions also stirred the

*The painting of HMS Kelly approaching Namsos, with Lord Mountbatten's cap and sword.*

*A contingent of Kelly survivors returns to Norway to present a picture of Kelly to the town of Namsos where she took part in a daring evacuation in the early part of World War 2. From left to right: Fred Lucas, Vernon Shaw, Tug Wilson, Captain Dunsterville, Ron Hall, Rocky Wilkins, John Morris and Harry Lord.*

imagination of the Norwegians and the people in the United Kingdom. What a Navy Britain had in those days! There was a magnificent bunch, an extremely large number, of brilliant destroyer Captains ready for the fray. Like the Battle of Britain pilots who were to make history for their exploits later, the destroyer Captain Ds and the commanding officers in their Flotillas performed superbly, whether it was out in the oceans with the convoys or fighting the German navy around the coasts of Northern Europe.

One of Mountbatten's fellow commanding officers in the 1st Destroyer Flotilla when Mountbatten commanded *Wishart* was Captain B. A. W. ('Wash') Warburton-Lee. Warburton-Lee commanded the Flotilla Leader, HMS *Hardy*. With his sister ships HMS *Hunter* and HMS *Havoc* he made his way in snowstorms and bad visibility to Narvik harbour at dawn to inflict damage on merchantmen and have a running battle with the German navy. *Hardy* opened up with gunfire and used torpedoes, sank the German commodore's ship and caused heavy damage. Warburton-Lee was under direct instructions from the Admiralty in London who told him: 'You alone can judge whether in these circumstances attack should be made. We shall support you whatever decision you take.' Warburton-Lee was determined to do as much damage as possible and, not content with his first foray, he went into Narvik a second time. More German destroyers appeared and in a ferocious fight *Hardy* was at last disabled and Warburton-Lee killed. He was awarded the Victoria Cross posthumously. Admiral Sir Andrew Cunningham said on several occasions that *Hardy*'s Captain was one of the best destroyer officers to have served under his command. He was a pal of Mountbatten.

Many of *Kelly*'s active service ratings as well as some of the officers had former shipmates in the gallant *Hardy*. It was the same with HMS *Cossack*, whose Captain, Philip (later Sir Philip) Vian would eventually command the Navy in the D-Day assault on Normandy. *Cossack*'s bold action in

Norway roused the nation and Captain Vian became a household name in the early months of World War 2 when the cards were stacked against Britain. For weeks the Navy had searched for the 12,000-ton German supply vessel *Altmark*, whose parent ship *Graf Spee* had been scuttled after the stirring Battle of the River Plate. It was believed the *Altmark* held prisoner 300 British Merchant Navy seamen whose ships had been captured and sunk by German raiders on the high seas. Eventually the *Altmark* was spotted off Trondheim before she entered Jossing Fjord, a 1½-mile-long inlet, and anchored. Territorial rights were complicated but eventually *Cossack* got her orders to go in — and go in she did indeed, in the style of our Navy in Nelson's or Drake's days. *Cossack* entered the fjord at ten o'clock at night and placed herself alongside *Altmark* with the famous cry from the boarding party: 'The Navy is here!' There was little resistance. By midnight the rescued British seamen were safely aboard the *Cossack* and shortly found themselves at Rosyth instead of in prisoner-of-war camps in Hitler's Europe. It was better than singeing the King of Spain's beard. *Hardy*, *Cossack*, *Kelly* and dozens more should never be forgotten.

MINISTRY OF DEFENCE

MAIN BUILDING, WHITEHALL, LONDON, S.W.I

TELEPHONE WHITEHALL 7022
in Wellington
4th March 1965

CHIEF OF THE DEFENCE STAFF

My dear William,

In Sydney I came across another of our shipmates, Norman Simmonds, who served as a young AB from the second commission to the time the ship was sunk.

He had not heard of the Reunion Association but was very keen to join and get news of his former shipmates.

I enclose a cutting about our meeting. He is at present self employed as a stove enameller.

In Wellington I met two further Kelly survivors. The first one, Gamble, joined as a boy at Chatham in September 1939 and only left early in 1941. He had never heard of the Kelly Reunion Association.

The second one, Stewart, tells me he is a member of the Association, but I give you both their addresses over.

I also met Quale again at Auckland in good form. His address is as you doubtlessly know:

Please write to Gamble

yours sincerely

Mountbatten of Burma

FIRST SEA LORD,
ADMIRALTY,
LONDON, S.W.1.

### KELLY REUNION

### MESSAGE FROM FIRST SEA LORD

I am very sorry that I cannot be with you this evening, particularly as I should like to have expressed to you all my pleasure at the strides the Association has made in the last few years. I congratulate all concerned on the good work they have put in.

I am glad to have been able to put two more **Kelly** survivors in touch with our Secretary as a result of my recent visits to Australia and New Zealand.

We flew over the exact spot where the **Kelly** went down 15 years ago and I was happy once more to pay a silent tribute. I was also glad to be able to lay a wreath with my wife on the memorial last November at Hebburn, where we met a number of survivors and relatives. The grave is beautifully looked after by our friends in Hebburn.

I now send you all good wishes for a successful evening in 1956 and look forward to the next reunion which I hope I shall be able to enjoy with you.

Chapter 13

# The heroine of Plourivo

One night in January 1941 *Kelly* was on patrol in the hazardous western end of the Channel. She was working out of Plymouth with other ships of the 5th Flotilla doing sweeps and escorting fast British minelayers operating off the French coast in the vicinity of Brest, then one of the most important of the ports occupied by the Germans. *Kelly* was west of the Channel Islands not very far off Brittany. It was nine o'clock, the night was dark and the sea was calm but the wind was freshening. *Kelly*'s crew were at Action Stations.

The first indication of something suspicious came with a small blip on the radar screen in *Kelly*'s plotting room. The destroyer's bridge was told of the object, not many yards away on the starboard side. As *Kelly* sailed past it was thought for a moment that the radar had thrown up a Nazi E-boat lying stopped. Mountbatten ordered his searchlights turned on to what was revealed to be a 20-ft fishing vessel painted white and with one sail. The fishing vessel was heading north-west but was practically stopped. *Kelly*'s pom-poms were already trained and fired a couple of bursts over the little vessel. It was a mistake and Mountbatten, annoyed, at once rang the cease-fire gongs.

Ordinary Seaman Bill Dunn, who had spotted the vessel on the radar, was ordered to go to the main deck of *Kelly* where he was within hailing distance of the little boat. As it neared *Kelly* he shouted: 'Who are you? Where are you going at this time of night?' There were five occupants of the boat and their leader replied in English that they were French fishermen. From the bridge Lord Mountbatten ordered, 'Tell them to come alongside.' They were taken aboard via a rope ladder, then *Kelly* switched off her searchlights, went 'Slow Ahead' together, put on speed and left the fishing boat behind empty and adrift. The French-speaking Bill Dunn was placed in charge of the escapees, for that is what they were. The group of gallant Frenchmen had come away from their homes near Paimpol under the noses of the Germans and were determined to get to England to join General de Gaulle's Free French. Far from being a fisherman, their leader was a distinguished French aristocrat, Count Henri de Mauduit, whose Château du Bourblanc was only five miles from the fishing village from which they had dodged the Germans and set sail for

*While HMS* Kelly *was on night patrol in the English Channel she picked up a party of five Frenchmen in a fishing boat who were making their way to England to join the Free French forces. The leader of the party, seated at the top of the table, was Count de Mauduit who was an important person in the French colonial service.*

freedom. They knew nothing about *Kelly* or Mountbatten but were delighted to be aboard a British warship. Their luck was in.

It was not long before de Mauduit and his compatriots were led to 'someone very tall, the Captain, who said in excellent French: "I am happy to receive you here since you want to join General de Gaulle"'. Lord Louis shook their hands and added: 'I cannot take you immediately to England because I'm on patrol on the way to Brest to escort a ship'. The Frenchmen were invited to the wardroom, made comfortable in arm-chairs, with crew members on sentry duty, and they opened a large basket they had brought with them containing sandwiches prepared by the Count's wife and bottles of cognac and champagne which they offered to share with Dunn.

Count de Mauduit's story was a dramatic one. He had been a French colonial administrator on the Ivory Coast when he heard of the declaration of war and then the defeat of France in 1940. He was determined to get back to France and fight against the Germans. Although the demarcation line between Vichy France and his home in Brittany was said to be impenetrable without a pass, he got on to a train and arrived home without any trouble. While the Countess de Mauduit, Betty — Scots-born and brought up in the USA — was preparing to use their large old château up on a hill on the Cotes-du-Nord to shelter British airmen and other allied fighters on an escape route back to Britain, her husband decided, if he could, to get to London to put himself under the orders of de Gaulle. In the few weeks he was at home in his château he discussed his plan with his wife who agreed. He found a man in nearby Paimpol on the coast who owned a fishing boat. It was not too difficult to put to sea since the Germans allowed fishing expeditions by day as they were useful for food supplies, but boats had to return by dusk. Two young men from a local school of navigation joined de Mauduit and the boat's owner. They spent a day fishing to allay suspicion and at nightfall instead of returning to Paimpol they sought the shelter of a small island to avoid German launches checking the coast for boats not already back in port.

Because of sandbanks and pitch darkness it was a difficult departure but a good wind got them to the open sea. They heard overhead German planes returning from bombing raids on the United Kingdom and this strengthened their resolve to get into the struggle as soon as possible. They pointed their craft north-west to get away from the approaches to Jersey and Guernsey, which were also occupied by the Germans, but their two young navigators were way out in their dead reckoning. When HMS *Kelly* met them they thought they were but twenty miles from the English coast and had hove to in order to achieve a landfall in Devon or Cornwall in daylight. In fact, when they encountered *Kelly* they were still not far from France and they would have been lucky to have escaped detection by German vessels much longer. One of the gunshots from *Kelly* landed close by in the water and rocked the boat. They were blinded by the destroyer's searchlights and they thought the dark shape which towered nearby would crush them. De Mauduit was greatly relieved when he heard the voice of Bill Dunn. He recognised that Dunn's French was 'coloured by a strong Scottish accent' like his wife's.

During two days aboard *Kelly*, when they learned from the crew that the Captain was a relative of King George VI, they were allowed to stroll freely round the decks. Back in Plymouth Lord Louis said: 'I regret I cannot help you any more as I am obliged to deliver you into the hands of the port authorities.' Before leaving their 'host' they drank a toast to 'victory' in champagne from their basket, kept a bottle of cognac, and left the other bottles for *Kelly*.

Ashore, the freed Frenchmen were taken 'very pleasantly' to prison and put up for the night. They gave the prison governor the bottle of cognac and the governor's wife in exchange took them tea and biscuits. Next day de Mauduit and his companions were taken by train to London by two policemen. They were 'overwhelmed by the kind attentions of other travellers'. In London, the head of college premises where they were interrogated gave de Mauduit half a crown to buy cigarettes. The five Frenchmen were massively questioned about the German occupation of

*The five escaping Frenchmen from Paimpol are questioned in* Kelly's *wardroom. From left to right: a cadet, Count de Mauduit, Jean Chadron, a cadet and Leon le Bouedec.*

the Brittany coast. The Count's companions eventually were enrolled in the Free French Navy while de Mauduit, who was able to give his questioners the names of relatives in London, his sister and his wife's cousin, was taken to meet de Gaulle at the General's London headquarters in Carlton Gardens. After a month de Mauduit was sent by de Gaulle as Governor General of Equatorial Africa. This did not please him at all. He didn't like 'kicking his heels' for eighteen months in Africa but managed to become attached to one of his colleagues returning to London. From then he became associated with Colonel Remy, the French wartime resistance hero, doing dangerous work in his home country. He trained to be a parachutist at Glencoe in Scotland and was dropped in France 24 hours before the D-Day landings.

The Count's adventures were only half the story of the de Mauduits' wartime bravery. He came into the *Kelly* Reunion Association story in May 1961 after Lord Mountbatten had met him again. Mountbatten had been honoured with the Freedom of Paimpol. He told Rocky Wilkins: 'Paimpol is now "twinned" with Romsey and Count de Mauduit came over with the delegation from Paimpol. He kept talking about his adventure with the *Kelly* and when I told him that there was an annual reunion dinner he asked if there would be a chance of him being able to come over and attend one as he would be quite willing to pay for his dinner.' So both the Count and Countess de Mauduit met the *Kelly* survivors at the following year's reunion. The Count made a point of saying to Bill Dunn (who during the war became a Lieutenant in the Royal Navy) that he recognized his voice as the French-speaking Scotsman who hailed him and his friends in the Channel twenty years before.

He said to Dunn, 'You must all come back to France'.

Dunn asked, 'Who?'

De Mauduit said: 'The crew'.

Dunn replied: 'There's an awful lot'.

The reply was: 'It doesn't matter how many there are. Bring them back to France.'

Lord Mountbatten was invited too but he wrote to de Mauduit thanking him for the invitation 'which I found on my return from a visit to Haile Selassie in Addis Ababa and a visit to the Isle of Wight to be installed as Governor by the Queen'. He added that the date of the *Kelly* Association visit to France 'is the very date on which I have been invited

*Kelly survivors visit the Count and Countess de Mauduit in France.*

*The Count and Countess de Mauduit standing by a chestnut tree which was planted in Paimpol by Mountbatten.*

by the Queen to go to Balmoral so I am afraid I can't accept'.

Ex-Lieutenant Bill Dunn, Rocky Wilkins and others went to the château. There was a large party of thirteen *Kelly* Association members, some accompanied by their wives. De Mauduit laughingly made two provisos with Dunn. First he reminded Dunn that when the Frenchmen disembarked from *Kelly* they also left five bottles of cognac. When he visited the château Dunn could return the cognac! Bill Dunn took five bottles of Scotch. The second condition involved a giant chocolate cake. When her husband was to make his escape from France his wife included among the provisions she packed a giant home-made chocolate cake. After the war he told his wife the *Kelly* crew had enjoyed the cake and the Count had also told his friend Remy the same fib. The truth was this, said de Mauduit: 'The cake was too big. Here we were trying to escape with this handicap of the chocolate cake. I threw it into the first ditch when we had left the château and got down the road a bit. But don't tell my wife.'

'"By jove", the Count's wife said to me', Bill Dunn recalls, '"I heard you enjoyed the chocolate cake!" "Not half we did", said I.'

For their visit as guests of the Count and Countess the *Kelly* contingent flew to Jersey and then went to Dinard where they were met by the Count who had seven large cars waiting to take them the hour's drive westwards along the coast to his château. It was a large rambling place with barns and outhouses, centuries old, which the visitors thought looked like Colditz. They were greeted with drinks and sweets and shown to their bedrooms with four-poster beds. They dined that night in the great hall with a sumptuous menu specially prepared by the Countess. The whisky was opened and many other drinks as well. In their honour the Countess had created a '*Kelly* Club' in the château for the duration of the holiday. The *Kelly* visitors were taken below to see Henri de Mauduit's magnificent

*The Chateau du Bourblanc, home of the Count and Countess de Mauduit, from which the Countess helped stranded Allied airmen to escape across the Channel.*

cellar and there was a bottle of one of the finest clarets for each to take home.

It was not until the day after their arrival that the *Kelly* men learned the true story of Betty de Mauduit, the Heroine of Plourivo, whose name was celebrated on the Cotes-du-Nord and throughout France. As far as she had been concerned France's defeat in 1940 was only a disastrous episode in a war which she was quite certain would end in Hitler's Nazis being crushed. By the time her husband had arrived back from Africa Hitler had given up his plan to invade Britain and Betty was quite certain it would not be long before the RAF would repay what the Luftwaffe was doing to Britain by bombing factories of the Third Reich. If some airmen were shot down and came knocking at her door for help, she asked, how could she possibly send them away? Her husband agreed and Betty joined the Resistance.

It was thanks to their dog's nosiness that, between two floors in the old château, a 'secret' space big enough to hide several crews from British bombers had been revealed. In fact Château du Bourblanc became an important last stop on one of the escape routes back to England. At one time up to 36 British and Allied airmen at a time hid from the Germans in Betty's home. During the day the fleeing airmen had to lie low in their hideout. They dared not smoke in case the Germans paid a call because the smell of smoke would have given away their presence, so they had to emerge from the château into the night air for a cigarette. There was a network of Resistance men and women who led the airmen in small groups to the château then to the last links in their escape route. They were got out by submarine and fast launches and a Lysander aircraft regularly flew in and out of a nearby covert landing ground, occasionally bringing the same day's English morning newspapers.

Although the Germans became curious about the château they did not take over there while Betty de Mauduit was in residence. But, the *Kelly* men were told, to allay suspicion German officers were entertained there to dinner on occasion, dinners that were more like banquets. There was even one meal when Betty, who had hardly any staff, actually persuaded two Allied pilots on the run to act as butlers and waiters at the Germans' table. They got away with it by using nods and gesticulations without saying a word to the SS officers, who were made happy with food and plenty of drink.

But eventually Château du Bourblanc's secret came out. Betty was in the kitchen making a christening cake for somebody in the tiny village below the château when a handsome young German officer stepped into the kitchen, clicked his heels, saluted and told Betty: 'Madam, I have orders to arrest you. We understand you are assisting Allied fliers to escape.' Betty endeavoured not to look surprised and turned to a twelve-year-old girl servant saying: 'Anne Marie, the carrots are cooked,' at the same time asking the officer: 'Would you like to stay for lunch?' The young German said he was honoured. The little girl servant left the kitchen, got on her bicycle and went hastily to warn the village of Plourivo with the words: 'The carrots are cooked, the carrots are cooked'. Colloquially in that region it meant the game was up. It was the code phrase telling the trusted locals that the Countess de Mauduit had been arrested.

After the young officer and his guard ate lunch the search party combed the château. No escapees were found but they discovered the secret hide-out and evidence that it had been occupied recently. When the message 'The carrots are cooked' reached the village Resistance workers it was a signal for them to go into action. The airmen were taken out of the secret room, through the false floor of a gigantic wardrobe, down a ladder and into a long tunnel which had been made centuries ago when the château was built. While the young German officer and his small guard ate their splendid lunch in the banqueting hall the airmen upstairs had been smuggled away. The lunch was too good and the search too late.

Betty de Mauduit was taken off to Ravensbrück concentration camp near Potsdam, the largest in Germany for women internees, where she suffered privation, cruel treatment and torture. She was kicked off a top bunk, her back was badly injured and she was unfit for any work, but had she ceased work she would have faced extermination. Her fellow prisoners realized how important a person she was and practically carried her to work, hiding her during working hours and taking her back to the living quarters afterwards. The women were engaged carrying bodies of fellow prisoners who had been gassed because they were unable to work. They were forced to take the dead for cremation in the incinerators. This grim work went on for many months. The action of Betty's fellow prisoners saved her life, she said. Her imprisonment lasted three years, and she was released when the American Army entered the concentration camp. Because she said she had lived in New York the Countess was sent to the United States but she was reunited with the Count after four years' separation. To their great joy Henri de Mauduit marched down the Champs Elysées with the Free French Forces when Paris was liberated.

Bill Dunn, who did the interpreting, and Rocky Wilkins who, it turned out, was the man who fired the pom-poms over the sailing vessel and was hauled over the coals by Mountbatten, maintained close friendship with the de Mauduits. Dunn, who after the war became a successful miller near Glasgow, was in contact with the Edinburgh Festival authorities about this brave Scots-born woman, who was awarded the Legion of Honour and the Croix de Guerre. He felt she should have some recognition in Scotland for her exploits and contribution to the Allied Victory. He thought: 'Here is a woman who should be honoured and invited to "close down" the famous tattoo on one of the evenings'. Unfortunately Betty de Mauduit became too ill to travel and like her husband is now dead.

MINISTRY OF DEFENCE

MAIN BUILDING, WHITEHALL, LONDON, S.W.I

TELEPHONE WHITEHALL 7022

CHIEF OF THE DEFENCE STAFF      1st July 1965

My dear Wilkins,

.How nice of Count de Mauduit to invite a party of members and their wives to spend a weekend at his Chateau during September. Do let me know what happens about this.

When I visited the Joint Services Staff College at Latimer on the 25th June, I heard that there was a member of the KELLY's ship's company with a furniture removal firm who tried to see me, but came to the College just too late. I wonder who it was? I am sorry to have missed him.

This letter requires no answer, of course.

your sincerely

Mountbatten of Burma

---

(Translation of letter from Le Comte H. de Maudit)

29th September 1965

Allow me to send all my thanks for the photograph which you dedicated and which Mr. Wilkins brought with him on your behalf. This touched me very much and I am most grateful to you.

All our friends of the Kelly left us on Monday and the house now seems very large since their departure. It was a great joy and a real pleasure for us to receive them. We hope that they will have happy memories of their all too brief visit to Bourblanc.

Everything went off very well and even the weather spoilt us with the warm sun.

We sincerely hope that this first visit to Brittany will not be the last and that it is the prelude to future similar reunions.

---

1st October 1965

Thank you so much for your letter of 29th September with your interesting account of the visit of the Kelly Representatives.

I have also received a long and enthusiastic letter from Wilkins, with a map showing the routes along which you took the party to Brest, etc., and an account of every detail of their visit, including a copy of the menu the Countess de Mauduit produced for the temporary "Kelly Club" which you kindly installed for the visit!

How nice of you to hope that this might be repeated in the future; I am sure that there is nothing which the Kelly survivors would appreciate more.

I am sending a translation of your letter and a copy of this reply to Wilkins for the Kelly Re-union members.

With my kindest regards to Countess de Mauduit and yourself.

Le Comte H. de Mauduit,

---

BROADLANDS,
ROMSEY.
HAMPSHIRE.

TELEPHONE
ROMSEY 33

31 July, 1965.

Dear Wilkins,

Thank you for your letter of 15 July which I found on my return from a visit to Haile Selassie in Addis Ababa, followed by my visit to the Isle of Wight where The Queen installed me as Governor.

I also enclose a translation of a letter that the Count De Mauduit sent to me and a copy of my reply to him. When you go there please don't fail to convey my personal good wishes. It might amuse you to use the phrase "from the Squire of Romsey" to "the Squire of Paimpol".

yours sincerely

Mountbatten of Burma

Chapter 14

# 'We could not go on being lucky'

When Lord Louis arrived back home after Crete for a brief respite from Naval duty before taking up a new job, he wrote a letter to his sister Louise, Queen of Sweden, telling her in great detail of his escape. Mountbatten and his sister, who was eleven years older than him, were in regular contact by post until she died but the letter about *Kelly*'s fate was something extra. It amounted to close on 4,500 words. Not only was there detail about the actual battle off Crete and how it came about, the personal letter was more imaginative than a Captain's official report of proceedings, the official and more formal account which Mountbatten sent to his Commander-in-Chief in the Mediterranean and to Admiralty. Mountbatten did not include anything which might be regarded as 'classified' but to Queen Louise, whose husband's country was neutral, he revealed his personal feelings and described many of the most stirring incidents that occurred during *Kelly*'s destruction, how he himself became a survivor and how some of his men perished. It was the kind of letter any sailor might wish to have written home to a dear relative. The length and content reflected the sheer energy of the man. There can rarely have been such a personalized account from such a distinguished combatant in wartime.

Mountbatten wrote hoping Louise had realized that the German radio announcement that *Kelly* had been sunk with all hands including her Captain was 'enemy propaganda'. He said his wife Edwina had been worried until news got through to London that some *Kelly* people had been picked up, whereupon the Admiralty contacted her and 'put her out of her misery'. He told his sister that their 'stupid governess', because she believed German propaganda, brought his daughters Patricia and Pamela out of school in New York to tell them he was missing and they had been worried children for 24 hours. It was, however, a bit of a miracle that nearly half of *Kelly*'s officers and men were picked up, he said. There was a domestic touch when 'Dickie' told Louise that, when news reached Malta of the beginning of the Crete battle and he realized *Kelly* and his ships would be taking part, he called on Admiral Ford and gave him a suitcase containing a uniform suit, blue, and a suit of white uniform, pyjamas, underclothes, toothbrush, etc. He told the Admiral that if the *Kelly* were sunk, as seemed quite probable, and if he were picked up, as he hoped he would, he 'would be presumably taken to Alexandria' and he would be grateful if his suitcase would be put into the next plane from Malta to Alexandria.

Mountbatten explained to his sister that he was aware that the 'very latest and finest' destroyers would be used off Crete for rearguard action in the most dangerous and exposed position and they would be the most likely to be sunk. Also, after 21 months of intensive activity in war, it was unlikely that the *Kelly* could go on having lucky escapes. Describing his experience off Crete he said one of the two ships with him, *Kipling*, sustained defective steering gear. The letter to his Royal sister added: 'The little cherub who sits up aloft and looks after us poor sailor men must have put the *Kipling's* steering gear out of action for it was due to this incident that we owe our lives'. He told Queen Louise that a large caique proceeding to Crete was sunk with 'the wretched Germans jumping into the water in full marching order'. In other circumstances the enemy soldiers would have been picked up but even at 30 knots it was doubtful if *Kelly* could get into position in time to carry out the task of bombarding a German-occupied airfield. After dawn next day *Kelly* and her sister ship *Kashmir* avoided bombs from a German aircraft and Mountbatten stated: 'I sent for my breakfast on the bridge and I continued reading C. S. Forester's book about my favourite hero, Hornblower, called *Ship of the Line*'.

The sun was well up, the sea was calm and it was 'a lovely Mediterranean day' when they saw ominous black objects, revealed to be the dreaded Stukas, with a reputation of diving almost vertically on ships then

**Below** *A near miss by German bombers as the 5th Destroyer Flotilla was on the way to Crete in May 1941.*

**Bottom** *This photograph, taken from one on Mountbatten's flotilla on the way to Crete shows HMS Kelly dropping depth charges on a German U-boat.*

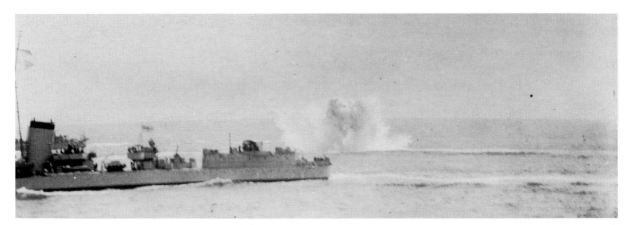

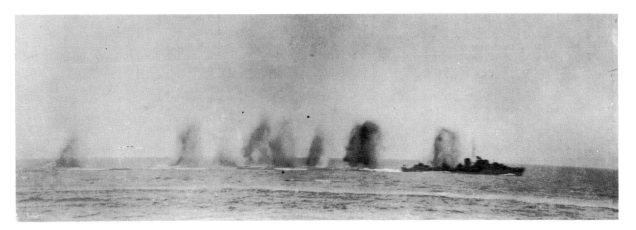

*HMS Kelly avoiding a stick of German bombs during an attack by German aircraft off Crete.*

releasing their bombs when they were so low they could not miss. Full Action Stations were sounded and *Kelly*, with her guns firing, dashed 'Full Ahead' and went to starboard, then port as Mountbatten tried to avoid the bombs by forcing the bombers to dive deeper and steeper. One bomber was shot down, then to his horror Mountbatten saw the third or fourth wave hit the *Kashmir* somewhere amidships and 'she was finished'.

Then Queen Louise was told how *Kelly* perished. One of the Stukas came lower than the others while *Kelly* was turning at over 30 knots under full helm. The bomb was released so close to the ship that it couldn't miss. It hit square on X gun deck and killed the crew of the twin 4.7-in gun mounting. The next wave was coming in and Mountbatten gave the order 'amidships' and then 'hard-a-port' but *Kelly* only listed over more heavily to port. 'All ships list outwards under full helm, at full speed, and this list was getting worse. I gave the order "stop engines" and then heard the coxswain shout up the voice pipe "Ship won't answer the helm. No reply to the engine room telegraphs!" Then I realized that we were for it. The next wave of Stukas had started their dive towards us and I remember shouting "Keep all guns firing", an unnecessary order for all the guns continued to fire until the guns' crews were actually washed away from their guns.

'I realized the bomb must have torn a gaping hole down near X magazine, as we had lost our stability and were rolling right over. I suddenly saw the water rise on our port side in a raging torrent of over 30 knots and thought "Whatever happens I must stay with the ship as long as I can. I must be the last to leave her alive." We were over beyond 90° now and I climbed up on to the distance correction indicator of my station keeping gear, which I had invented and which was fitted in the Flotilla. With my arms I clung round the gyro-compass pedestal. And then the sea came in a roaring maelstrom. I saw officers and men struggling to get out of the bridge, then I took an enormously deep breath as the water closed over my head. The awful part was that even after we were upside down, we continued to race through the water, though of course at a rapidly decreasing rate.

'Somehow I managed to flounder and work my way across the upside-down bridge until I got to the bullet-proof bridge screens. Here I had to pull myself under, and up to this moment it was horribly dark. A faint glimmer of daylight appeared on the other side of the bridge-screens but the water was churning round and I could distinguish nothing. I suddenly felt my lungs were going to burst and that I would have to open my mouth unless I could somehow keep it shut. With my right hand I gripped my mouth in a vice-like grip and with my left hand I held my nostrils shut. It was a fight of willpower. Would my hands obey me and keep my mouth and nose shut longer than the reflex action which would force me to open them and swallow a lot of seawater?

'I had my Gieves waistcoat on, but had not blown up the rubber ring which is fitted to the waistcoat. This was lucky because it made it easier for me to get out from under the bridge, but now I had to kick hard to fight my way to the surface. Slowly, infinitely slowly, the water got brighter and brighter and then suddenly, with lungs bursting, I broke surface. I gasped for breath, but the next moment I saw the stern of the ship approaching us with both our great propellers revolving in the air. They looked as though they were going to come right over and hit us. I saw the Navigator, Lieutenant Maurice Butler-Bowden, with his back to the ship. I yelled to him to "swim like hell" because I was afraid that the propellers would hit him. We both managed to get clear but only by a matter of six or seven yards!

'At this moment, up bobbed one of our stoker Petty Officers, a great character and a bit of a humorist. He looked at the "pilot" and then at me and then produced a typically cheery crack. "Extraordinary how the scum always comes to the top, isn't it, Sir?" I looked around. I could see one Carley raft, which someone must have had time to release before the ship turned over. I saw men all around me in the water and yelled out "everybody swim to the raft".

'I suddenly noticed I still had my steel helmet on and this seemed ridiculous in the water so I took it off and threw it away. I pulled the mouthpiece and tube out of my waistcoat and blew up the rubber ring. That made it easier to stay afloat. Then at that moment, suddenly and unexpectedly, a row of splashes appeared between me and the Carley raft;

*Survivors from HMS Kelly in a Carley float before being rescued by HMS Kipling.*

then with a roar one of the Stukas shot overhead with her machine-guns firing at us. I bitterly regretted throwing away my tin hat; you have no idea how naked one feels in the water without one when one is being machine-gunned.

'By now I had reached the raft and gave orders that only the wounded were to be allowed inside the raft; those who were not wounded were to hold on outside, and those for whom there was no room would hold on to the men who were holding on to the raft. The dive bombers came again and again, a hail of machine-gun bullets swept by, this time hitting some of the men around the raft. As men died, I had them gently taken out of the raft and men recently wounded put in to take their place. It was a gruesome and unpleasant business, and yet the sea was calm, the sun was shining and it reminded me of so many bathes I had had in the Mediterranean in the days before the war.

'My eyes were stinging and my mouth had a bitter acrid taste and looking around I saw everybody's face smothered in heavy oil fuel, looking like negro minstrels. This added greatly to our discomfort and to the unpleasantness. I thought it would be a good thing to start singing to keep up people's courage and so I started that popular song "Roll out the barrel" and the others soon joined in, which seemed to help.'

Mountbatten continued: 'Then the miracle happened'. *Kipling* appeared at full speed to their rescue. *Kelly* was just afloat and started to go as *Kipling* approached and he called 'Three cheers for the old ship'. Lord Louis told everybody to swim to the scrambling nets and himself towed a very badly wounded man who was bleeding freely, but by the time he got him as far as the *Kipling* he was obviously dead, so he let him go.

'As soon as I got on board, I went up to the bridge. I was soon in command of my Flotilla and the *Kipling* was under my orders, but naturally I did not interfere with the Captain, that is Captain Aubrey St Clair-Ford, who is a brave, brilliant and very competent man.' *Kipling* then picked up *Kashmir* survivors, a much more difficult job for she had

*Kelly turns over and is sunk after being hit by Ju87 dive bombers. Nine officers and 121 of her ship's company were lost.*

gone down far more slowly than *Kelly*, and as a result there were more survivors in and around five rafts. Hardly had they got opposite the first raft and stopped the engines than German bombers reappeared. Every time *Kipling* went back to a raft, the same thing happened.

'Finally, I told him (Captain St Clair-Ford) to lower his fast motorboat which could then go round collecting the survivors from each raft and would be able to come alongside the *Kipling* in whatever position we were, without having to try and manoeuvre the whole ship alongside a Carley raft. Hardly had the boat reached the water than he came to me and said "There's another Junkers 87 diving at us. I'm afraid I shall have to go ahead out of it." I shouted to the men in the waist to "cut the falls" of the motorboat. This was necessary because the fast motorboat is not a "sea boat". It is normally only lowered in harbour. There is no quick-release hook but only a big single shackle with a screw-pin which takes half a dozen turns to unscrew. There was no time to do this. That is why I told them to cut the actual rope falls which were holding the boat. A man with a knife dashed up the foremost falls and cut them. I shouted "Cut the after falls, you bloody fool!", because I knew what was going to happen. I had personally supervised a course of all the engineer officers of my Flotilla at the Experimental Oil Fuel Establishment at Haslar, to ensure that they should be able to increase speed at a far greater rate than had been customary. The *Kipling* was no exception. Her 40,000 horse power was applied with such speed that the ship leaped forward and the bows of the motorboat were driven under. My cry to cut the after falls had been heard by my own First Lieutenant, Lord Hugh Beresford, and the First Lieutenant of the *Kipling*, John Bushe. Together they leaped to the after falls at the moment when the ship had gathered such speed and the heavy motorboat had sunk so deep in the water that the after davit was pulled right over and seemed to crush them as the falls tore away and the boat sank in the sea together with the two First Lieutenants. Hugh was one of my oldest friends. He was a Midshipman with me in 1927 in the *Queen Elizabeth*. He was a great-nephew of Papa's great friend Lord Charles

*HMS* Kipling's *boat picks up survivors from the* Kashmir.

*Survivors aboard HMS* Kipling *on their way back to Alexandria.*

Beresford. I think this incident hurt me more than any that day.'

*Kipling*'s Captain remarked that without the motorboat, rescue work was now going to take a very long time and hoped the aircraft did not get there before they picked up all the *Kashmir* men. Mountbatten replied that that was his responsibility and told him to go ahead.

'With great skill and great courage,' Captain St Clair-Ford nosed his way from one raft to another in between the persistent air attacks. It was a long and painful business and after two hours some of Mountbatten's own staff officers asked him whether he would consider allowing the *Kipling* to leave the rest of *Kashmir* survivors and proceed to Alexandria. 'They pointed out, with complete justification, that the *Kipling* now had on board all *Kelly*'s survivors, more than half of the *Kashmir*'s survivors and it was becoming more and more difficult to pick up the remainder and avoid being hit by the bombers. I decided that we should stay. After three hours, there was only one more raft to be picked up and this proved particularly difficult because the attacks were getting worse. After consulting the Captain, my staff came back and urged that the right decision was to let the *Kipling* go before she was sunk with the loss of an additional five or six

**Above** Kelly *and* Kashmir *survivors crowd the decks of* Kipling *on the way to Alexandria.*

hundred lives. I decided we would stay to pick up all we could. I felt it would be better for us all to be sunk together than to leave our Flotilla mates struggling helplessly in the water without any prospect of being saved.'

At last *Kipling* was able to turn for Alexandria. Her own damage prevented her from doing more than half speed, so they limped home at fifteen or seventeen knots, the messdecks and upper decks everywhere crowded with survivors, many of them wounded and in poor shape.

'I went round with a notebook and pencil which I borrowed,' Mountbatten wrote, 'to get particulars of the more severely wounded and to find out which of their families they wanted me to send messages to, to say that they had been saved. I found that my Leading Steward, Camenzuli, had been killed and my Petty Officer Steward, Micellef, had been injured and badly burned. I was particularly sad about this for they were the only two of the original Maltese retinue who had volunteered to stay with the ship when the remainder were released on our not going to the Mediterranean.'

The attack was still going on. *Kipling* managed to dodge the bombs but Mountbatten said many near misses came so close that everybody on the bridge was drenched with the spray. *Kipling*'s guns' crew had been augmented by some of the best gunnery ratings from the *Kelly* and the *Kashmir* who helped to fight off the bombers. Finally the Germans gave up the attack and *Kipling* steamed on through the night.

'As we entered Alexandria harbour, everyone who could still walk

**Top left** *Survivors of* Kelly's *pom-pom crew. From left to right: (back row) Jack Cole, Sub-Lieutenant Hutchinson, Sid Mosses, Roy Reed, (front row) Rocky Wilkins, Leading Seaman Waite and Able Seaman Wilcox.*

**Left** *Members of HMS* Kipling's *crew after rescuing their flotilla mates from the Mediterranean.*

crowded out on to the upper decks. There must have been between four and five hundred crowding every inch. The Mediterranean Fleet, which had only got back shortly before us from the battle, were moored close together in harbour. All the ships' companies cleared lower deck and gave us a heart-warming cheer as we steamed past. At the landing stage I was met by the cheery grinning face of our nephew Philip, who had come to meet me. He roared with laughter on seeing me and when I asked him what was up, he said: "You have no idea how funny you look. You look like a nigger minstrel!" I had forgotten how completely smothered we all were in oil fuel.'

Lord Louis enquired about his suitcase, which would be so handy, but it never turned up. Later enquiries showed that the RAF 'had been too clever by half'. A printed label with his name and Broadlands address on it was still attached to the suitcase so, disregarding Admiral Ford's orders to take it to Alexandria, they flew it straight back to England. So Mountbatten had to go, like everyone else, and buy some ready-made clothing. That evening, the surviving officers of the *Kelly* had a dinner party. 'We had all been a very happy mess and now nine were missing and only eight of us present. And yet the evening was a tremendous success. We reminisced about the happy times of the commission. We talked in turn about each of those who were absent in terms of warm friendship and affection. It was rather as though they were just temporarily away and not gone for good. The next day came the painful business of saying goodbye to the survivors of the ship's company.'

When the moment came to shake hands with each of them, said Mountbatten, it was almost more than he could bear. 'I somehow felt this really was the last of the *Kelly*, for while the ship's company were gathered together, her spirit appeared to survive, yet I couldn't help feeling her

*Mountbatten goes ashore at Alexandria. At the bottom of the gangway are the Commander-in-Chief Mediterranean, Admiral Sir Andrew Cunningham, and Mountbatten's nephew Midshipman Philip Mountbatten, now Prince Philip.*

*Wounded from the Battle of Crete being taken to hospital in Alexandria.*

spirit would survive, because we had all loved the ship so much and were such a happy band of brothers. I have never known a ship with such a tremendously high ship's spirit and I don't suppose I ever will again.'

In spite of his grim experience, fighting his ship, dodging the ferocious bombing and gun attacks, his concern for his men who had gone down with *Kelly* or died in the water by his side and his anxiety for the wounded, throughout his long epistle Mountbatten ignored any sufferings of his own. He escaped flesh wounds but like his colleagues he was affected by swallowing oil which injured eyes and skin. The ordeal in the sea and the shock put many of his officers and crew out of action for months. Some went to hospital, and did not go to sea for some time, some did not get to sea in warships again. Not so Mountbatten. His physical and mental fitness, his calmness, his inspiring leadership were marvelled at. After a short stay at Alexandria with the Commander-in-Chief of the Mediterranean Fleet, Sir Andrew Cunningham, he was ready to continue the battle.

Lord Mountbatten told Queen Louise how he was sent home by Admiral Cunningham, the journey taking more than a fortnight. When he got back, he reported to Prime Minister Winston Churchill, and gave an account of the battle. He concluded: 'To my utter delight, I have been appointed in command of a fine new ship and will soon be back again in the battle at sea. I have something extra to fight for now. I have to pay back an enemy who butchered my men in the water after he had sunk the ship.'

BROADLANDS,
ROMSEY,
HAMPSHIRE.
SO5 9ZD.

 TELEPHONE
ROMSEY 3333.

6th February 1970

My dear Wilkins,

To my great surprise I have been awarded the
Humanitarian Award of Variety International which
I am to be handed in a ceremony in Puerto Rico on
Friday 8th May.

One of our Frigates, the JUPITER, is being
sent there to participate in the ceremonies and
I am told that they have commissioned Mr. John
Terraine, whom you met when he was writing the script
for the Television Series of my Life and Times, to
write the script for my "citation" which is being
read in sections by famous actors.

The sponsors of this show, Sir James Carreras
(British) and Mr. Mike Frankovich (American) recently
met and decided that they would like to include an
Able Seaman from the KELLY to read the portion dealing
with the KELLY.

If they were to send you an invitation would
you be able to accept? An all expenses paid trip
would be arranged in order for you to be there on
the 8th May for the Ceremony.

If you accept then I will inform all concerned
so that you may get an official invitation, and I
will ask you to get in touch with Mr. John Terraine
to make a date to discuss with him the actual text
of the script about the KELLY which you are going
to be asked to read.

Please let me know as soon as possible whether
you would be prepared to accept this invitation.

yours ever
Mountbatten of Burma

---

BROADLANDS,
ROMSEY,
HAMPSHIRE.
SO5 9ZD.

26th May 1970

My dear Rocky,

Thank you for your letter of the 20th May and for sending
me the copy of the script from which you spoke at the Humanitarian
Award Dinner at Puerto Rico. I am very happy to have this for my
archives.

I enclose a copy of my letter to Sir James Carreras from
which you will see I am trying to get the other script as well.

I am glad to have the account in your letter of the vicissitudes
which the Kelly Committee had to meet to get the dinner going at all to
keep in my archives. What a wonderful show you all put up and how
proud you can all be of the result.

yours ever

Mountbatten of Burma

---

BROADLANDS,
ROMSEY,
HAMPSHIRE.
SO5 9ZD.

TELEPHONE
ROMSEY (0794) 513333

4th December 1975

My dear Rocky,

I recently took part in a BBC television programme
entitled "Think In Oceans" which was the story of the Admiralty
Boardroom. They offered me a fee of £25 but I have renounced
this and told them to send it direct to the HMS KELLY Reunion
Association Fund, to help build up our funds for our reunion next
year when we hope that Prince Philip will be able to come.

yours ever
Mountbatten of Burma

---

BROADLANDS,
ROMSEY,
HAMPSHIRE.
SO5 9ZD.

TELEPHONE
ROMSEY (0794) 513333

30th December 1975

My dear Rocky,

I was offered a £500 subscription by
Conoco Limited for presenting their awards recently
and I asked them to make out the cheque to the Kelly
Reunion Association and enclose it herewith.

This now means you have £525 in the kitty
towards the cost not only of the 1976 reunion but also
that in 1978 hopefully.

Please let me know some time how you
propose to use this money.

With all best wishes for 1976.

yours sincerely
Mountbatten of Burma

Chapter 15

# A 'sure kill'

Personal experiences at Crete written for Mountbatten's archives included those of one gunner who bagged a German aircraft, Petty Officer Ted West, the enthusiast for Oerlikons. The first of the German Stukas to attack *Kelly* screamed down in an almost vertical dive towards the ship's port side and West had it squarely in his sights. When the plane was a third of the way through its dive West opened fire and his tracer shells went right into the enemy aircraft. Pieces flew off the Nazi and West knew it was a 'sure kill'. *Kelly*'s gunners engaged Stukas as they dived in succession. He recalled seeing a great column of flame shoot from the after 4.7-inch guns and Lieutenant Kidson saying 'Keep firing. We've been hit aft.' West had a stoppage in his Oerlikon and unstrapped himself from his gun, cleared the stoppage and continued firing without strapping himself to the gun again. Another Stuka dived and again West had him squarely in his sights.

'It was like shooting at sitting ducks', he thought, when suddenly the sea came up and hit him. 'I remember the feeling of being plucked into the depths, a violent blow on my legs which did not seem to hurt at all, then being twirled round and round and down and down. I held my breath until my lungs seemed to be bursting. I heard bells ringing in my ears and saw flashes of red lights in front of my eyes. I thought "So this is what it's like to drown". Next I remember I was floating on the surface of the sea with the sun shining in my eyes. There was a tightness about my throat which I did not understand until I put my hand there and found it was the strap of my tin hat which was hanging from the back of my neck. I got rid of that and the duffle coat which was weighing me down and had a look around me. About a hundred yards away *Kelly* was upside down.'

Although West had a lifebelt it wasn't blown up. 'You could not fire an Oerlikon with an inflated lifebelt on,' he said. It was a while before West saw the first signs of life. It was the destroyer's Petty Officer Yeoman of Signals swimming towards him. West said 'Good morning, lovely weather for a swim isn't it?' His colleague replied with 'something unprintable' about the Germans. One by one other survivors, eight or nine of them, grouped round the raft, looking a sorry sight, covered thickly with fuel oil. There was a hail of machine-gune fire from a low-flying Stuka. West thought his best chance of survival was to swim away from the large groups. He couldn't imagine German pilots wanting to waste ammunition on a lone swimmer even if they saw him. Twenty miles away he could see the mountains of Crete and wondered whether he could swim that far. He still had his shoes on and decided not to kick them off because if he was picked up and taken prisoner he would need shoes. (He actually kept the shoes as a souvenir and still had them after the war.)

As he rose on the crest of a wave, West saw *Kipling* which had parted company from the Flotilla the night before because she had steering gear trouble. *Kipling* made straight for the capsized *Kelly* and rammed her. 'I thought afterwards that it may have been intended to open her up so that some of the trapped men in her could get out.' (Mountbatten added a correction: It is certain that she collided with the wreck of the *Kelly* by accident in trying to get nearer to the Carley raft. Twenty-four Stukas had finished their attack and those that had not been shot down had returned.)

West's graphic personal story told how *Kipling* had barely started picking up survivors before she had to fight off new attacks, tearing away at full speed, guns blazing and zig-zagging, taking avoiding action. *Kelly* was down by the stern, her bows sticking into the sky with one lone survivor sitting on top. 'Slowly she settled deeper into the water and finally slid below the waves ... So she ended her life, after being mined, in collision, torpedoed and now finally gone. In all from the time the bomb hit the after gun to the time she capsized fifty seconds had elapsed. For her to finally sink took some time.'

For Petty Officer West there was nothing to do but 'wait for a miracle'. Even though Crete looked near, it would have been hopeless to try to swim that far. Although it was May the water was not exactly warm and he started feeling cold. He estimated he and others were in the water between three and four hours when the miracle happened. 'Sure enough, coming towards us was *Kipling*. I am sure no Channel swimmer could have done better than I did. I reached her side and was thrown a heaving line. At the same time I saw another swimmer I recognized as Lieutenant Robin, one of our officers. I passed the line over to him and said, "After you, sir". He passed it back and said, "No, after you".'

Rescue nets were over the side of *Kipling* but try as he would West's legs refused to function. He had to be hauled on board and the tot of wardroom whisky did him the world of good. West also graphically described how *Kelly*'s First Lieutenant and *Kipling*'s motorboat crew lost their lives. As the motorboat was lowered to the water in an attempt to speed up the rescue of *Kashmir* survivors, another dive bombing attack started. *Kipling* gathered speed and the motorboat buried her bows in the sea and was torn from the davits.

There was all-round praise for the gallantry of *Kipling*'s Captain and crew in staying in the vicinity for so long and picking up so many *Kelly* and *Kashmir* survivors against the tremendous odds. West said, 'As we sped away I felt extremely sorry for the few remaining survivors left behind. One man standing up in a "skimmy dish" saluted as we went by. I thought, however, "It is on the cards we shall be with you again soon". It was not to be so.' (Here again Lord Mountbatten, who was painstaking in his quest for the fullest correct details about Crete, wrote a correction: 'I think we left hardly any survivors of the *Kashmir* behind. Two or three men were in a whaler and the one in the "skimming dish" was picked up by the whaler

*Lord Mountbatten and some of his senior officers board the Admiral's barge to scatter the ashes of Chief Petty Officer West at sea.*

and the whole lot managed to get back to Crete and in fact I saw the coxswain of this whaler in Australia after the war and he told me that they had all survived, which is a great relief for I did not wish to leave anybody unaccounted for.')

West's story went on to tell of the continued German attacks and the near misses as *Kipling* got away from the scene. In their rage at missing with their bombs, the Nazi pilots machine-gunned the crowded decks of *Kipling*. The men were drenched by huge spouts of water but not hit. They endured rows of sparks flying from the steelwork as the bullets struck. Even so West introduced a touch of humour. 'Shortly before the last attack started corned beef sandwiches had been distributed. I was standing near A gun when they came along. There was no time to eat them, however, so they were put under a shot mat out of the way. During the machine-gunning I went flat on this shot mat, so with my added weight they became "pressed beef" sandwiches with a vengeance.'

Ted West was awarded the DSM. When he died his ashes were taken to sea and scattered off Portsmouth in accordance with his wishes. Lord Mountbatten and other *Kelly* colleagues accompanied his widow to sea in an Admiral's barge loaned by the C-in-C Home Fleet for this special tribute arranged by Mountbatten.

A large proportion of men who lost their lives in warships sunk in both World Wars perished because they were trapped below decks and unable to escape. One of the worst places to have been in when *Kelly* was struck was the engine room. Those at Action Stations on the upper deck and bridge had a better chance of survival than those operating the powerful engines in the bowels of the ship. Turning over in a matter of seconds with the machinery still at full throttle was a terrible experience. It was a miracle that any of them got out alive. John Robinson of Scunthorpe told of the last fateful moments off Crete and how he got out of the upturned ship.

Like the others, he had a long night at Action Stations when *Kelly* was bombarding Maleme airfield and at 03:55 after a sandwich and cup of ki he went below for the morning watch. Everything was running smoothly at a speed of about 25 knots when at 06:00 Action Stations sounded again. The revolution indicator rang. 'I opened up the throttles and in two or three minutes the speed increased to well over 30 knots. Engineer Commander Evans came down to his usual position and informed us that a wave of enemy aircraft was coming up astern. As we did not get a lot of gen down below during action Commander Evans had stationed Leading Stoker Doyle at the engine room hatches to keep us informed. By this time the boiler room crews had regained what small amount of pressure they had lost, so I continued to open up the throttles until they were wide open.

'The attack started and we began to turn at full helm as a bomb exploded close by. In a destroyer turning at high speed and at full helm it was necessary to hold on to something handy. This went on for almost two hours, twisting and turning. How many near misses we had I do not remember. A few minutes before 08:00 Doyle shouted down to say *Kashmir* had been hit and had sunk very quickly. Knowing I had lost some revolutions owing to the continuous turning, I had just time to make a quick check and we were making sufficient revs for just on 34 knots.

'At about 08:05 just as we started to turn there was an extra loud explosion. I thought it might be a very near miss. The ship continued to list to port. Both steering motors went off the board. The chief engine room artificer went aft to try and restart them but I saw him coming back along the port gratings and looking towards me he shook his head. The bridge telephone rang. Commander Evans went to answer it but only got a lot of incoherent talking so he hung up. All this time the ship was going over to port. Everyone was holding on to something. I myself was standing at the starboard throttles, holding the wheel, my feet gripping the plates. The ship was nearly on her beam ends. Instead of her coming back again she gave an extra lurch and went right over.

'My feet slipped away from the plates but I managed to retain my hold on the throttle wheel. Water was pouring in through the hatches. After I felt it reach my feet and then up to my chest I let go of the throttle. There was a loud roaring noise which sounded like a steam pipe fractured. The lights gradually dimmed. Then we were in complete darkness. There was a loud rumbling noise which might have been machinery breaking loose. After swimming about for a few minutes I felt what I knew to be one of the ladders leading up to one of the two hatches. I tried to pull myself up the ladder but the rush of water entering the engine room just washed me back. After coming to the surface again I thought "This is it". For all I knew the ship was then ready for making its final plunge. Strangely enough I was not afraid. "If this is how it has to be then there is nothing I can do about it. Anyway it won't take long."

'Then treading water, waiting for the end as it seemed, I happened to turn round and saw a luminous disc of greenish light. This I instantly knew to be the other hatchway and it could not be as much submerged as the other one. "There's a chance", I thought, and made for where I guessed the ladder would be. Just as I got near it a shadowy form reached it before me. So half pushing him and pulling myself down the ladder I got through the hatch, across the deck, and with lungs just about bursting, broke surface a few feet away from the ship's side while a few feet away from me was an engine room stoker, Tom Rogers. There were a few bad moments; while crossing the deck I got caught up in some lines that could have been boat falls or guard rails. After what seemed hours and feeling utterly exhausted what with diving deep whenever I heard machine-guns and fighting off frequent bouts of cramp I was picked up by *Kipling*.'

Machine-gun attack from aircraft gradually ended and eventually, as darkness fell on the evening of the tragic day, high level attacks ceased as the *Kipling* drew further from the German air bases. *Kipling*'s crew and her survivors anxiously scanned the skies and the count of separate German attacks totalled a mammoth 108. The men from *Kelly* and *Kashmir* as well as their rescuers in *Kipling* hardly believed their luck in holding out in the retreat to Alexandria. With darkness there was some relief and relaxation. Most were far too tired and uncomfortable to eat and all they wanted was sleep. Many were in a pretty bad state, wounded and covered with oil, some urgently needing medical attention, everybody terribly shocked, eyes hurting severely. There was a doctor on board but urgent treatment in hospital was required by many. During the night five of the wounded died and Lord Mountbatten, after one of the most dreadful days any Naval officer had ever faced, performed the burial services. *Kipling* herself had developed a list through the flooding of compartments caused by near misses and she was running out of fuel. Next day, still some hours out of Alexandria, *Kipling* ran out of oil and came to a complete stop. A minesweeper arrived with fuel. While re-fuelling went on the little vessel passed over urns of tea and loaves of new white bread. For the survivors nothing had ever tasted so good. For many it was the first food and drink to pass their lips for fifty hours.

As HMS *Kipling* passed through the breakwater at Alexandria, warships' officers and men cheered loudly. It was said: 'If ever anybody deserved such a reception it was the Captain and the men of the *Kipling*.' A fleet of ambulances awaited the wounded and those who did not need hospital attention filed into buses and away to Dhaikelia airfield where each ship's company was mustered and the sad count of survivors carried out. More than half of *Kelly*'s complement was absent.

In wartime, names of casualties took some time to filter through to the newspapers. Seven weeks after Crete at a time when heavy demands were being made on the obituary columns of *The Times*, that newspaper carried in a single day no fewer than four personal tributes, each of them signed 'L.M.'

Lieutenant Commander Lord Hugh Beresford: 'even as a midshipman in the *Queen Elizabeth* showed every sign of following in the footsteps of his illustrious great uncle Admiral Lord Beresford. He was undoubtedly the best-liked of the younger officers in HMS *Kelly*. Much of his service career was spent in destroyers and he was First Lieutenant of the *Hostile* and the *Codrington* before joining the *Kelly*. He set himself the highest possible standard in every walk of life. He lived up to it himself and in expecting others to do likewise was rarely disappointed. Although his heart and soul were in the Navy he found time to take a very active interest in the Boy Scouts. No one was better liked by both seniors and juniors all of whom will miss him very much.'

'After two years in the West Indies Lieutenant M. V. Sturdy came home and commissioned the *Kelly*. It is rare for an officer to make his

*'It is rare for an officer to make his
mark so young' wrote Mountbatten
of Lieutenant Michael Sturdy who
lost his life at Crete.*

mark so young. Michael Sturdy was an outstanding figure. Tall, good
looking with irrepressible good spirits, he could be counted upon to keep
everyone cheerful under the most adverse conditions. He was an efficient
officer, popularity equally great in the wardroom as on the lower deck.'

Surgeon Lieutenant V. J. R. Sheridan: 'He had more small ship
experience than most medical officers having gained his DSC in China
gunboats. He was very popular both in the *Kelly* and the 5th Destroyer
Flotilla generally. When the *Kelly* was torpedoed in the German minefield
on 9 May 1940 the sickbay was wrecked and all lights failed. Dr Sheridan
tended the wounded under great difficulty by the light of a torch. Off
Crete the *Kelly* went too quickly to enable him to help once more with the
wounded. His loss will be keenly felt by his many friends.'

Then 'L.M.'s' personal tribute to Paymaster Lieutenant Commander H.
J. Reeder: 'Apart from three years as Assistant Secretary to the
Commander-in-Chief of the Nore and undergoing a secretary's course,
he served continuously since 1933 in Flotilla Leaders, first as Secretary to

Captain D, 1st Destroyer Flotilla, then during the war as Secretary to Captain D, 5th Destroyer Flotilla. It is no exaggeration to say that he had won for himself a unique position in those two Flotillas as commanding officers in all those Flotillas will be the first to concede. He had every quality in the highest degree, charm, tact, efficiency, courtesy and loyalty. He was liked and admired not only by his messmates and shipmates but by all his Flotilla mates. Few if any accountant officers can have seen more scrapping than he and none can have exercised so great and good an influence as he did. His loss will be felt not only by his friends in the Accountant Branch but by the whole service.'

The 'Paybob' who was the Secretary to Captain D5 was an important man for Mountbatten to lose. It was 36 years later that Mountbatten came in contact with Reeder's son, by then also a Lieutenant-Commander, M. J. Reeder of Chichester. Mountbatten wrote saying he was sorry Reeder was unable to get to Mercury for a Kelly Squadron Open Day. 'I thought I would write you a separate line as I understand you are the son of my great friend and secretary.' He told Lieutenant-Commander Reeder that he was so impressed by the way his father had helped Captain D1 that as soon as Mountbatten was appointed Captain D5 he immediately wrote to him and asked him if he would join him. 'He accepted and did a really wonderful job and it was a tragedy that he should have been lost when the Kelly was sunk at the Battle of Crete. Had he stayed with me I am sure we would have gone right through to the top. I had great difficulty in finding a successor and in fact tried half a dozen different supply officers when I became Chief of Combined Operations. None of them came anywhere near the competence and charm of your dear father.

'Then when I went as Supreme Allied Commander, South East Asia, the First Sea Lord, Sir Dudley Pound, resigned on ill health and died shortly afterwards, so I nabbed Lieutenant-Commander Ronald Brockman. He came to me as my secretary in South East Asia with the Acting rank of Captain, of course, and remained with me ever since. Even on promotion to Rear Admiral and Vice Admiral he never left me and finally ended up with a KCB, a CSI and a CBE.

'I mention this only because I had looked forward to having a joint career with your father along the same lines, of which I was robbed by his sad loss in the Kelly.'

BROADLANDS
ROMSEY.
HAMPSHIRE.

TELEPHONE
ROMSEY 3333

12th March 1973.

My dear Rocky,

I saw Micallef and Baldacchino
during my visit to Malta and we talked
about you and the Reunion.  They brought
the model of the "KELLY" and offered to
return it, but I said they could keep
it for the present while they hold the a
Reunion out there, but they must eventually
return it to you.

I don't believe I ever sent a copy
of my sister's biography which is remiss
because it contains my own personal account
of the sinking of the "KELLY".  I am
sending it herewith.  You may care to show
it to other members as convenient, but the
copy is for you to keep personally.

Yours sincerely

Mountbatten of Burma

---

From:  Eric Merrill, M.B.E.                    **British Railways Boar**

222 Marylebone Road
London NW1 6JJ
01-262 3232
Telex 24678                                    Controller, Public Relations and Publi

Earl Mountbatten of Burma,
Broadlands,
Romsey,
Hampshire,
SO5 9ZD.

y/r
o/r  302-8792                              Date 5 October 1973

Dear Lord Mountbatten,

Your letter to the Minister for Transport Industries about the
nameplates of the locomotive "Kelly" has been passed to the
Board and on to me as being responsible, among other things,
for museums and historical relics.

We are not keen to hand over such nameplates because, once
agreement to do so is given, the requests snowball and we
could either offend someone or be bereft of nameplates.

However, we will hand over the "Kelly" nameplate - I say
nameplate because we have only one.

I shall be grateful if in any publicity attaching to this you
will as far as possible make it clear we regard this as a very
special case.   No doubt you recall we have already handed
over the nameplates from "The Royal Navy Reserve 1859-1959".
I await the attacks from the Army and the Royal Air Force!!

Yours sincerely,

Eric Merrill

---

BROADLANDS,
ROMSEY,
HAMPSHIRE.
SO5 9ZD.

TELEPHONE
ROMSEY (0794) 513333

20th November 1973

My dear Rocky,

You will be interested to hear that the "KELLY" locomotive
nameplate has been delivered to me at Broadlands.    They could
only find one, the second one having been lost or stolen.

As you know they particularly don't want any publicity on
this matter so I am keeping the nameplate here and if you like will
bring it up to the next re-union dinner.

yours ever

Mountbatten of Burma

---

BROADLANDS,
ROMSEY,
HAMPSHIRE.
SO5 9ZD.

TELEPHONE
ROMSEY (0794) 513333

22nd January 1974

My dear Rocky,

I am leaving on the 23rd for two months on a visit
to China ( Peking, Shanghai, Hangchou, Canton) and then
to New Zealand after which I join the Royal Yacht BRITANNIA
for the Queen's Pacific Cruise.

Meanwhile, I should tell you in confidence that I
would like to bring my oldest grandsons, the Honourable Norton
Knatchbull aged (26), and the Honourable Michael John Knatchbull
( aged nearly 24), but I also will bring my great nephew the
Prince of Wales, if he is back in time and can get away from
his ship.

As he has not yet got the necessary leave, it is
essential that the possiblity should not leak to the press.

However, I think it is only fair to warn to members
of the KELLY reunion in strict confidence that there is a
fifty fifty chance that H.R.H. will come along to the dinner,
and I am sure you will have a record turn out if he comes.

yours ever

Mountbatten of Burma

# Chapter 16

# Combined Operations

One of *Kelly*'s ratings, Paddy Milton, went into Combined Operations and became commanding officer of an infantry landing craft. Mountbatten was proud of him and sought to locate him for the reunions. In fact Mountbatten inspired hundreds of young men who went on to take vessels of one sort or another in Combined Operations. A great many potential RNVR officers did their compulsory sea time in destroyers before going to HMS *King Alfred* for final training and when they became Sub-Lieutenants opted for appointments in destroyers. I was one. I was waiting at the HMS *Victory* mess in a brand new uniform with a half stripe when the appointment came. It was to join HMS *Broke* replacing the First Lieutenant, Peter Scott — yes, *the* Peter Scott. HMS *Broke* had been out in the Atlantic chasing U-boats and escorting convoys and she had had a rough time. 'Where is she now?' I had to ask excitedly. She was barely a mile away in Portsmouth Dockyard. When I got there *Broke* was in dry dock for a much-needed refit. Lieutenant Peter Scott had gone quickly to MTBs in E-boat Alley based on Dover. He had left a message asking his successor to please send on his belongings which included painting materials and cameras. *Broke* was left with only a few ratings. They were there to man the guns at night to assist in the defence of Portsmouth against German bombers which threatened the great Naval base at the time.

My spell with *Broke* did not last long. She was in for a long stay and I certainly would never be First Lieutenant. It got around that Mountbatten had said that the next best thing to destroyers was Combined Operations because there was absolute guarantee that you would get extremely close to the enemy. Mountbatten said that almost all the chaps awaiting appointments after 'passing out' made destroyers their first choice and Combined Operations their second. As there weren't many appointments going in destroyers Mountbatten said, so it was alleged, his Combined Operations scooped the cream of the officer entry. Some young officers thought: 'Mountbatten can tell that to the Marines!' Secretly Mountbatten referred to his fledglings in Combined Operations, certainly those in LCTs (Tank Landing Craft), as 'Commissioned Bargees' and we would all have loved to see him try to handle LCTs (especially those fitted, believe it or not, with two right turning screws) in order to see what sort of a hash he made of it. Anyway, we who got through landings at Sicily and Salerno, Anzio and Elba, and the South of France and those who invaded Normandy had an exciting time rubbing shoulders with the enemy as Mountbatten promised.

My 'commissioned bargees' story led to Lieutenant-Commander Trevor Blore writing a book with that title when he described the impertinent landing on the Isle of Elba made solely by 'flat bottomed bastards' because the channels were so shallow-mined by the Germans that it ws impossible to have destroyer and big-ship fire support. Some LCTs even carried Goums*, their wives and their pack horses. They must have scared the locals as much as the occupying Germans.

Mountbatten was loved in Combined Operations and everybody was sad to see him go to South East Asia. One of the best appreciations of Mountbatten after his death was written by Commander Rupert Curtis, DSC, RNVR, who landed Lord Lovat and his 1st Commando Brigade at Ouistreham in Normandy on D-Day. He wrote an article for the London Flotilla Bulletin, published by the Association of Reserve Officers of the Royal Navy who still pay subscriptions to be members and have high-powered winter lectures at the Naval Club and the 'In and Out' (the Naval and Military Club in Piccadilly). Rupert Curtis, in his tribute, which was written on behalf of all Reserve Officers, said:

'I remember being inspected by Mountbatten in the fairly early days of Combined Operations in late 1942 when the landing craft forces were still young and unfledged. I was serving in an LCT Flotilla under Geoffrey Snagge as part of Force J in Southampton. We needed someone to make us realize that our role was important to our country, that we had a great part to play in achieving final victory, for many of us who had been serving in convoy escorts and other roles found Combined Operations very much an unwanted, unglamorous Cinderella at that time. The presence of Mountbatten in our midst uplifted our hearts and no one from the youngest rating could fail to realize that we were in the presence of a very gifted man and leader.

'The debt which the nation owes to him in his period of service as Chief of Combined Operations is probably not sufficiently realized. Churchill's directive to him in October 1941 was that he should turn Britain from a bastion of defence into a springboard for attack. Taking the torch from the hand of Sir Roger Keyes, he mounted Commando raids from Vaagso to St Nazaire and played a major part in planning and preparing for the North African landings. But today the Dieppe raid of August 1942 is regarded by some as a blemish on his record, an unnecessary failure which should never have been embarked upon. The slaughter of the Canadians and the relative failure of the operation gave support to this view. The frontal assault without sufficient fire support should have been avoided, but it was forced on Mountbatten against his judgment. However, the lessons learnt were beyond price and they probably laid the true

---

*Goums Morocains were fierce and colourfully robed Moroccan troops founded in 1908 as a local police force of volunteers. In World War 2, 22,000 of them fought in Italy and France. They took with them their mascots — goats with 'golden horns'. When Morocco became independent in 1956 the Goums Morocains formed the nucleus of their country's army.

foundation for the success of the Normandy landings.

'From Dieppe sprang the notion of building a prefabricated port in England and towing it piece by piece to the French coast and planting it there, so confirming Churchill's earlier thoughts on the project. Mountbatten saw to it that every lesson was studied and the answers found. He pursued his path with imagination and immense energy and knitted Navy, Army and Air Force together to fight as a band of brothers and as one unified force, a lesson which we had never before learnt in our history. He developed the philosophy for landing a vast army on a heavily defended coast and supporting it so that victory would follow. He was among those who urged us to go for Normandy and not for the well-nigh impregnable Pas de Calais, however inviting the shorter route might be. But before he could see the Allies reap the rewards of his vision he was called upon to shoulder even greater responsibilities.'

BROADLANDS,
ROMSEY,
HAMPSHIRE.
SO5 9ZD.

TELEPHONE
ROMSEY 3333

3rd July 1972

My dear Rocky,

I am writing to thank you and your most efficient Committee
for the wonderful arrangements you made for the KELLY Reunion
Association Dinner onboard the President.

I believe this was a record attendance of actual survivors
and it was a most splendid evening and I do congratulate you and thank
you all.

The high-spot for me was of course getting the E-boat
steering wheel back so very unexpectedly.   I have written to Scorer
but as I don't know his address I enclose the original letter for you to
post on and a carbon copy for your files.

Yours ever

Mountbatten of Burma

---

3rd July 1972

This is the second time that you have scored a
bull's-eye on me with a real surprise; the first was the
White Ensign and the second now is the E-boat steering
wheel.

I, of course, knew of its existence as all of us
did in the ship but I never knew what had happened to it
and I never expected to see it again.

It was thus a real thrill when you and Rocky
Wilkins handed it over to me at the dinner.

Mr Scorer,

---

BROADLANDS,
ROMSEY,
HAMPSHIRE.
SO5 9ZD.

TELEPHONE
ROMSEY (0794) 513333

7th December 1972

My dear Rocky,

My Private Secretary, John Barratt, telephoned to you on
my instructions asking you to make contact with him as soon as
Micallef arrived in London.   I had in fact kept an hour clear on
the afternoon of the 20th November to receive him and his wife
and indeed you and your wife at 2 Kinnerton Street as I was up in
London on that day.   Unfortunately, you failed to ring up and make
contact and so the invitation could not be extended to you.   I am
sorry about this misunderstanding.

I have spoken personally to the Queen about the arrangements
for the visit of her butler (Micallef) and her housekeeper (Jessie Grech)
to the Silver Wedding Service.   They were both invited at the same time
and Her Majesty rather imagined they would come together and keep each
other company.   However, Micallef said he would like to bring his wife
and Jessie wanted to bring her niece.   Her Majesty gave instructions for
invitations to be sent to all four

Yours sincerely

Mountbatten of Burma

---

BROADLANDS,
ROMSEY,
HAMPSHIRE.
SO5 9ZD.

TELEPHONE
ROMSEY (0794) 513333

8th June, 1973

My dear Rocky,

I found Ted West's stories very human and interesting.
He got one thing wrong about the story of the SCHARNHORST and
GNEISNAU because, in fact, the KELLY was leading a Division of
the Fifth Destroyer Flotilla from Londonderry to Gibraltar at that
moment and we were warned from the Admiralty that the SCHARNHORST
and GNEISNAU had been sighted heading for St. Nazare.   I immediately
put the telegraphs to "full ahead" and gave the order "hard to port" and
started out for Brest being certain they would have gone there.   We
went off at 32 knots in company and arrived while the lights were still
on and hopefully ahead of the battle cruisers.   Unfortunately they must
have slipped in just before us so as daylight broke we had to head for
home.

Yours ever

Mountbatten of Burma

Chapter 17

# 'In Which We Serve'

Noel Coward's film *In Which We Serve* made *Kelly* famous throughout the world. It was made entirely because of his friendship with Lord Louis which started between the wars. Mountbatten always wanted Coward to talk to his *Kelly* survivors about the making of the film but on the one occasion when Coward said he could make the reunion he was acting in the West End and could not get away to make the promised speech.

The two were great friends from 1924. Noel Coward used to spend holidays at sea with 'Dickie' or stay in the Mountbatten home in Malta. Life for Coward was carefree and peaceful. It is said that he spent some of his time in Malta at the piano composing his great song 'Mad dogs and Englishmen'. In 1934 he stayed with the Mountbattens prior to going on a summer cruise when Mountbatten was Captain of HMS *Daring*. He fitted in well with the household like a member of the family and acted as social secretary for cocktail parties and such like, not averse to taking the mickey out of some of the Naval crowd who in those days didn't agree with such parties on a Sunday and declined invitations for the Sabbath. Mountbatten complained to Coward that he had no interest in and knew nothing about the Army yet he had written a 'tremendous glorification of the Army in the play and film *Cavalcade*'. What about giving the Navy a break? 'Yes', said Coward. 'The moment I get a good story I'll do it.'

When World War 2 started Noel Coward visited Mountbatten in *Kelly* quite frequently, having drinks in the wardroom and walking round the ship talking with the crew. When Mountbatten returned to England after Crete, Coward went to see him (it was June 1941) and said: 'Dickie, I've got the idea of a naval *Cavalcade*. It will be the story of the *Kelly*.'

According to Mountbatten, he said to Coward: 'It's out of the question. It's the stupidest idea I've ever heard.' To begin with, Mountbatten said, the story of *Kelly* was not at all a glorious tale. It was very ordinary. *Kelly* had been doing what all other destroyers had been doing. 'We've been mined, bombed, torpedoed, everything you can think of and we ended up by being sunk.'

Coward replied that that was the whole point; it was what was going on throughout the Navy at that moment. 'That's what the people want to know about.'

Mountbatten's story was that he said: 'Go ahead, do another destroyer.'
Coward said the only destroyer he knew about was *Kelly* and
Mountbatten said: 'Well, invent one.'

'I can't do that, I don't know what goes on at sea,' Coward went on.

Then stated Mountbatten: 'I said "If you swear you won't give anything
away and change things so you can't recognize *Kelly*, all right you can go
ahead".' Mountbatten's far from convincing story continued: 'Well, he
didn't. I don't know whether it was his fault or not, it leaked. It was
supposed to be a secret. I did say this to him: "What part are you going to
play?" He said he was going to play the part of the Captain. I said: "There
is one thing you must be quite certain about. If you are going to play the
part of the Captain you are not going to be a hero. You are just going to be
one of the ship. The heroine is the ship. You must have a Chief Petty
Officer and an Ordinary Seaman and their families!"

'So Coward had as the chief bo'sun's mate none other than Bernard
Miles, and Ordinary Seaman "Shorty Blake" played by Johnnie Mills, two
of the greatest stars in the British film world. That went reasonably well
but in due course he said he'd reached the stage where at Denham Film
Studios he had a full-scale model of "HMS *Torrin*" (the destroyer in the
film) and he wanted to borrow a ship's company. So he asked the Second
Sea Lord if he could have a ship's company off a destroyer that had been
recently damaged and was paying off, with the clothes they wore at sea.
They went down for a week and they were looked after very well and that's
why the ship's company in the film always looked so very genuine.'

Mountbatten loved telling more about *In Which We Serve*. Coward

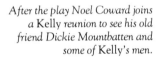

*After the play Noel Coward joins
a Kelly reunion to see his old
friend Dickie Mountbatten and
some of Kelly's men.*

*Some jokes at a reunion dinner from Bernard Miles who was one of the stars of* In Which We Serve.

invited the Second Sea Lord from the Admiralty down to the studios and Mountbatten went also. The Admiral was shown the mock-up destroyer and said he wished Coward had asked him if they could borrow a real destroyer's motorboat. Coward was too polite to say the motorboat they had was in fact borrowed from Naval stores!

Then the Admiral was asked if he would like to see some of the film 'rushes' of shooting the previous day. In the 'rushes' shown there was a very dramatic scene where the chief bo'sun's mate's wife was killed when her home was hit in the blitz of Plymouth. Her niece, married to an Ordinary Seaman, had been sheltering under the stairs and escaped. 'Shorty Blake' arrived in the Chief Petty Officer's mess where he was asked if there was any news from home.

'Shorty' replied yes, that the girl had had her baby.

The Chief Petty Officer said 'Good'.

Blake said the girl had had the baby after the blitz.

The Chief said: 'Oh, she was all right then?', and went on 'I hope my wife's all right', to which 'Shorty' said: 'I'm sorry. I'm afraid she was killed.' Mountbatten, who liked to recall all these details from the film years afterwards, said: 'This was beautifully done, typically underplayed by two great film stars. But you know what? The Admiral declared: "I say, how right you were to ask for real sailors. No actors could possibly have done that!"'

For Mountbatten, *In Which We Serve* exactly fitted his ego. But the Admiralty considered such a film was important for the morale of the Navy and the nation. Far from being fictitious, one of the best-known film critics of the day concluded unkindly that: 'Here was Mountbatten playing Noel Coward'. In years to come other film producers sounded out Mountbatten about a new '*Kelly*' film but he would have none of it. He thought Coward's film was a masterpiece.

BROADLANDS,
ROMSEY,
HAMPSHIRE.
SO5 9ZD.

TELEPHONE
ROMSEY (0794) 513333

25th April 1974

My dear Rocky,

I am delighted to note that the response from our shipmates for the Reunion Dinner has been so great even without their knowing the date. Thank God the date has now been fixed for Saturday, 8th June which will suit me, personally, particularly well as I have to be in London to take part in the Rehearsal for the Trooping of the Colour as Colonel of the Life Guards.

I will ask the Prince of Wales to wear a monkey jacket, the same as me, as we are both on the active list. I would like to bring my eldest grandson, the Hon. Norton Knatchbull, who is a year older than the Prince of Wales and a great friend of his as well.

I hope you will keep in close touch with my private secretary, John Barratt, about the question of members who cannot attend owing to the high cost of tickets because I think that on this occasion I might be able to arrange for a friend of mine to produce some money to help out with this problem. We certainly want to get the biggest possible gathering of genuine members of the ship's company for His Royal Highness as it is a pretty unique honour getting him.

yours ever

Mountbatten of Burma

---

BROADLANDS,
ROMSEY,
HAMPSHIRE.
SO5 9ZD.

TELEPHONE
ROMSEY (0794) 513333

8th September 1975

My dear Rocky,

I am so sorry about the death of Ginger Meekings and I enclose a copy of my letter to his widow.

I shall look forward to seeing the sixteen members of the KELLY Association at the MERCURY on the 20th September and I gather one or two of you are going to sea in the Admiral's Barge for the commital of West's ashes.

I presume that you will be bringing the picture that West was going to give, with you and will hand it over for me to make the presentation. I do, however, require to have a few notes about it so that I know what to say in my speech. Could you let me have them please.

I hope you are going to get a letter from Vice Admiral Sir Ian McIntosh inviting you to go to the Press Conference onboard HMS BELFAST on the 11th September, to launch the appeal for preserving the last destroyer in the Royal Navy, HMS CAVALIER at Southampton.

He will fit you into the party. I hope you will be able to come since you represent the only surviving destroyer association.

yours ever

Mountbatten of Burma

---

BROADLANDS,
ROMSEY,
HAMPSHIRE.
SO5 9ZD.

TELEPHONE
ROMSEY (0794) 513333

26th May 1976

My dear Rocky,

I really must congratulate you and Shaw and indeed all concerned with the magnificent arrangements for the KELLY Reunion Dinner on the 22nd May.

I arrived in good time to meet everybody and have a talk before the First Sea Lord and Prince Philip arrived because I knew I would have to leave fairly early. However, there was a great muddle about our departure because Prince Philip was anxious to offer a lift to Joanna in his car so I came up to see her off and I, at that time, was going to stay on to say goodbye. Then his car wasn't there so we sent Joanna off in my car. She just missed the train but caught the next one.

Then Prince Philip said he thought there would be an anti-climax if we now went back again and mixed, particularly as the Queen was waiting up to see us when we got back, and wondered whether it would be accepted if he was to withdraw at this time. That is why we had to put out a call for you and Shaw to come to the gangway to say goodbye because Prince Philip was so anxious not to go without telling you in person how much he had enjoyed himself.

By this time I had lost my own car and the only way to get to Windsor Castle was to go with Prince Philip in his car, so I am afraid I left much earlier than I have ever done before but on the other hand I am 76 and not very much good at staying up for the dancing. Still I would have liked to have stayed just to tell you again how wonderful I thought all the arrangements were and how delighted everybody was.

I know my grand-daughter, Joanna, was absolutely thrilled and particularly asked me to thank you personally for everything.

Will you please thank Howgate very much for those wonderful flag signals he painted on all the cards. I am keeping my cards in the archives here.

I am glad you agree to do without a Toast Master another time; I think he only gets in the way and you and I can do the Toast Master's job between us and save some money.

yours ever

Mountbatten of Burma

---

20th July 1976

My dear Rocky,

I am happy to tell you I have at last been able to find a white uniform which I had over the period of the war and hope to be able to present this in person to the Maritime Museum in Malta, as I hope to be going out next February for the Trooping of the Colour by 41 Royal Marines Commando.

The visit, of course, has not yet been arranged so must be kept secret.

yours ever

Mountbatten of Burma

Chapter 18

# Reunion dinners

*Kelly* reunion dinners could never be the same without Mountbatten. The survivors became fewer as the years passed but the numbers at the dinners grew rather than diminished. Friends and relatives of survivors came as guests and were joined by the Royal princes, Prince Philip and the Prince of Wales; and distinguished Naval officers, many of whom had served with Mountbatten in the 5th Destroyer Flotilla, including the Ashmore brothers, Admiral Sir Edward Ashmore, who was in *Jupiter* and who became First Sea Lord, and Admiral Sir Peter Ashmore who was in *Kipling* when she rescued Mountbatten off Crete and who later became Master of The Queen's Household. Actors John Mills and Bernard Miles who played in the film *In Which We Serve* joined Mountbatten and his shipmates; so did Alan Price, the pop singer from Tyneside who created a musical play about *Kelly* staged at Newcastle upon Tyne.

The *Kelly* Reunion Association never had a formal constitution. Ratings who served in *Kelly* were full members and officers became associate members but none other than Lord Mountbatten played any part in the association's management. Originally there was a committee of London members who met regularly to organize the annual dinners, the annual Remembrance Day pilgrimage to Hebburn to commemorate their colleagues who died in the North Sea, and fund raising activities to pay for dinner guests. Since the first days Rocky Wilkins did most of the work and Vernon Shaw was treasurer but more and more Mountbatten had a hand in directing policy. However, Mountbatten always suggested ideas and possible guests to Wilkins and was never dictatorial. Eventually Mountbatten was invited to be President and no reunion organization has had the luck to have a more enthusiastic or influential figurehead. He personally arranged the attendance of VIPs.

There was the usual formality about toasts and, Mountbatten being a stickler for etiquette, even gave Wilkins written advice about drinking toasts aboard HM Ships. 'A dinner held on board *President* (at which a member of the ship's mess was present) may be regarded as a mess dinner in which case the following rules applied:

'1 The loyal toast to Her Majesty the Queen may be honoured sitting down provided that the band does not play "God Save The Queen"

**Right** *Mountbatten is piped aboard HMS President.*

**Below** *Old shipmates and friends for forty years — the President of the Kelly Association, Lord Mountbatten, and the Secretary, Rocky Wilkins.*

*At a Kelly reunion Prince Philip meets Stoker Garner, the man who said 'Extraordinary how the scum always comes to the top, isn't it, Sir?' as he broke surface after Kelly's sinking at Crete.*

because if it does everyone present is obliged to rise.

'2 Once the Queen's health has been honoured sitting down, it is bad form to stand up for any lesser toast; it follows that all other subsequent toasts must be drunk sitting down.'

There was formality about the toasts, to 'the Captain' and always to Absent Friends made by an ex-*Kelly* rating. There the formality ended. In the earlier days there was a toastmaster but Mountbatten suggested to Wilkins that they do without a toastmaster. 'You and I can run it between us and save money.'

In the most humorous way Mountbatten very much held court sitting next to whoever might be the principal guest, with Rocky on the other side of the chief guest whether it be the Prince of Wales or the First Sea Lord. Mountbatten put his stamp on the spirit of the occasion. Everyone looked forward to the Captain's speeches. When he was First Sea Lord and Chief of Defence Staff he asked the ladies present for their forebearance while he gave his former shipmates a rundown on the present defence situation. He said he always tried to make his *Kelly* dinner speeches different but they inevitably included long references to the history of *Kelly* 'because we are here tonight to commemorate our gallant ship'. On one occasion without a single note he spent 45 minutes detailing *Kelly*'s escapades from the first day of the war until the final moments at Crete. He would go into statistics, repeating the numbers killed and wounded both in the North Sea and at Crete. But he told the funny stories as well as the grim facts. There was a good deal of banter fostered by Mountbatten himself. He liked, for example, to make the man who used the word 'scum' when he broke surface stand up and be counted.

**Above** *Mountbatten introduces Prince Philip to his former shipmates.*

**Right** *Lady Mountbatten arrives with her husband for a Kelly dinner aboard HMS President on the Thames.*

Mountbatten liked to revive the comment which, he had told his sister, was made by the Duke of Edinburgh after Crete. Every *Kelly* Association member knew the story of what happened when the survivors reached Alexandria. Mountbatten never stopped telling them — when HMS *Kipling* arrived at her berth, waiting on the quayside was his nephew Prince Philip who was a Midshipman serving in the Mediterranean in the battleship *Valiant*. He was said to have smiled and said: 'Hello uncle. You look like a "nigger minstrel".' Prince Philip got the opportunity of denying this when he was prevailed upon to speak as a guest at a *Kelly* dinner. He said he referred to his uncle's eyes looking like 'curried eggs!' Prince Philip must have been right. As one officer said, Lord Mountbatten had plenty of time on the journey in the *Kipling* to have his face cleared of the oil he had collected before being rescued. Prince Philip made his dinner audience laugh when he jokingly said there were advantages and disadvantages to being related to successful officers. The more successful they were the greater the disadvantage because if an uncle was not doing that well there was always a chance of doing a bit better.

The fact that he had never seen *Kelly* did not affect the issue. 'I lived under her and under *his* shadow for quite long enough as it was. I couldn't do anything without being told: 'That's not right. That's not the way it was done in *Kelly*!' Prince Philip fitted in excellently with the happy mood of a *Kelly* dinner presided over by Mountbatten. 'I didn't get away with very much', he said. 'You know what they say about "this young man will go a long way". Well I went all the way out to the East Indies. Blow me down he was there! I did escape him for a short time in the Pacific. Later on I

*The Captain remembers former times with some of his lower deck shipmates.*

went to the Mediterranean and blow me he was there. And it's very nice to be here and here he is too!'

Lord Mountbatten loved to refer to the Prince of Wales in his reunion speeches. He told one dinner: 'His Royal Highness is now commanding officer of HMS (that means "His Mother's Ship") *Bronington*.' After the Prince made his first appearance at a *Kelly* reunion his great uncle jokingly referred at the next dinner to the Prince's speech. 'We asked him to tell us something about the modern Navy which he'd been in only a year or two. We're looking forward to having him here again so he can tell us what more he knows!'

It was typical of Mountbatten that whether he really recognized an old shipmate or not he never failed to give the man the impression that indeed he was remembered well by his former Captain. 'He continued to have a marvellous memory for faces even when he was well into his seventies', said Rocky Wilkins. 'But if he spotted someone at the dinner whom he recognized as being a 'Kelly', or wasn't sure, he would ask me who was the rating sitting over there, what was his job on board. He jotted the details down on a piece of paper and later in the evening he would make sure he would talk to the man personally with "How are you? You are Simpkins, how are you getting on?"'

*Kelly* reunions started with a 'stag' dinner. It was successful from the start. It was presided over by one of the senior ratings, a Chief Yeoman who was a signals chief and very close to Mountbatten in wartime. 'When the next reunion was discussed the question of wives attending was brought up. The Chief Yeoman was firmly against womenfolk attending

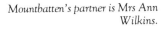

*Mountbatten's partner is Mrs Ann Wilkins.*

**Above** *Mountbatten's granddaughter Amanda, one of the many members of the Mountbatten family to attend Kelly reunion dinners.*

**Left** *A bouquet for Lady Mountbatten at a Kelly reunion dinner at the Royal Overseas League.*

*Lady Mountbatten meets a Chief
Petty Officer Signals, one of her
husband's 'trade'.*

*The Mountbattens take the floor
aboard HMS President.*

*The Mountbattens share a joke with Rocky Wilkins.*

and the vote went with him', Wilkins said. 'However, someone asked "How about Lady Mountbatten?", who was a great favourite among the crew because of her many kindnesses. The chiefie and everyone else with him agreed that Lady Mountbatten should be invited to attend. So I wrote to Lord Louis to ask whether his wife would like to attend. Then she 'phoned up herself to ask whether the ratings' wives were going to the dinner. When she was told no, she said: "Well, if you think I'm going to be the only woman present you have another think coming".' Rocky went back to the committee with Lady Mountbatten's proviso and that settled it. The other wives were invited and so eventually were daughters and granddaughters, Lord Louis' descendants as well.

Lady Louis was presented with a large bouquet of flowers. She thanked Rocky. 'She said it was a very nice gesture but that some florists had the habit of sticking wire up the stems of flowers which caused them to perish in a day or two. "Please don't give me a bouquet in future. Why not put a little posy or spray on each lady's place including mine. That will be much better".' Mountbatten got to know the womenfolk as well. *Kelly* reunions became family affairs with Mountbatten taking the dance floor with Lady Louis and ratings' ladies.

The popular 'Scrounger' Scorer, the man who was able to present Mountbatten with *Kelly*'s battle ensign and the E-boat steering wheel recovered from the smashed-up *Kelly* when she arrived at Hebburn, wrote privately to Mountbatten and suggested that there should be some award to Rocky for his work for the *Kelly* Association. Mountbatten wrote an appreciative letter saying awards were not available for such work as

**Right** *Mountbatten relaxes with a cigar at a Kelly dinner.*

**Below** *Another relic for Mountbatten. At the 1972 reunion he was presented with the steering wheel of E-40, which torpedoed Kelly in 1940, by former Ordinary Seaman Ralph Scorer.*

running reunion associations. But he came back with his usual simple and precise advice. He suggested to Scorer that the members might decide to give Rocky some suitable memento. He told Scorer he entirely shared with him the feeling of gratitude for Rocky Wilkins' work over the years. 'I'm afraid there is absolutely no way of getting his magnificent work recognized officially because, of course, there are not hundreds but literally thousands of reunion organizations all over the country and I am associated with about twenty of them. There is always somebody who gives his whole spare time to running them and none of them ever gets recognition because it is not done as a service to the public or to a charity but it is a social service for shipmates, etc. I know they do not qualify for a decoration. What happens in the case of other reunion organizations is that when the time comes an appropriate piece of silver is usually given to the man who has given all his time to it. I would be perfectly happy to arrange for an appropriate silver box to be made with the *Kelly* Arms on it and an appropriate inscription which you might care to think about. A box specially made like this would cost £70 and would be quite valuable. I would make myself responsible for placing the order and paying the bill provided you could organize on a secret basis without Rocky knowing about it a subscription list from as many different survivors as possible. The whole point would be that in the inscription we should say "Subscribed by (the number) of your fellow shipmates", or words to that effect. If you can organize this through some members of the committee I will gladly stand the difference between the money raised and the cost of giving Rocky a gift like this.' The members in fact organized a 'Rocky Benefit Night' and Rocky's thank you present was a gold cigarette box inscribed with the Mountbatten of Burma signature.

*The Captain gets back his battle ensign after 25 years. Mountbatten had not seen Kelly's battle ensign since she was torpedoed in the North Sea. It had been kept in store at the Tyneside shipyard and was presented to him at the reunion dinner in 1966.*

**Above** *'Rocky Benefit Night'.
The Association said thank you to
Wilkins with a gold cigarette box
in 1974.*

**Right** *A Kelly contingent
presents a bell to the landlord of
the 'Kelly' pub at Hebburn on
Tyne where the famous ship was
built.*

In addition to the mementoes in Lord Mountbatten's 'ship's passage' at Broadlands and in the *Kelly* corner in the Malta War Museum in Valetta, many *Kelly* survivors established museums, some with bars, all with photographs of Mountbatten, in their own homes. Brewers have spread the Mountbatten image by naming pubs after him or the *Kelly*. It started with a '*Kelly*' pub at Hebburn to which Mountbatten sent a signed photograph of himself by Karsh; the 'Lord Louis' at Southampton had a model of *Kelly* made with advice by the Imperial War Museum and this model has now gone to '*Kelly*'s' Hotel at Gosport, a town familiar to thousands of naval men. '*Kelly*'s', used by the *Kelly* Association as its southern headquarters, has a Naval and military history museum full of *Kelly* material and photographs. The 'Royal Station' Hotel at Newcastle upon Tyne, where Mountbatten stayed during *Kelly*'s construction and repairs at Hebburn and on his post-war trips to the area, has a Mountbatten lounge, and now London has its own 'Mountbatten' Hotel, formerly the 'Shaftesbury' Hotel in Covent Garden, which has a *Kelly* model and features aspects of Lord Louis' life from his first taste of action at sea in Lord Beatty's flagship and including Burma and South East Asia as well as Lord and Lady Mountbatten's historic task in India.

At the last reunion dinner he attended, Mountbatten was presented with a navy blue sweatshirt inscribed with the *Kelly* badge and 'The Fighting Fifth' emblem. He took off his jacket and went away in his shirt sleeves, impressing everyone by his apparent fitness. The dinner audience waited for a few minutes while he donned the sweatshirt. The gift was the idea of some of the *Kelly* ratings' wives. Mountbatten was very much attached to it and was wearing it when his boat was blown up off the Irish coast. It helped identification and was produced at the inquest.

*'Who's for a pint?' asks the Captain. Lord Louis draws the beer at the opening of the 'Lord Louis' pub in Southampton.*

*HMS Kelly and Mountbatten are celebrated at 'Kelly's' Hotel near the waterfront at Gosport, Hampshire. The whole bar is a naval 'museum' with a special Kelly corner. It is regarded as the southern England headquarters of the HMS Kelly Reunion Association.*

*Bottoms up — a pint goes down well.*

*Mountbatten wearing his 'Fighting Fifth' sweatshirt which was designed by Mrs Ann Wilkins. The flowers were brought from Malta for his granddaughter Amanda but as she had to go back to university without them they were presented to Ann Wilkins. Behind Mountbatten is Lord Hutchinson QC who was serving as a Sub-Lieutenant on Kelly at the Battle of Crete and (left) the Kelly Association treasurer, Vernon Shaw.*

★   ★   ★

'The Navy's not so good as it used to be!' All the old salts and sweats say this about whatever Service they were in. When Rocky Wilkins and his shipmates started saying this, that the discipline wasn't what it used to be and the young men in ships today had it far too comfortable compared to the pre-war days, Mountbatten decided that survivors should go to sea and experience the modern Navy for themselves. So the lucky *Kelly* men have been guests in several modern warships. They took a trip in the North Sea in HMS *Kent*, the missile destroyer, on one of her last trips before she was taken over for training purposes. They dined in the wardroom and used the officer's bar and decided that there was certainly a far better choice of food for the ratings thanks to modern cafeteria messing facilities. In HMS *Kent* they visited the various messes, Chiefs', Petty Officers' and ratings', nowadays fitted out with bars outmatching almost anything ashore. Although the daily tot of rum has gone forever (which the 'Kellys' thought was too bad) they were impressed not only by the vastly different equipment on board today but also with the technical quality and high standard of training of the lower deck men. Because of the highly technical nature of the job for both officers and ratings today, there has to be a far greater understanding and a closeness that makes the relationship different from that of the old days. In HMS *Kent* one of the ship's officers conducted a live broadcast so the *Kelly* men could tell the crew first-hand stories about the *Kelly*'s activities, about the sinking at Crete and how they each survived — and what a great Captain they had in Lord Louis.

*Kelly men go back to sea aboard HMS* Euryalus. *Here are the 'Kellies' in their rig of the day with some of the younger members of the warship's crew.*

**Above** *In the wheelhouse of Euryalus — Nobby Hall at the wheel with Rocky Wilkins and Tug Wilson looking on.*

**Left** *Back in the 'hot seat' after forty-odd years. Able Seaman Wilkins at the gun with some of his ex-Kelly colleagues.*

*Kelly* parties have been guests aboard the carrier *Invincible* in which Prince Andrew served in the Falklands conflict, in the Class 42 destroyer HMS *Exeter* when she was the new Leader of the 5th Destroyer Flotilla, and to shore establishments including HMS *Heron* and her naval airmen at Yeovilton. They had a letter from Captain R. N. Woodward of the destroyer *Glasgow* inviting half a dozen of them to spend a week at sea in his ship in the Channel. The Prince of Wales remembered that there are some *Kelly* men who like to go back to sea and 'fixed it' with the Captain. In the *Glasgow* they had dinner with officers and their wives and were given their own cabins. During the week they were guests of all the messes from the Junior Rates' to the Chief Petty Officers' and took part in the ship's exercises, rigged out in modern survival and anti-flash gear. Rocky Wilkins, as an ex-AA rating, ws given the task of firing a 30 mm gun. As usual presents were exchanged. The *Kelly* men each received a ship's crest, tie pins and cap tallies and handed over a *Kelly* Namsos print. There was a surprise signal to the ship from their President, The Prince of Wales: 'Believing this to be the night on which you are entertaining a "mob" of old "Kellys" to dinner in the wardroom, please would you pass my very best wishes to all of them and say I hope they enjoy their stay on board as much as I did. No doubt they will miss having their characters humorously dissected before their eyes by the Buffer and the rest of Sods Opera Team.'

**Left** *There she goes — Rocky fires the guns again.*

**Below** *It wasn't like this forty years ago! The Kelly contingent go ashore by helicopter.*

BROADLANDS.
ROMSEY.
HAMPSHIRE.
SO5 9ZD.

TELEPHONE
ROMSEY (0794) 513333

8th September, 1977

My dear Rocky,

Thank you for your letter of the
1st September which I found on my return from a
visit to Germany.

I had an account of the KELLY Musical
from Commander Turnbull and Ralph Scorer and I
have also had a copy of the programme but I am
glad to have another one which has been sent to
me by the Press and Publicity Officer of the
South Tyneside Borough Council.    Perhaps if
you are in touch with them you will thank them
sometime as I presume they sent it on your account.

I must say I would be delighted to have
a copy of the script if you can get it for me.
It is an almost unique honour to have had a musical
about a destroyer.

I quite agree that you should go ahead
with the 1978 Reunion and will provisionally mark
down the 20th May in my engagement diary.    If
you have any difficulty with the Commanding Officer
of the PRESIDENT let me know.    I would like to
bring my second granddaughter, the Honourable Amanda
Knatchbull with me as the visit of her elder sister
Joanna proved such a success.

Thank you also for sending me the
photograph of my uniform in the Malta War Museum.
The "shoe trees" are certainly the type I still use
though they are maybe an odd thing to put in a
Museum!

I shall look forward to seeing you at
the MERCURY's Open Day on September 17th.    I shall
be coming over for a short while and would like to
have an opportunity of meeting the 14 members and
their wives if you would make a point of introducing
me to them.      I hope to be accompanied by my
goddaughter, The Marchioness of Hamilton, who may
be one of a party staying with me at Broadlands and
may be driving me over.      Her grandmother was my
brother's sister-in-law.

Yours ever

Mountbatten of Burma

---

28th August, 1977

Thank you so much for your letter of
the 13th August which I found on my return from a
month with my family at my place in Ireland,
Classiebawn Castle, to which no mail was forwarded.

How very nice of you to have written
to give me that excellent account of the musical
play about the KELLY which you attended.

Ralph Scorer also wrote me an account
which will supplement yours.    I shall place both
in my Archives, in the KELLY files, as I think it
must be unique for a destroyer to have a musical
play produced about her.

I am sorry that the news media did not
pay more attention to Sir Bernard Miles laying
the wreath at the KELLY Memorial in Hebburn.

Commander James Turnbull,

---

BROADLANDS.
ROMSEY.
HAMPSHIRE.
SO5 9ZD.

TELEPHONE
ROMSEY (0794) 513333

3rd October 1977

My dear Rocky,

Thank you also for the copy of "HEADLINES".    I have
ordered some more copies to give to my grandchildren.

I am particularly grateful to you for having got another of
the mess deck stories, this time by Sid Mosses.    I agree with you that
these stories are intensely interesting and I do hope you will be able to
get the others to continue to write memories of their service in the KELL

I hope you had a good time in Portugal.

Yours ever

Mountbatten of Burma

Chapter 19

# *This Is Your Life*

Tricking Lord Mountbatten onto *This Is Your Life* was the popular programme's biggest coup. It happened in April 1977. A whole year of planning was necessary and the producer, Jack Crawshaw, had to have a lot of allies, not least the Mountbatten family and relations whose blessing was vital before research started. There was a visit to Broadlands for background while Mountbatten was overseas. The *Kelly* Association was in on the secret too and, while Prince Philip knew about it, the Queen did not.

For the presenter, Eamonn Andrews, the critical moment came, as always over the years of the programme, when he had to confront Lord Mountbatten with the words: 'This Is Your Life'. Hidden from Mountbatten were 180 guests including a dozen of his relatives gathered at Thames Television studios in London with 30 million expectant viewers waiting for the surprise personality.

Andrews has had many anxious moments while waiting with his big red book. With Lord Mountbatten, Andrews' palpitations were a great deal worse than normal. Mountbatten was the biggest catch the programme had ever landed. When he said 'Earl Mountbatten of Burma, This Is Your Life!' the presenter's heart stopped, an icy trickle ran down his spine. 'What do you mean?', demanded Lord Mountbatten. Then he caught on and Andrews was mightily relieved as they walked down the stairs to the waiting audience. Mountbatten melted and smiled and said 'Well I'll be …'

It had taken eight years to get a member of the Royal Family. Jack Crawshaw knew that Mountbatten had a sense of humour and the family agreed that the idea might appeal to him. There were surprises other than seeing his family. Mountbatten was greeted by Dame Vera Lynn, the wartime forces' favourite whose broadcasts once filled the messdecks of *Kelly*; Danny Kaye had been flown from Hollywood, and the one-time boy star Jackie Coogan recalled how Lord and Lady Louis with Charlie Chaplin featured in a home-made movie in California in the 1920s. If they had stayed in Hollywood the Mountbatten couple could have become film stars, Coogan said. The television surprise was hailed by the newspapers, 'Eamonn collars the Earl' was one headline. Mountbatten did not waste any time in getting a copy of the programme for his Broadlands library.

There was also a Fleet Street story: 'Did Mountbatten know the "Your Life" secret?', suggesting that the Earl was likely to have a copy of the film at his home and declaring that he was not fond of ad-libbing 'which would have been necessary were the thing a total surprise. He likes to be prepared.' As it was, Eamonn Andrews and producer Crawshaw later explained that they had first approached Mountbatten's son-in-law Lord Brabourne, a noted film producer himself. The stars of the show, the television critics wrote, were the audience including members of the Burma Star Association and *Kelly* shipmates. Later Mountbatten told his *Kelly* men what it was like to be on the opposite side of the surprise. Any speculation about him being in the know about *This Is Your Life* was firmly squashed in the kind of sparkling wit with which he excelled. Not only was he double-crossed by his own family, who had agreed when the show was mooted that he was not to be told, but by everybody else including the 'Kellys'. Rocky Wilkins was so intent on keeping the secret that he 'confided' in his old shipmates that the *This Is Your Life* victim was to be Admiral Burnett. Mountbatten told his *Kelly* men later: 'The family asked Prince Philip's advice and he was told not to tell anybody. The Queen complained a bit she didn't know about it beforehand. I said "Well, Philip knew about it three months ago". He said "I was told not to say anything about it so naturally I didn't tell her". That is keeping secrets, isn't it?', declared Lord Mountbatten.

Mountbatten said that the family had been all in the Bahamas together on holiday. During one of their picnic parties somebody asked whether he had remembered it was Pamela's (his younger daughter's) birthday on 19 April. '"Very well", I said. "Pammy, I will take a party to the theatre and we'll go along to a restaurant and have a reunion for your birthday." She said: "Well, I'll come along to the dinner but instead of going to the theatre I would like to have two of the episodes from the TV series of your

*Mountbatten greets old shipmates at the television studios on* This Is Your Life.

life and times, because my three children are too young to have seen it''.

'Lord Brabourne said this would be easy because Thames TV had the films. We are both friends of Howard Thomas, the Thames TV Chairman. If he could lend us a projection room we could take the family to see it. So that was agreed. We then had an argument as to which episode we would have. But I was completely taken in, it sounded so honest. When we got back Lord Brabourne reminded me, "You haven't forgotten you are coming to Thames TV tonight". I said: "So I am". He said: "Well, the family's gone up there and I am just starting a meeting, I'll pick you up on the way". So he picked us up. He then turned round to my private secretary, John Barratt, and said: "Would you like to come along?" He said: "Yes, all right, I don't mind".

'When we got near there he thought it was a bad show that I should go in with a big bouquet and a gift-wrapped parcel [for Pamela] so he said: "By the way, Howard Thomas is just launching a book and he has asked if he could have a photographer take a photograph of you as you come in for his publicity. Do you mind?" I said: "No I don't mind". "Well in that case we'd better put the bouquet and parcel in the boot — you can give them to her afterwards." I said: "All right" — even then I didn't suspect anything. Then we arrived too early. We went round the block. I said: "This chap's going round the block". "Oh no!", he said. We finally arrived at exactly 8:15.

'Howard Thomas opened the doors. I said: "Howard, what's that little group of people over there? Is that your family party for your book?" He said: "No, no. In fact, it's your family." I said: "They ought to be in the projection room". "No, they said they would like to wait for you." I went over and I saw this large group, and being wise after the event, I thought they were a bit clean and tidy. The boys had had their hair combed. They all looked exceptionally tidy. So I kissed the girls and patted the boys and said: "Well, let's get going". And at that moment a sinister figure appeared from behind one of those big pillars in the foyer with a big red book. So I

*There was a big turnout of Kelly survivors in the television audience when Mountbatten was captured for* This Is Your Life.

said to Howard: "Is this your book you're doing publicity for?" He said: "No, it isn't". And then this ghastly fellow said: "Earl Mountbatten of Burma, This Is Your Life" and I didn't know what he meant. I said: "What the hell d'you mean?" And then, as I had never seen the programme — well I had once … doing a little contribution with Bob Hope who'd helped me in a charity — I knew it existed and a fellow called Andrews did it. And suddenly I realized what had happened! Luckily I remembered there were children present so I didn't say anything!

'We were then led into the auditorium and there I saw all your ugly faces and all the medals and it struck me that it was a much more serious business than I'd thought. They had the Burma Star people there, they had prisoners of war, shipmates, friends, everything. At this time thinking "how the hell I was going to bring this thing to an end?" and I was going to choose my moment. The family all sat down on one side. There were a lot of empty seats the other side and then he introduced the family. Then he said: "Now there are eight of your grandchildren here but two, your two eldest granddaughters are not here". I said: "Yes, Joanna. Joanna is in Sydney, Australia, trying to get a job on TV. She's a thousand miles away so you won't get her, and as for Amanda, the young one, you certainly won't get her, I only left her three days ago in Nassau, when I flew back to England and she left me there to fly up to Boston to spend a weekend with an American boyfriend. She said: 'I am sorry I shan't see you again Grandpa for some while because after that I am going straight back to university'." And then the door opened and they walked in! Now let me tell you. I was pretty shocked at seeing Joanna because I couldn't think who put up the money to fly her back — but then I saw this girl, whom I had always regarded as pure as the driven snow. Never heard a wrong word sully her lips. Never had she told a lie. And now she'd told me a whopping lie! And there she is this "wretched" girl. Well, that was it. Then I must say I went back and I realized I was "had".'

*Mountbatten and Kelly survivors on the stage with Eamonn Andrews. On the right is one of Mountbatten's old friends from Hollywood, Danny Kaye.*

Chapter 20

# Boy stoker who left his post

The story about the *Kelly* stoker who never attended a reunion dinner was one which upset Mountbatten, Rocky Wilkins and the rest of the *Kelly* Association. It resulted in what Mountbatten told Wilkins was the first adverse publicity the ship ever had. It was Mountbatten's wish that every single officer or rating who served in *Kelly* should be in touch with the Association and attend reunions if at all possible. There is abundant evidence in the Earl's letters to Rocky and others of his desire to be reunited with all the men who served with him in the destroyer. It was Mountbatten who got the Admiralty to supply lists of *Kelly* men who survived the actions and in the years between the loss of *Kelly* and formation of the Association many had changed addresses so were not contactable. In his world travels nothing delighted Mountbatten more than an unexpected meeting with one of his old crew. He rediscovered them in several countries and put them in touch with Wilkins.

In the film *In Which We Serve* Richard Attenborough (now Sir Richard) played the part of a young stoker who left his engine room post in the action when the ship was severely damaged by a mine. The actual stoker, who was only seventeen when the incident happened in the North Sea, *did* arrive in London intending to attend the first reunion at the Royal Overseas League. However, at the last moment he decided not to enter the dining room and apparently stood watching the dinner in progress through the glass panels of the door until just before the meal ended. He quietly disappeared and has not been seen by his shipmates since that day. Rocky was more than once reminded by Mountbatten to try and get hold of him and Lord Louis hoped Wilkins would pursue his efforts with Navy Records. Actors who played in the film, including Sir John Mills and Lord Miles (Bernard Miles) attended reunions and became honorary members of the Association. Mountbatten wrote to Attenborough saying that everybody wished he would attend a dinner. He mentioned the stoker, and said he would see if the man could not be persuaded to attend a reunion — particularly if Attenborough would be there. Nothing came of this. Attenborough did not attend a reunion.

Eight years later, in 1978, Rocky Wilkins, to try to please his Captain, was still endeavouring to trace the stoker. He sought the aid of *Navy News*, the periodical read by a great number of Naval and ex-Naval men. Unfortunately, the information given by Rocky to *Navy News* appeared without the prior knowledge of Lord Mountbatten. It was a well-meaning effort by Wilkins but the facts reporting the man's name were repeated in a daily newspaper and the story found its way to the *Sunday Express*. It was a story that was bound to attract the attention of a news editor. The *Sunday Express* chief reporter wrote in a long story that the ship's company of *Kelly* were a proud and close crew, moulded that way by their commander 'a no-nonsense but humane officer who was to achieve world-wide acclaim as Admiral of the Fleet Earl Mountbatten'. Together, the *Express* stated, they survived mines, bombardments and other enemy attacks until finally succumbing off Crete.

The newspaper told how the stoker — it was early in the ship's career — momentarily lost his nerve and dashed up a ladder from the engine room. Now attempts to find him, backed by Earl Mountbatten, had upset the crew and some had been 'angered', although Earl Mountbatten had been reported as saying he wanted to tell the man that all was now forgotten. The *Sunday Express*, which correctly and responsibly eliminated the stoker's name from the story, could not get a comment from Mountbatten, who was on holiday in America at the time. His secretary said, however, that he did not believe Mountbatten would have initiated a move to find the man and make his life a misery by telling everybody he had deserted his post. The Editor of the *Sunday Express*, Sir John Junor, followed up the story in his own notable column 'Current events' and strongly criticized Lord Mountbatten.

The stories disturbed Mountbatten. He told Rocky Wilkins that they must discuss how they were going to handle the adverse publicity. He had not seen what Rocky gave to *Navy News*. Rocky had not sent a draft or discussed it with Mountbatten's secretary, John Barratt. Both Mountbatten and Barratt had enough experience of publicity to realize it would cause a storm. 'I can't leave this episode untouched on in my speech', Earl Mountbatten wrote. 'I naturally don't want to harm you in any way because you were certainly doing your best, so I would propose to say something on the lines that the Captain of the ship always takes full responsibility for anything done by the ship's company. In this particular case I was entirely instrumental in getting the attempt to find [the man's name] started and I knew that the *Navy News* was going to be asked to help, but I did not see, until weeks later, exactly what was said in the *Navy News* which caused all the trouble. If I had seen it I would have changed the wording so as to omit the story about his deserting his post and merely say we wanted to have a 100% of the survivors together once more, and give him a very warm reception to our reunion. If you have any objection to my talking along these lines please ring up ... and let me know what you suggest. May I say, finally, how very sorry I am that you should have had so much adverse publicity; the first adverse publicity that the dear old *Kelly* has ever had! I know you were doing your very best and I just think it was lack of knowledge of public relations that led you into the trap of saying something which the papers could take up. I certainly intend to take the full responsibility along the lines I have suggested unless you have any other ideas.'

At the subsequent dinner — whether the ex-stoker saw the stories or not is not known, but he did not communicate with Rocky Wilkins —

Lord Mountbatten again made it clear to everyone that he told Rocky he ought to try to trace the shipmate. Unfortunately, Rocky had not sent the story to Mountbatten first. The *Sunday Express* endeavoured to have a reporter at the dinner but he was not allowed in and this, as it turned out, might have been unfortunate because Mountbatten gave a detailed account of how, obeying orders with which he did not agree, he took his ship into a minefield. He tried to pretend it wasn't a minefield, he said, but he knew it was and he was more frightened than the stoker was. A mine grated under the bridge, then it grated under the engine room 'which must have been very frightening because the engine room was right down to about the bottom' and the 'poor' young stoker moved away from his post, which was wrong. The mine then grated under the wardroom but did not go off until it got between the propellers. 'It threw most people off their feet. So no wonder he was frightened. I was too. But I had to do something about it so in fact I had him up. I cautioned him. A caution to him and a caution to me for not having impressed my personality on the ship's company better so they realized they couldn't do that. I made a tub-thumping speech. I said, "I can tell you that you will never get the order to abandon ship from me. The only way you'll get out of *Kelly* is if she sinks below your feet."' Mountbatten went on to say that the stoker was '... a gallant fellow. He won the Distinguished Service Medal in another action so all we want is to find him. If you ever find him bring him along and say how very welcome he will be here.'

There was applause from *Kelly* men for what they considered to be a magnanimous speech. Coming from their old Captain, though, it did not surprise them.

Although he was judged to be at fault in his honest endeavour to trace the stoker, Rocky Wilkins wholeheartedly considers that Lord Mountbatten's side of this disagreeable matter should be stated. He still does not fully understand why Mountbatten should have persisted in asking him to trace the stoker. It could be that Mountbatten felt some latent remorse for admonishing the teenage lad and really wished to express some forgiveness nearly forty years later. He stresses that Mountbatten repeated that he rebuked the young man but also rebuked himself for failing to impress himself and his personality on the lad. But Mountbatten, like all of them, genuinely wanted to see the stoker back with the rest of the ship's survivors, Rocky says. It was also interesting to learn that Mountbatten had seemingly made some enquiries himself, enabling him to reveal to the *Kelly* men that the chap had been awarded the DSM for some heroic action in his later career in the Navy, a fact which hitherto had been unknown to his *Kelly* colleagues. Rocky also emphasizes that, so far as he himself was concerned, his friendly relations with Mountbatten continued. In his subsequent dealings with Mountbatten there was no malice or rancour on either side. After Lord Mountbatten's full and frank statement at the dinner the affair was never mentioned again.

**22nd May 1978**

Everybody present at the KELLY Reunion on the 20th onboard HMS PRESIDENT missed you very much but nobody more than I, myself, and my next grand-daughter, Amanda, who had heard so much from Joanna about her sitting next to you last time.

I hope that your arthritis will soon be better and that you will be all right again.

Please accept my sincere thanks for those lovely flowers from Malta which were presented to me at the dinner. I meant my grand-daughter, Amanda, to take them with her but she had to go by train to her university and had nowhere to put the flowers. So she gave them back to me and then I thought that I would make a public gesture on behalf of us both, so I passed them on to Anne Wilkins with best wishes from you and from myself. I hope you agree with this.

Mr G. Micallef,

---

BROADLANDS,
ROMSEY,
HAMPSHIRE.
SO5 9ZD.

TELEPHONE
ROMSEY (0794) 5133...

16th October 1978

My dear Rocky,

Thank you for your letter of the 6th October which I found on my return from Balmoral.

I am so glad that your suprise party turned out to be a genuine surprise as happened tome when all of you double crossed me!

I note all the rest that you say in your le* and shall look forward to hearing from you again.

I note that you are experiencing the same as have done about retirement, that there seems to be m to do!

I have recently written a foreword for the I of HMS PROVIDENCE and Genesis Publications Limited I made the cheque out for my fee of £320 to the HMS KI Reunion Fund and I enclose it herewith.

Yours ever

Mountbatten of Burma

---

BROADLANDS,
ROMSEY,
HAMPSHIRE.
SO5 9ZD.

TELEPHONE
ROMSEY (0794) 513333

30th September 1978

My dear Rocky,

I see you have at last been caught, like I was, by your own family and that your niece, Valerie White, is springing this surprise on you.

No Able Seaman in the history of the Royal Navy has done so much to perpetuate the history of his own ship with the ship's company and, indeed, with the media than you have.

Your original conversation with the late Able Seaman Godfrey Winn started the ball rolling. He was a wonderful author and a great friend of our family and he obviously helped you to get the KELLY Reunion Association under way.

Since then it has gone from strength to strength and you have had the most remarkable set of VIPs attending your dinners and they seem to get better and better.

How you manage to produce so many survivors each time is a permanent wonder to me but it always makes me personally have a very happy and nostalgic evening and I certainly hope that this evening, which is a Rocky Benefit will be a pleasant surprise and a great success.

I send you my very best wishes for the occasion

Yours ever

Mountbatten of Burma

---

BROADLANDS,
ROMSEY,
HAMPSHIRE.
SO5 9ZD.

TELEPHONE
ROMSEY (0794) 51...

22nd June 1979

Dear Rocky,

Thank you for your letter of the 20th June which crossed my last letter.

First of all I thank you and the KELLY Association for your birthday wishes for my 79th birthday which I very much appreciate.

Will you please thank the widow of Dusty Miller very much indeed for the cap tally she sent me which I am delighted to have.

Yours ever

Mountbatten of Burma

Chapter 21

# *The Prince's sea time*

Prince Charles first met the *Kelly* Association at the reunion dinner in 1974. He had already heard plenty about the old shipmates in his conversations with Lord Mountbatten. He even knew some of their names. As early as the previous year Mountbatten told Rocky: 'I hope to bring one or two grandsons and possibly a great nephew to this dinner, but it depends whether they are free. For the moment therefore this must be kept to yourself.'

Later, but still several months before the dinner, he reminded Rocky: 'I will also bring my great nephew the Prince of Wales if he is back in time and can get away from his ship'. As the Prince had not yet got the necessary leave it was essential that the possibility should not leak to the Press. However, Mountbatten added that it was only fair to warn members of the Association 'in strict confidence' that there was a fifty-fifty chance that HRH would attend the dinner and 'I am sure you will have a record turn-out if he comes'.

When it was certain the Prince *would* attend, Mountbatten said he would ask the Prince 'to wear a monkey jacket, the same as me, as we are both on the active list'. He also asked Wilkins to keep in touch with his private secretary, John Barratt, about the question of members who could not attend owing to the cost of travel and tickets. 'I think that on this occasion I might be able to arrange for a friend of mine to produce some money to help out with the problem. We certainly want to get the biggest possible gathering of genuine members of the ship's company for His Royal Highness as it is a pretty unique honour getting him.' Lord Mountbatten did not think Prince Charles' name should be on the official toast list unless he agreed, but thought the Association might perhaps persuade him to say a few informal words nearer the time.

To everyone's delight not only did Prince Charles enter into the spirit of the reunion, enjoying himself thoroughly, but he made the speech of the evening. Added to the fun there was banter and interruptions between Lord Mountbatten and the Prince and some of the former ratings. Prince Charles said the *Kelly* Association was a most extraordinary institution, a lot of it due to Rocky Wilkins, who sat next to him. 'I actually managed to get his name right and I didn't even serve with him!' (A tilt at Lord

*Prince Charles meets the 'Kellies'
at a reunion dinner.*

Mountbatten who liked it to be known that he knew the name of every man who served under him in *Kelly*.)

The Prince of Wales said he couldn't emulate Lord Mountbatten's feat of a magnificent half-hour oration and didn't know nearly as many jokes as Admiral Philip Burnett whose speech preceded his own. When the Prince said he relied on his own jokes, Mountbatten chipped in: 'You can tell them, can't you?' Prince Charles quipped: 'Not since you were rude about it!' The Prince said his great uncle had asked him to talk about the present Royal Navy. A few weeks previously he had completed nearly a twelvemonth afloat, sailing almost round the world as an active Naval officer. He talked hilariously about his own experiences and his talented off-the-cuff speech delighted his audience, not least the womenfolk.

'The last four months till the end of April I was in the Pacific. Last year I was on the West Indies Station for seven months, which was the greatest possible fun. In the Pacific we were about the first Royal Naval ship to go across it for some considerable time because they don't go there much now for various reasons. But the ship, HMS *Jupiter*, was on the Far East Station and I joined her in Singapore which is somewhere I'd never been before. But I'm sure quite a lot of you have been there and imprinted your names on Bugis Street. I won't give the details in case the wives ... [Laughter drowned his words. Singapore's Bugis Street was a haunt of sailors, full of bars and girls.] But it has changed a lot I think since the war.

'We went from there across the Java Sea and down to Brisbane and on the way we had a distress signal in the middle of the night. I was on watch, at two o'clock in the morning I believe it was, and it gave the position of this ship and I thought this is very exciting because it must be at least a hundred-thousand-tons tanker and we were in for a fantastic amount of salvage money. So I called the Captain and he came up on to the bridge and I said: "Sir, we must go and find this ship — it is really very, very exciting — salvage money and all that sort of thing, and can't we go up to 28 knots and go and find it?" So he said "Come on then, all right, off we go". So we steamed in a southerly direction and when we got there we sent the helicopter up as we've got helicopters nowadays and the Fleet Air Arm have to be kept busy and we went over and had a look. Believe it or not, it wasn't a hundred-thousand-ton tanker but a small barge — a tug with two barges which had jack-knifed and got stuck on a coral reef. So I should think our combined salvage money would have amounted to about ten quid.

'From there we had to go through a minefield — that was very exciting — an old Second World War minefield — and we had to come out backwards at four knots and it took four hours to get out! We then went on to Brisbane and that was fun. We had two days there, the only two days of sunshine and reasonable weather since Christmas. The day after we left the heavens opened and they had the biggest storm they had had for years and it flooded the whole countryside. Thank God we missed that! It was said that so bad was the weather and so awful were the floods that there were snakes travelling on the backs of sheep down the rivers!

'We went on to New Zealand where I joined my parents and my sister in Christchurch for the Commonwealth Games and that was extremely enjoyable. It's a marvellous institution, the Commonwealth Games. But it is in a terrific spirit and it really is a great example of what the Commonwealth can achieve, and it all went off extremely well. Then we

**Right** *Prince Charles and Lord Mountbatten talk to former Kelly crew members. On the left is 'Scrounger' Scorer, the man who retrieved Kelly's battle ensign and the E-boat steering wheel.*

**Far right** *The Prince dances with Mrs Gwen Dewall, one of the survivor's wives.*

went on and I left the Queen in the Royal Yacht and then back to sea in an opposite direction. We arrived in Fiji, I think it was. A marvellous country and happy to have been a colony of Great Britain's — they're independent now — where they welcome you as long-lost friends. They're one of the few countries that voluntarily decided to become a colony. They asked Queen Victoria for protection because they were fighting each other and got fed up with it. From there we went on to Samoa which is a splendid place and also to Tonga, which is very notable for the fact that they have enormous people there. The King is the biggest man you have ever seen which is extremely appropriate for a sovereign. He's bigger than anyone else. So I've got to do something about it!'

The Prince described his adventures at a yacht club during a call on the Pacific voyage. 'All these enormous women tried to dance with me. And one who was particularly large came up to me and said: "Aah's been told to introduce … Aaah's been told and now Aah's got you!" It was like dancing with several spare tyres! I managed to escape from her clutches. We went on to Hawaii, a very exciting place indeed. We spent a week in dry dock and the Americans were incredibly efficient. I played polo in front of about 5,000 people, which doesn't often happen. We then went on across the Pacific, exercising with two American destroyers. We had on one occasion a sports afternoon on board *Jupiter* and representatives from each American ship came on board. One of the officers from an American ship — he was talking to me on board — "OK", he said, "So you're going to be King one day". So I said: "Yes, yes …". "So what kind of a deal is that?", the American officer asked. I said: "I'm not sure. I'll let you know when I find out!"

'Anyway, we arrived in San Diego, the enormous American naval base in California — a vast number of American ships there. Again they were incredibly helpful, kind and almost overwhelming in their hospitality. And sailors, as you all know only too well, sailors still are and always will be the same kind of people. Some of the sailors when the Americans came on board were saying: "You see the hangar there, that is where he keeps his polo ponies". "Not really", they said. "We knew he was important but we didn't know he was that important."

'From there we went on to Acapulco in Mexico which was again a very enjoyable place. I did this fascinating thing, I don't know whether you've ever seen on the television. You go parachuting behind a boat and you start on a sort of deck floating in the sea, you put on this parachute harness and the boat is somewhere out there and the man says "Stand back from the edge", and you literally take a running jump as the boat moves off. And I succeeded. I went straight up to about 400 ft and went round the bay. Very exciting and I looked down and I was wondering what the hell was going to happen if the bloody rope snapped.

'Then we went through the Panama Canal which is something I was very glad to have done, and we then ended up in San Juan. I don't know if you have ever been there, but it is one of the nastiest places I have ever been to. I have been there several times before. We always end up there. We do exercises with the American Navy. I hardly dare tell you but I met two splendid people from Liverpool. They came on board one evening when I was on duty. And in the wardroom of our ship, we can in most frigates, you can draw the curtain across the middle and you can have a dining section in one part and a sitting-out section in the other. And it makes the best nightclub in the business. You can turn the tape recorder on and we were doing this and this splendid small lady, she was only very, very small indeed, from Liverpool, came up to me and said: "This is a ladies' excuse

*A picture of the Kelly ship's company for the Prince of Wales. It was taken in Malta two days before Kelly was lost at Crete.*

*'This is the man we call
"Scrounger" Scorer' Mountbatten
tells the Prince of Wales.*

me". And I said: "Oh, is it really?" And she dragged me and gripped me very very tight and we were dancing away furiously and she said: "Oh. Y're luvly, y're luvly". She said: "Give us a kiss". She said: "I can write ten pages to my Mum about you. Give us another kiss", she said. I said "No, no! No, no!", I said: "That'll be twenty pages now will it?" She said: "Yes". That is one of the perils of meeting ladies from Liverpool in Puerto Rico.

'We then continued back across the Atlantic and fortunately escaped without any disastrously rough storms or anything, got back at the end of April much to everybody's joy and relief. I remember I was photographed on the flight deck of HMS *Jupiter* entirely alone amidst a sea of people all greeting their wives and there was a great headline saying "The lonely Prince". It was all very very sad. I've made up for it since then!'

BROADLANDS,
ROMSEY,
HAMPSHIRE.
SO5 9ZD.

TELEPHONE
ROMSEY 0791 51333

23rd July 1979

My dear Rocky,

Thank you for your letter of the 19th July.

I am so sorry I could not get to the MERCURY's Open Day on Saturday but the trouble was I had a party who came down specially for business discussions at Broadlands.

A recent gathering of some thousand members of the Burma Star Association came to Broadlands and after going round the house I met them and talked to them and they included, curiously enough, a man who had served in the KELLY in the first commission and who had attended one of the first Reunions but never attended one again. He had obviously lost touch.

John Barratt kindly made a note of his name and address which I attach on a separate piece of paper for you to follow up.

As regards Finch's medals: I am afraid I don't agree at all with your remark in paragraph 3, about a large sum of money to be paid for campaign stars and medals which were awarded at the finish of Service.

He never had to pay for any of the original issue which were given to him free. If he loses them that, I am afraid, is his own responsibility. You can well imagine the trade that could be done in war medals, which fetch quite a lot in shops, if people were to say they had lost their set and wanted a fresh *free* set and then went and sold them.

I am afraid it would start a real racket. I am sorry but I couldn't agree to even try and get that changed. Nor could I succeed.

However, as I am hoping to get a reasonable sum of money from the sale of the latest KELLY prints, if that money is enough to pay for your dinner and you can manage to keep back £39.98 to get Finch's medals, that would be a reasonable proposition for we know him to be honest and they might be given to him, perhaps, at our next KELLY Reunion dinner, if the Committee agree.

I have seen the artist, Myers, and he has been to Namsos and spent several days there. He spent an entire night in the fjord off the town to see what it looked like by the midnight sun. He also found photographs taken of the blaze at the time, so he even knows what the flames looked like and he seems to have made a very good sketch. I have approved it and hope he will soon do a finished production which will then be turned into prints.

The artist and I will both sign them and they hope to sell them for a reasonable sum of money and the profits will all go to the KELLY Reunion Association which should set you up for the rest of your life, I hope.

Yours ever

Mountbatten of Burma

---

26th July 1979

I was so sorry to hear that you have been unwell and am writing to send you my very best wishes.

I do not know whether you have heard from Rocky Wilkins recently but the KELLY Reunion Association continues as strong as ever.

Last October I returned to the Hebburn Yard on Tyneside to celebrate the 40th anniversary of the launching of our beloved KELLY and a large contingent of KELLY survivors, headed by Rocky Wilkins, came along to support me.

It was a wonderfully nostalgic occasion and to mark the anniversary I was presented with a cartoon type drawing by a local artist depicting incidents in the life of the KELLY. I was also given several small prints of the drawing and enclose one herewith as I feel it might amuse you.

A local woman also wrote a charming poem entitled 'The Spirit of the KELLY' and I enclose a copy of that in case you haven't seen it.

With all best wishes.

Mr. Herbert Phillips

---

COMMONWEALTH WAR GRAVES COMMISSION
32 Grosvenor Gardens, London S.W.1
Téléphone: SLOANE 0751
Telegrams: COMMGRAVE LONDON S.W.1

Ref.: CM 77

8 September 1971

A J Wilkins Esq
Secretary
HMS Kelly Re-Union Association

Dear Mr Wilkins

According to the official history HMS Kelly was sunk 40 miles off Crete. Those of the ship's company who were not picked up have no known graves but the sea. They are commemorated on the Naval Memorial at their manning ports, most of them at Chatham. None of the 18 identified Naval and Marine graves in Suda Bay War Cemetery, Crete, are from the Kelly.

Yours sincerely

Director-General

Chapter 22

# *Funeral*

Mountbatten himself suggested certain of the arrangements for his own funeral. He did not forget his shipmates from *Kelly*. Seven years before he was killed he wrote to Rocky Wilkins saying: 'It has occurred to me that representatives of the HMS *Kelly* Reunion Association might like to be invited to my funeral whenever it does take place. If this is so and you could confirm that some would like to come and possibly walk in the procession I will arrange to lodge your letter with the Lord Chamberlain to make sure that an invitation is sent at the proper time.' He asked Wilkins what he thought of getting one of the members, possibly Ralph Scorer, to carry *Kelly*'s ensign on a flagstaff in the procession. 'Scrounger' Scorer, a breezy character from the hills of County Durham, retrieved both the E-boat steering wheel and *Kelly*'s battle ensign from the wreckage of the vessel when it arrived at Hebburn for repair after the North Sea torpedoing.) He had made a surprise presentation of them to Mountbatten twenty years later at a reunion dinner in HMS *President*. Mountbatten asked Wilkins to keep what he wrote confidential as they didn't want the newspapers 'to hear of such unusual plans'. Rocky was asked to 'tell only two or three of his most intimate and reliable associates'.

Lord Mountbatten cannot have imagined the magnificence, scale of, or the world interest in his funeral. As it turned out, it would have exceeded his expectations and gratified him immensely. It took place a little more than a week after the shock to the world of the explosion off Mullaghmore and, as usual on these great occasions in the capital, the detailed preparations were made to perfection, though they were not entirely to the satisfaction of Rocky and his *Kelly* colleagues.

Rocky Wilkins got a telephone call inviting him to attend a conference conducted by a Major-General at Horse Guards on the Friday of the week preceding the funeral, Lord Mountbatten's body having been brought from Dublin airport to lie at Broadlands and at Romsey Abbey before being taken to London. Representatives of military and civil organizations involved from home and overseas were present and Wilkins promptly asked why it was that the *Kelly* survivors were so far back in the funeral procession. He would have thought, he stated, that they should have been

**Above and left** Lord Mountbatten's funeral. Kelly survivors march through Whitehall to the service at Westminster Abbey. Some came to London without being sure of an admission ticket but all were able to attend.

**Below** Kelly survivors at the memorial service for Lord Mountbatten at Romsey Abbey. One of his former shipmates, Tug Wilson, reads the lesson.

nearer the cortege than was scheduled, at least leading the ex-Servicemen's contingents, whereas the 'Kellys' followed such as the British Legion, the Royal Naval Association, the Royal Marines Association, men who served in Asia, the Life Guards and many other groups. 'We were the very last', he said. 'The only people who followed us were the standard bearers from Romsey. I was told by this officer that when State funerals are run by the Army the most honoured guests are placed in the rear of the procession. "The *Kelly* survivors are the most honoured guests".'

For the first rehearsal, participants had to be at Wellington Barracks by 04:00. The day of the funeral they had to be in position at 08:00. Tickets were allocated for 24 members of the *Kelly* Association but, although there was no chance of additional tickets, *Kelly* survivors, including former stewards who had flown at their own expense from Malta and others from far-distances — had arrived without being invited. To give Rocky more worries the 24 tickets from the Lord Chamberlain's office were sent to his old address and were 'lost' until the day before the funeral. Rocky spoke to the Association's Vice President, Admiral Burnett. What were they going to do about the extra shipmates? They had all arrived in the 'rig of the day', *Kelly* blazers, badges and medals. 'Who was I to turn them away?', Rocky asked. 'Anyway, it was a case of "Take a chance and fall in behind".' So, although some men were well over seventy and Rocky pointed out that the two-hour march was going to be a test of stamina for the oldest, the 24-ticket limit was ignored. Thirty of them joined in to record their tribute. They proudly marched on the crowded route via Whitehall to the Abbey and with no trouble at all sailed through security, officials and ushers. Their 'uniform' was their passport. Rocky had even laid on their usual professional photographer.

*Countess Mountbatten lays a single rose on the grave of her father in Romsey Abbey with surviving crew members of HMS Kelly looking on.*

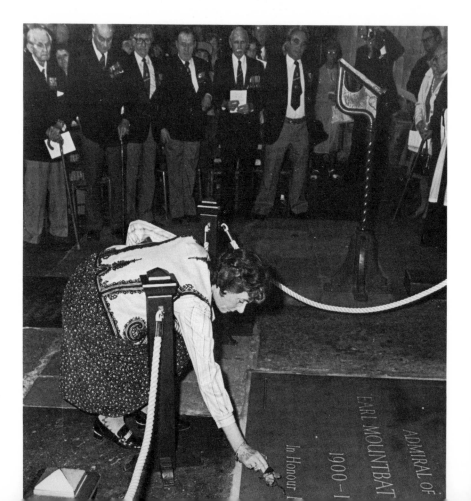

Chapter 23

# The Prince takes over

The Prince of Wales presided for the first time at the *Kelly* dinner in May 1980. For him it was an unenviable task addressing his great uncle's men, but the Prince carried it out superbly. He paid eloquent tribute as did others. The Prince made it a jolly evening. He said Lord Mountbatten would not have wanted that particular reunion to be miserable. He caused murmers of satisfaction when he assured the *Kelly* survivors that he was proud and honoured to take over the leadership of the Association. He looked around the tables at the men who had served with Lord Mountbatten, in their sixties, seventies, some of them in their eighties, and joked: 'It looks as though I shall be the last member of this Association!'

As one of the survivors said: 'The Prince is a real "chip off the old block"'. He meant that he is exactly like his father the Duke of Edinburgh in his mannerisms and his sense of fun, while the Duke is so much in the mould of Mountbatten, the uncle who took such a profound interest in his nephew's upbringing and career, not least Prince Philip's long Naval service. The Prince of Wales is great company with a sparkling sense of humour. It is doubtful if he could act as freely, informally and unconventionally at any other function as he did at this one. There has never been and there probably cannot be again any lower deck organization as close to the heir to the throne as this one.

After the meal was completed the Prince raised his glass and said: 'We drink the Loyal Toast sitting down. Ladies and gentlemen, the Queen.' Then he announced: 'Now you may all smoke — if you must'. There were a few nervous coughs, then some fumblings for cigarette packets and lighters and some people lit up, it seemed a very few. Like his father, and Lord Mountbatten, who used to enjoy an occasional cigar but did not smoke in his later days, the Prince is a non-smoker and his abstinence has probably set an example to many of the nation's young people.

He reminded the *Kelly* men that he had been Captain of a very small ship, the minehunter HMS *Bronington*, about three or four years previously. 'About the only thing that happened when I left that ship, instead of an association being formed, they put me on a wheelchair and hung a lavatory seat round my neck and then they pushed me over the side.

'One of the great things about the *Kelly* Association was really, as the result of a war, you shared in a kind of adversity which those of us like myself who have been brought up in a generation that hasn't known war of and kind, which obviously is a relief, can't quite understand. [The Prince was speaking before the Falklands War.] But it does produce a kind of spirit which is quite unique. That is one of the reasons why this Association has gone on for as long as it has.'

About the only adversity he could recall having shared in HMS *Bronington* was one memorable occasion, off Holyhead, Anglesey, when they were doing an exercise, and managed to anchor on an underwater telephone cable. This was something the Navy is not supposed to do. On the chart little wavy pink lines here and there signified where these cables were. The cable on which they anchored linked Wales with Ireland! They spent a long time trying to pull the thing up, which had the effect of merely raising the cable off the bottom and dropping it down again. Nothing would shift it. To begin with, there were great jokes going around. There were pipes made over the ship's broadcast saying: 'Shore telephone call in the cable locker'. They thought of sending divers down but eventually decided to slip the ship's anchor and release the cable. Afterwards, letters started appearing from the Admiralty saying: 'Don't do it again'.

Lord Mountbatten, said the Prince of Wales, believed it was not the *Kelly*'s exploits that made her unique and allowed the Association to grow up, but that extraordinary spirit of comradeship. No Captain in the Royal Navy ever knew his ship better. Lord Mountbatten knew all his shipmates intimately. He knew their best qualities, their weaknesses and all the other things that helped him control his ship's company. 'Sadly, in my day in HMS *Bronington*, because of the drafting system which there is nowadays, half the ship's company in the ten months that I was on board left; so, maddeningly, just when I was getting to know people, they all shoved off.'

Prince Charles thought the *Kelly* Association might be interested to hear a little of what some of those who had not survived thought of their Captain. Many letters were written to Lord Mountbatten after the *Kelly* sank, several from the families of those who went down at that battle on 23 May 1941, 39 years previously. The first one he read was from a father:

'I wish to extend to you on behalf of my wife and myself our thanks for your letter and photographs and it is a great comfort to us to know that you yourself do not forget and feel for us and we can quite understand now why our dear son the last time he was at home always kept telling us how proud he was to be serving under you and if I may use his own words "what a grand fellow and shipmate" you were.'

Another letter the Prince quoted:

'I hardly know how to express my thanks to you for your kindly thought and action in sending the photograph of HMS *Kelly*'s crew. No one man in a thousand would have thought of it or bothered to have gone to all that trouble. But you are, as my son always told me, a perfect gentleman and you will always hold a warm spot in my heart for your kindly act.'

A third letter was written by a brother:

'I have been asked by my mother to thank you for your letter and for the photograph of HMS *Kelly*'s ship's company. This further evidence of your kind thought for the bereaved relatives of those lost in HMS *Kelly* gives proof that the men are not forgotten by their Captain. This fact, I am sure,

*The photograph of the ship's company of HMS Kelly, taken two days before she was sunk, which Mountbatten sent to many of the bereaved families.*

has helped them to bear the weight of their grief.'

After Lord Mountbatten died, the Prince personally received over 2,500 letters from people all over the world, quite apart from those letters the Queen received, and his father and members of his family. The Prince was deeply touched by all of these and tried as hard as he could to reply to them. Throughout all the letters the theme was the same: that Lord Mountbatten above all else cared for people as individuals and took the trouble to think of them, of their lives and problems, and to consider things which many other people did not. This, Prince Charles said, went a long way and meant that people really did love him.

'Now your Captain is dead. And we have all lost a very special friend. I at any rate have lost someone who was like a second father to me and the world has lost a particularly great statesman. I am sure that you all remember after your return to Alexandria, after you had been picked up and he came to say goodbye, and I thought that it would be worth just reading what he said to you then, you probably remember it, but for those of us here who haven't heard it before, it is well worth reading. He said "I've come to say goodbye to the few of you who are left. We have had so many talks but this is our last. I've always tried to crack a joke or two before and you have all been friendly and laughed at them. But today I'm afraid I have run out of jokes and I don't suppose any of us feels much like laughing.

"The *Kelly* has been in one scrap after another but even when we have had men killed, the majority survived and brought the old ship back. Now she lies in 1,500 fathoms and with her more than half or our shipmates. If they had to die, what a grand way to go. So now they all lie together with

*Mountbatten talks to the girls and boys of HMS Mercury.*

the ship we loved and they are in very good company. We have lost her but they are still with us. There may be less than half the *Kelly* left, but I feel that each of us will take up the battle with even stronger heart. Each of us knows twice as much about fighting and each of us has twice as good a reason to fight. You will all be sent to replace men who have been killed in other ships and the next time you are in action, remember the *Kelly*. As you ram each shell home into the gun, shout 'KELLY', and so her spirit will go on inspiring us until victory is won. I should like to add that there is not one of you that I wouldn't be proud and honoured to serve with again. Goodbye, good luck and thank you all from the bottom of my heart.''

'Well, despite the shattering shock of Lord Mountbatten's death, he has, I think, left behind such a great example for all of us to follow. And I know this has been one of the things that I found about his death which has been enormously helpful, that, although one does miss him terribly, instead of thinking about it all the time, I found that I thought to myself of all the things that he did which suddenly came back to me. The marvellous things he thought about. The people he cared for. His intense thoughtfulness; again treating people as individuals. And his moral courage, which is a great example for us to try and follow if we can. And also his open-mindedness — and above all else, I value that, I think, more than anything else.

'Even in his old age, he could always understand new ideas and accept the sort of things that many people would not accept or try to understand. He was always fascinated with flying saucers, for instance, and I remember many an article and so on he would cut out and read and send to other people who didn't always share his enthusiasm. I did I must say because I think they're fascinating. But I think he would also want us to be positive above all else in our approach towards the future. He never looked back — well, he did on these occasions, obviously, because it was a marvellous chance to reminisce but I know he would want us to work towards a greater understanding throughout the world and particularly in a country like Ireland. But I know that one of the things that I am most anxious to try and do is to make sure that he didn't die in vain. I don't quite know how. It is one of the most difficult things in the world to know where to begin when you aren't a politician. It is bad enough when you are. But I do so want something positive to come out of this and all I can say is that I shall do my best where I can and one of the ways I want to try and work is through the United World Colleges, which was another of his great loves and passions in his life — this Association and the United World Colleges — and I seem to have taken them both on.

'I hope that I can be worthy of the *Kelly* and what is left of her. So, ladies and gentlemen, let's drink to that extraordinary ship, that very special ship, and as we do, let's remember, let's do as her Captain urged and shout out her name so that her spirit will go on inspiring us and future generations. ''KELLY!''.'

One of *Kelly*'s officers, Commander James Turnbull, welcomed the Prince as the Association's new President, together with the Association's other guests who included the commanding officers of HMS *President* and HMS *Mercury*, Lord Mountbatten's grandson Lord Romsey, Sir John Mills, civic leaders from the Medway — *Kelly* was a Chatham-based ship — Lord Mountbatten's former private secretary John Barratt, Mark Myers the artist who painted the picture of *Kelly* entering Namsos and Sir

Donald Gosling, Chairman of the White Ensign Association. The Prince presented all *Kelly* survivors attending with Mark Myers' Namsos picture.

The dinner over, the Prince took the opportunity of chatting with all the *Kelly* men and many guests. He had a pint of beer at a bare trestle table while the dinner tables were being cleared from the deck in HMS *President* to make room for the dancing which followed. Lord Mountbatten had danced there with his wife and some of his shipmates' wives. One survivor's pretty teenage granddaughter will probably forever regret that, when asked by the Prince for the first dance, she was so flustered and shy that she stammered some excuse and the Prince soon found another partner.

★ ★ ★

The Prince of Wales had an unexpected and pleasant surprise for *Kelly* men and their ladies one day in the summer of 1981. As had been the custom for a number of years, survivors made their way to HMS *Mercury* at East Meon, Petersfield, Hampshire, a few miles from Portsmouth. *Mercury* is the Royal Navy's communications and navigation school and in the early 1970s the New Entry Training Squadron was renamed the *Kelly* Squadron as a tribute to the destroyer and Mountbatten and his men.

*Prince Charles and Rocky Wilkins chat at HMS Mercury.*

*Prince Charles and Lady Diana Spencer at HMS Mercury a few days before their wedding.*

Lord Mountbatten used to drive across from Broadlands on the annual open day to take the salute at a march-past of new entries and at the tail of the march-past he was delighted to watch his old crew members step smartly past.

On 25 July Prince Charles, in place of his late great-uncle, agreed to take the salute. While the *Kelly* men waited with hundreds of others, including parents, relatives and girl friends from all over the country who went to see the young men parade, there came an announcement which thrilled them all.

Totally unexpectedly, the Prince had decided to bring his fiancée, Lady Diana Spencer. Minutes after the news went round a helicopter of the Queen's Flight, piloted by Prince Charles, arrived overhead and landed on the lawn of the mansion used as the officers' quarters. There was huge applause as a smiling Lady Diana took her seat in the front row of the spectators. She looked shy and beautiful. Everyone was excited and delighted, particularly the womenfolk, for this was the first time almost everybody present had seen the young lady who the following week at St Paul's Cathedral was to become the Princess of Wales and our future Queen. Although the royal bride's visit was at short notice, HMS *Mercury*'s staff coped superbly. So did the Band of the Royal Marines, Commander-in-Chief Naval Home Command, from Portsmouth. After those stirring Naval marches, 'Hearts of Oak', 'A Life on the Ocean Wave' and 'Rule Britannia', as the *Kelly* men marched past the Prince on the rostrum the bank struck up 'Get me to the Church on Time', Stanley Holloway's song from *My Fair Lady*. Lady Diana appreciated the tribute, she blushed a little and broke into the smile which is now known the world over.

After the ceremonial divisions the Prince and his bride-to-be met the *Kelly* party in the wardroom for drinks. Lady Diana joined and chatted with the clusters of *Kelly* ladies. She gave them a close look at her engagement ring but said: 'You can look at it but don't touch it!' The couple did a walkabout in the spacious grounds of HMS *Mercury*, stopping to talk with so many people that the sherry and the first course of the lunch in the large Petty Officers' mess had to be cut from the menu. The Prince and Lady Diana sat opposite one another at the 'top table' with 25 other guests, and shared with dozens of other visitors the simple lunch from *Mercury*'s kitchens comprising English roast lamb, baby carrots, broccoli spears and new potatoes — and, of course, 'Prince Charles Pudding' and 'Lady Diana Dessert!'

The couple had a polo engagement at Windsor that afternoon but before their helicopter took off and circled the cheering sailors and their families, Rocky Wilkins managed to say some brief words. He rose from his seat, next but one to Prince Charles, and placed a parcel on the dining table between the Prince and Lady Diana. He simply said: 'Sir and Your Ladyship. Here is your wedding present from the *Kelly* Reunion Association'. Lady Diana opened it at once. The present was a specially-made paperweight from Staffordshire and she said: 'Thank you all very much. How very, very nice.' Rocky and his wife had the honour of representing the Association at the wedding in St Paul's Cathedral.

*The bride-to-be meets Rocky Wilkins who presented her with a wedding present on behalf of the Kelly Association, a paperweight inscribed with the 'Fighting Fifth' emblem.*

Chapter 24

# *She belongs to Hebburn*

Every year since the *Kelly* Reunion Association was formed Hebburn-on-Tyne has welcomed *Kelly* survivors on Remembrance weekend. While the great national service went on at the Cenotaph in Whitehall and at war memorials throughout the Commonwealth, Hebburn has staged three services; one at St Cuthbert's parish church, another at the town's war memorial and a third at the cemetery where 27 members of *Kelly*'s crew, killed in the North Sea early in her career, are buried. In addition to their memorial there is now a tablet on the grave in memory of Lord Mountbatten's murder at Mullaghmore in County Sligo.

Each November a group of the *Kelly* Association arrives in the town to stay in Hebburn private homes, in local hotels or the 'Royal Station' Hotel in Newcastle which also commemorates the ship with a Mountbatten bar. Lord Mountbatten, with his wife Edwina, have joined the Remembrance services at Hebburn, so has their daughter Patricia, now the Countess Mountbatten of Burma, and officers and men. The most recent was as well attended as ever. *Kelly* survivors brought their wives and families and as usual it was a weekend affair, lasting from the Friday to Sunday. The commemoration commenced with a civic buffet reception given by representatives of the local councils and the Tyne & Wear Council. There was the regular visit to the Sea Cadet Corps headquarters by the River Tyne prior to the Sunday morning. To a local silver band, whose history goes back to the days when many industrial firms and every colliery in the area had its own band, and to the marching band of the TS *Kelly* Sea Cadets, British Legion members joined by Sea Cadets, other organizations and the *Kelly* survivors march — there are some nowadays who don't march any longer — to the handsome old church. Then they go on to the local war memorial and finally to the cemetery for the laying of wreaths. A wreath was laid on behalf of the Prince of Wales, another for Countess Mountbatten and a third on behalf of surviving *Kelly* shipmates.

Then came wreaths from the police, fire brigade, the shipyards and townsfolk who retain proud and affectionate memories of the *Kelly* crew members during wartime. The weekend concluded with a reception and a buffet at the immense club and headquarters of the Hebburn British Legion, with wartime photographs and letters being exchanged by the

*The Mountbattens at the* Kelly
*memorial in Hebburn on Tyne
cemetery.*

Hebburn people who built and repaired *Kelly* and made crew members
welcome in the industrial town on Tyneside.

Mr Frankie Firth, member of South Tyneside council and a civic leader
for thirty years, made a welcoming speech. He also spoke at the grave of
the *Kelly* survivors. Mr Firth remembered the days just before the war
when *Kelly* was building and crew members, most of them young lads,
lodged with townsfolk and were regarded as sons. They were welcome
again when *Kelly*'s exploits resulted in severe damage in 1940 when she
was torpedoed, and there were broken hearts when she finally went down
off Crete. One of the *Kelly* men, Jack Ellis, who married a local girl and
became a janitor looking after a block of flats, had just died. One Hebburn
lady was courting one of *Kelly*'s crewmen who perished. She never
married. She was sent a ticket for Mountbatten's funeral at Westminster
Abbey. Frankie Firth recalled events like this.

He remembered Lord Mountbatten from his first visit while the ship
was building to the last memorial service Mountbatten attended when he
remarked about the decline in employment in the area. At one time
Hebburn itself, much due to its shipbuilding and other heavy
manufacturing, had more jobs than it had population. But it had been
different on Tyneside for many years between the wars. Jarrow, next door
to Hebburn, was a particularly depressed area and much needed work had
come as a direct result of the Jarrow march in which the famous little
Labour politician, Ellen Wilkinson, was one of the leaders who made big
headlines in the newspapers as they marched down to London.

Frankie Firth was one of many who knew Lord Louis in his *Kelly* days
and again when he returned after the war to mourn his dead shipmates

buried in Hebburn. After Mountbatten's death his daughter, Countess Mountbatten of Burma, followed her father, took his place as the chief mourner at the cemetery and unveiled the tablet added in memory of Lord Mountbatten. She also opened the new headquarters of the Sea Cadets towards which Lord Mountbatten had given a cheque. 'A lovely woman, Lord Mountbatten's daughter, and she had a beer with us', said Firth. Hebburn hopes one day to see the Prince of Wales, now he is the *Kelly* Association's president.

That Saturday night, looking across to the north side of the Tyne from outside the *Kelly* Sea Cadet Corps headquarters, the river presented a sight reminiscent of the old days when shipbuilding on the river was thriving. Nothing much was happening at Hebburn on the south side. The Hawthorn Leslie shipyard where the *Kelly* was built had long since closed down and no ships are being built there now. The dry dock had closed ten years before. Hebburn still made a contribution to shipbuilding as prefabricated units were being produced for vessels damaged during the Falklands battle. On this Saturday night, two miles of riverside on the opposite bank — which has in the past produced many great vessels, warships, liners and cargo container — there were thousands of lights glimmering over and across the Tyne. Prospects on the Tyne may again look bleak but for the moment it was a case of an ill wind ...

One Hebburn man, who had been in the shipyards all his life and had seen both the good times and the bad, was reminded of an old man from further up the river beyond the Tyne bridges who had for generations kept a shop that sold almost everything you could imagine, only in the present hard times days went by without him seeing a customer. He was on

*Mountbatten as First Sea Lord and Lady Mountbatten with Mr Smith, Commercial Manager of Hawthorn Leslie in November 1955.*

*Lord and Lady Mountbatten meet some of the Hawthorn Leslie employees who built* Kelly.

television recalling the days when Tyne shipbuilding was prosperous in peace and war. The Naval yards had once been kept busy, first preparing when war was threatened then even more busy repairing during and after conflicts. This old man declared: 'If we don't have a war soon there'll be a crisis!' Hardly a soul would agree but Tynesiders appreciated what the old man had in mind.

The brilliant lights on the north bank of the Tyne lit up the shipyards where a great deal was going on replacing some of the famous names that became known and were seen almost daily on television during the tense months of the Falklands conflict. The *Sir Tristram*, the vessel which arrived back badly damaged, carried piggy-back on a Dutch cargo vessel, was being refitted by Tyne Ship Repairers, a new private firm that had carried on where the nationalized British Shipbuilders had failed. Swan Hunter were fitting out the *York* at the Walker Neptune Yard, to be ready for sea in a matter of months; higher up there was the new *Ark Royal*, and the river was busy replacing the destroyer types *Glasgow* and *Coventry*, lost in the Falklands. The 43,000 ton replacement for the *Atlantic Conveyor*, is a roll-on roll-off container ship of sophisticated design and mixed ability, as the shipbuilders describe her. In addition to these Falklands replacements they were fitting out a new highly modern ship for Cable & Wireless. 'It looks lively from this side of the river with the lights and the bustle, but it's all a mere fleabite to what the Tyne is capable of and direly needs', a former foreman welder remarked resignedly.

Mr Derrick Edmondson is one of the Hebburn people who had a *Kelly* man and his wife as guests for the weekend. He has a vivid memory of 1937 when he says 10,000 were working in the shipyards on the south side of the river. The destroyer HMS *Jervis* was also building in 1937 and two other famous destroyers, *Legion* and *Lightning*, were still in the shipyard when *Kelly* came back from the North Sea, almost sinking. Young Edmondson's first job was as a gateboy in the ambulance house at Hawthorn Leslie where all the traffic came in. His orders were that no person was to enter the shipyard through this gate. One day a Naval officer

*Lord Mountbatten inspects the TS Kelly Sea Cadet Corps in Hebburn, November 1955.*

whom he did not know arrived and asked if he could go through. There was a grille on the doorway and Edmondson firmly refused to let the officer in. So the officer went down to the main gate and walked back to the garage by Edmondson's gate where he garaged his car. It was Lord Louis. Edmondson was reprimanded by his boss because he wouldn't let the Captain of the *Kelly* in. But Mountbatten pointed out that the boy had been told not to let any foot passenger in and had done as he was told, 'therefore you can't complain about it'. So here was another Hebburn person who got to know first-hand what a fair man Lord Louis was.

The dockyard men still around in Hebburn recall many little incidents. A rating from another ship had been guilty of some misdemeanor. His punishment was to run several circuits of the dock in uniform each lunchtime. Some dockyard men used to sit and poke fun at the poor sailor. Lord Louis saw this and approached the rating's commanding officer. The punishment was not stopped but the *Kelly* Captain's intervention meant the runner was transferred to Hawthorn Leslie's playing fields where he completed his 'sentence' without embarrassment.

*The role of honour for those who died while serving in HMS Kelly is now kept at St Cuthbert's Church at Hebburn on Tyne.*

*The memorial in the churchyard at Hebburn on Tyne, Kelly's home town.*

News of Mountbatten's action spread and he was praised for his thoughtfulness.

Edmondson, who became an electrician and a research engineer and is now a lecturer in maths and electrical engineering, remembers the grim scene when *Kelly* came back after being torpedoed, with her decks awash and dockyard pumps going feverishly to keep her afloat. Instead of being warped into dry dock, the warship had to be dragged in with a locomotive attached to each side of her. It was only then that the shipyard workers — and Mountbatten and his men — were able to see the extent of the appalling damage. Once in the dock they could all see that the hole in her was so big 'two double decker buses could have got in'. They still marvelled, says Mr Edmondson, at the feat of getting *Kelly* back to the Tyne afloat and at the six months' repair job making her fit for sea again. Some shipyard people thought she might have been towed into an east coast port rather than be taken back to the Tyne, but this is what Mountbatten was determined to do. Others, including some Naval people senior to Mountbatten, thought *Kelly* should have been sunk or scrapped. The vessel was virtually without any keel to put her on blocks in the drydock and she had to be shored up and the ship's shell built up again. Everybody in the shipyard was amazed at the surgery which lay ahead. The worst task of all fell to the local undertaker, Mr Joseph Donnelly, a dozen sailors under the Torpedo Officer Lieutenant Goodenough and some dockyard workers who had to release the bodies trapped in the mass of twisted metal.

★   ★   ★

The Chairman of the British Legion Club, Bob Sanderson, was one of 400 who built the *Kelly* and twice worked on repairing the vessel as a joiner. He was the 'guinea pig' when Lord Louis' bathroom was being built. The Captain was a practical man. He wanted everything just so. 'I was the lad who sat in the bath and stretched out my hand for the soap dish to be placed so that it was just right for his lordship's reach!'

'When *Kelly* came back so badly damaged it was certainly suggested that she might well have been written off', says Sanderson. Mountbatten

*One of the last pictures taken of Earl Mountbatten as he salutes the memorial to his former shipmates who gave their lives for their country. Hebburn on Tyne, 1978.*

wanted his ship repaired as quickly as possible. 'He said: "I've got a good crew and I don't want to lose any of them"', according to Bob. 'He is supposed to have paid for the repairs himself.' The latter, although a good story, is apocryphal.

★   ★   ★

Another story about Mountbatten and the Tyne was told by Lieutenant Sam Armstrong who had been a CO of an LCG in the Mediterranean landings. Before he joined up Sam had been a legal executive with a firm of marine solicitors in Newcastle and it was while he was doing this job that he met Mountbatten.

Soon after Mountbatten commissioned *Kelly*, she was in collision with a merchant ship which was badly damaged. *Kelly* was also damaged and returned to the Tyne for repairs. Sam's firm was engaged to act for the merchant ship's owners. In due course an appointment was made for Sam to meet Mountbatten aboard *Kelly* to take a statement and hear his version of what happened. Sam duly reported aboard *Kelly* armed with charts, parallel rules, dividers and plenty of well-sharpened pencils. He was met at the gangway by the OOW and promptly escorted down to the wardroom where a pink gin was thrust into his hand and he was told that Mountbatten would be along shortly. About half-an-hour and several pink gins later Mountbatten came into the wardroom and said: 'Hello, old man, sorry to have kept you waiting. I hope my chaps have been looking after you. I cannot talk to you now. I have an important appointment ashore. Anyway it was entirely my fault, I take full responsibility. Charge it up to me. So nice to have met you. Goodbye.' He was gone. Shortly afterwards Sam staggered ashore and made his way unsteadily back to his office. He said they never did get a statement from Mountbatten.

After the Remembrance Sunday parade at Hebburn in November 1976, Commander James Turnbull, who was *Kelly*'s and the Flotilla's staff electrical officer, placed a wreath on behalf of Lord Mountbatten on the grave of the *Kelly* men buried there and wrote to Mountbatten immediately. He said there was a good turn-out of twenty members of the Association and the *Kelly* Sea Cadets made a splendid show. Many civic figures were at the church which was packed and the crowds at the graveside were as big as ever. However, there was one matter which Commander Turnbull and some members of the *Kelly* Association found 'somewhat disturbing'. Turnbull said: 'In the last couple of years an Orange Lodge has taken to joining the parade, complete with regalia and banners. In a town with such a large population as Hebburn I cannot help feeling that this is deliberate "coat trailing". So far we have ignored them but this year they pushed right up towards the grave, getting in the way of the Sea Cadets and crowding the civic leaders. I don't see what we can do, as we don't organize the parade. I am only there by invitation anyway.'

Lord Mountbatten wrote to both Commander Turnbull and Rocky Wilkins suggesting they put their combined views to him and suggest what they thought might be done about the problem — 'the situation is very tricky and wants very carefully thinking out'. The Earl said: 'Personally, I feel it is highly undesirable for an honoured name like *Kelly* to be associated with extremists of either side in Northern Ireland. I remember our First Lieutenant, Lord Hugh Beresford, was mortified when it was proposed that the *Kelly*'s church party should march behind an Orange band in Londonderry.'

It was true there was nothing the *Kelly* Association could do about this. As Commander Turnbull said, they did not organize the Hebburn parade. The Orangemen continue to take part. Fortunately, there has been no trouble in the town as a consequence.

HMS *Mercury*'s *Kelly* Squadron has kept up links with the Tyne where the destroyer was built and repaired. Ten years after the *Kelly* Squadron was given that name, the young recruits were given a new marching tune, *Blaydon Races*, the north-east's 'anthem' written by Geordie Ridley who died in 1864. It has become famous the world over and especially at Wembley Cup Finals when Newcastle United or Sunderland have played. It was sung aboard *Kelly* and Captain Lord Louis knew it well. Adaptation of *Blaydon Races* was the idea of Lieutenant-Commander Malcolm Farrow, when he was the officer in charge of the *Kelly* Squadron, and his administration officer, Lieutenant Mike Baker. Malcolm Farrow's father, a retired Naval Captain, was High Sheriff of Tyne and Wear.

Chapter 25

# A 'marvellous' district nurse

One day in July 1979, less than two months before Lord Mountbatten was killed, he received a letter from a district nursing sister in Hampshire which disturbed him. The district nurse, Mrs Norma Sendles, wrote from Church Crookham, near Aldershot, as follows:

'Dear Sir, I hope you don't mind but I am taking the liberty to write to you about one of my patients who I hope will be of interest and concern to you. Mr Herbert Phillips, of Farnborough, is at present being nursed at home 24 hours of the day. He is a terminal case of carcinoma, and is in constant need of strong medication to try to control the pain. However, each day, helped by a devoted wife, he dresses and washes himself and sits in his lounge. There are moments in his day when the pain isn't uppermost in his mind and then we chat about other things. During the war he served on HMS *Kelly*, his stories are numerous, moving and sometimes sad. He talks with such pride about those days and recalling them helps him to forget awhile his present situation. I have nursed many terminally ill patients, but Mr Phillips' dignity, forebearing and quiet acceptance of his illness is truly remarkable. I can only add that, if all the qualities of his character he possessed whilst serving on HMS *Kelly* and which he displays to me now, you were indeed fortunate to have such a man under your command.' True to her profession Nurse Sendles added: 'I trust what I have written about my patient's diagnosis you will treat with strict confidence as he is unaware of the true diagnosis. Yours sincerely, Norma Sendles, District Nursing Sister.'

The same day he received the letter, Mountbatten made enquiries of Rocky Wilkins, seeking to remind himself about Herbert Phillips, and within the week he sent off letters to both 'the marvellous' (as he described her) Norma Sendles and his very sick former shipmate.

To Herbert Phillips he wrote a careful letter: 'I was sorry to hear that you have been unwell and I am writing to send you my very best wishes'. He brought Mr Phillips up to date with *Kelly* Association affairs and told him it was continuing as strong as ever. He said: 'Last October I returned to the Hebburn Yard on Tyneside to celebrate the fortieth anniversary of the launching of our beloved *Kelly* and a large contingent of *Kelly* survivors, headed by Rocky Wilkins, came along to support me. It was a wonderfully nostalgic occasion and to mark the anniversary I was presented with a cartoon-type drawing by a local artist depicting incidents in the life of the *Kelly*. I was also given several small prints of the drawing and enclose one herewith as I feel it might amuse you. A local woman also wrote a charming poem entitled "The Spirit of the *Kelly*" and I enclose a copy of that in case you haven't seen it.'

Mountbatten expressed his gratitude to Nurse Sendles for sending him the sad news. He enclosed a copy of his letter to Herbert Phillips and told Mrs Sendles: 'He did indeed serve on board HMS *Kelly* and I remember him well. As a matter of fact he has attended a number of the *Kelly* Reunion Association dinners in the past but nothing has been heard of him recently and we were wondering what had happened. The tremendous courage and dignity he is showing in the face of adversity is so typical of the attitude shown by the entire ship's company of HMS *Kelly* and I have always counted myself very fortunate in having the good luck to serve with men of such high character.

'It is comforting to know that Herbert Phillips is being cared for by such a wonderfully understanding person and I am most grateful to you for having written to me.'

Poor Herbert Phillips was proud to receive his letter from Mountbatten. It was cherished by him and his wife. 'He was thrilled', said Mrs Sendles. But he did not live to know the fate of his old Captain. Herbert Phillips passed away soon afterwards, before Lord Mountbatten died at the hands of the IRA.

Whenever he was made aware of the deaths of his survivors Mountbatten was always prompt in conveying his condolences to wives and families. A typical letter to a widow in Kent in 1965 said: 'I have only just heard the sad news that your husband has passed on and I am writing at once to offer you my sincere sympathy. I know from my own bereavement how terribly one misses one's life companion and I, therefore, understand so well what you must be feeling now and wish to send a special word of understanding. I am sure your husband will be missed by all the members of the *Kelly* Reunion Association.'

In his letters to widows Lord Mountbatten invariably likened their loss to that of his own. 'Remembering how I felt when my own wife died I can well imagine how lonely you must now be feeling', he wrote to a widow in Somerset. He also was thoughtful enough to implant a feeling of pride in a widow and her family by adding such a remark as this: 'You said you had a cap tally of the *Kelly* in your possession and asked if there was someone who would care to have one. If you have not already given it to someone else I would be very happy to have it here among my collection of *Kelly* souvenirs. Please do not give it another thought if you have promised it to somebody else.'

★   ★   ★

Mountbatten's heart was touched by a moving letter from a girl whose father, an Able Seaman, perished in *Kelly*'s sister ship *Kashmir*. The girl's letter was not addressed to him but it had been forwarded because it was thought he might be able to help. It was a modest request. The girl said the month of May had not meant anything to her until she had come to realize that she had lost her father in May 1941. She had then been only seven years old and shortly afterwards her mother also died. Subsequently she began to find out things for herself and she had been reading about the battle of Crete. Her quest was to obtain a picture of her father's ship the *Kashmir*, photographs and the names of survivors if possible because, if they held a reunion, she would like to meet some of them. 'I must have something in my father's memory having been an orphan since I was seven.' Mountbatten took what steps he could to fulfil the requests of the girl, then aged twenty. He passed her plea to *Kashmir*'s former Captain and himself wrote her a letter saying: 'I was, of course, very near to the *Kashmir* the moment when she was hit. Then the *Kipling* picked up survivors from the *Kelly* and the *Kashmir*. I was among the former and I regret that your father was not among the latter.' He went on to tell the girl the battle of Crete was one of the toughest the Navy had to fight and, 'though I am extremely sorry that your father was among the many who were lost, all those in the *Kashmir* put up a splendid fight and I was proud to have her with me.'

Years before *Kelly*, when Mountbatten was in the battleship *Queen Elizabeth* in the Mediterranean, he managed to help one of his men to marry the girl of his choice. A Leading Telegraphist, Bill Primrose, fell in love with a girl but could not marry her, as she was a Roman Catholic, unless he changed his own religion. Unbeknown to the rating, the girl wrote to Mountbatten and asked if he could help. When he had followed up the girl's plea Mountbatten asked the rating to see him. He told Primrose he and not the girl should have raised the problem with him. Six days later the girl had a letter from the Archbishop of Malta saying she could be married to Primrose in the vestry of St John's Cathedral. Long after his Naval days were over Primrose made a point of introducing himself to Mountbatten and told him his wife had recently died, after they had had 45 happy years together.

★   ★   ★

Mountbatten demonstrated the human touch in the case of the association member who lost his medals. This man reported to Rocky Wilkins that he had written to the Ministry of Defence about his loss but had been told that the medals could not be replaced free of charge, and that he would have to pay nearly £40 for a new set. Rocky asked the man for the correspondence from the MoD and sent it to Mountbatten. Rocky didn't think it fair that a man who had spent six years of his life in the Service, had been awarded the medals and through no fault of his own lost them, now had to pay for replacements.

Lord Mountbatten didn't agree at all. He said the man never had to pay for any of the original issue which were given to him free. 'If he loses them that, I am afraid, is his own responsibility. You can well imagine the trade that could be done in war medals, which fetch quite a lot in shops, if people were to say they had lost their set and wanted a fresh free set and then went and sold them. I am afraid it would start a real racket. I am sorry, but I couldn't agree to even try and get that changed. Nor could I succeed.'

Having said that, Lord Mountbatten had an idea. He told Wilkins he was hoping to get a sum of money from the sale of prints of the latest *Kelly* picture. If the proceeds were enough to pay for the dinner, and the

Association managed to keep back £39.98p to buy a new set of medals, that would be a reasonable proposition for they 'knew the man was honest'. Mountbatten would have been in his element teaching his devotees a lesson about not losing medals prior to doing a volte-face and making a presentation of a brand new set. Sadly, his death did not permit it, but the man *has* got his medals, at no expense to himself.

Among the stories in the Broadlands collection of *Kelly* anecdotes sent to Mountbatten by his men is this one, reminding his Captain how he got the rating out of a mother's threat forty years previously.

'I used to visit my girl while on leave — it wasn't a serious affair. My lighthearted relationship came to an unromantic end when I received letters from an irate mother suggesting I was responsible for her daughter's delicate condition and threatening me with letters to my parents if I failed to do something about it. Being perfectly innocent of blame and suspecting that certain submariners on leave at the crucial time were the real culprits, I felt I was being made a scapegoat because I was the only boyfriend whose home and ship's address were known. The whole situation was making me very worried and alarmed and in desperation I confided in the Gunner. He advised me to request an interview with the Captain.

'I duly presented myself to his cabin and Lord Louis sat at his desk and looked searchingly at me. He asked me to tell him all the story and questioned me from time to time. He asked me eventually if my conscience was clear on the matter and I fervently and truthfully assured him that it was. He thereupon drew paper and pen towards him and told me to look over his shoulder to see what he was writing. The letter was to the effect that in time of war the morale and wellbeing of his ship's company were of supreme importance, and unjust and unsubstantiated accusations such as those of her present attack on me would not be tolerated and that, if she persisted, further action would be taken with the local police, signing it Lord Louis Mountbatten, Captain RN. No more correspondence was received and my relief was boundless as was gratitude to the "Old Man" who had rescued me from a tight spot.'

An Able Seaman named Harry Lord, from Birmingham, went up to the bridge with his little bag of tools wearing his tin hat with 'Lord' printed across the top. Mountbatten was sitting in his chair looking around watching Lord at work. He asked 'What's your name?' 'Lord, sir.' Mountbatten replied: 'Remember, there's only one Lord aboard this ship and it's me. Either take that off or put your initial the other side of Lord.'

The Association couldn't have chosen a more appropriate present for their old Captain than the one he was given to mark his retirement as Chief of the Defence Staff in 1965. He wrote to Wilkins.

'I was deeply touched not only by the kind thought in the members of the *Kelly* Reunion Association giving me a gift on my retirement from active duty, but I thought it typical of the whole intelligent spirit with which the Association is run that a present which will be really acceptable was chosen. My son-in-law, Lord Brabourne, who is a keen fisherman, when he saw the magnificent trout rod from Hardy's told me that the existing rod was so badly damaged that he was going to ask me to get another rod for the house in any case, so you can see what an extremely useful present you gave me, and it will be put to use at once.'

The same letter contained invitations to a Broadlands Garden Party for Wilkins, Wilson, Shaw and Lucas. *Kelly* officers invited were Rear Admiral Burnett, Captain Butler-Bowden and Captain Dunsterville.

★ ★ ★

Mountbatten, gregarious and happy among his officers, was not a great drinker, but when his ships were in harbour he always tried to accept invitations to visit other wardrooms in his Flotilla in order to have a courtesy drink with his officers. He was to visit one of his ships each Sunday morning and he was invariably accompanied by the Flotilla Signals Officer, the then Lieutenant Dunsterville, who used to warn the host ship about Mountbatten's tipple. Egg nog was a favourite and on one particular Sunday morning they went to *Kashmir*. Yes, Mountbatten would like an egg nog. They made one up for him. He sipped it and put it down. He sipped it again and promptly put it down again. That is all he did with the drink. The time came for Mountbatten and Dunsterville to go. They went down the gangway and started to walk along the jetty towards the next destroyer. There were footsteps behind and the Captain and First Lieutenant of *Kashmir* rushed to Mountbatten with sincere apologies. 'We're terribly sorry, sir', they said. The egg in the egg nog was bad!

★ ★ ★

'Shalom' was a greeting Mountbatten used over the years when he encountered Rocky Wilkins. It became a joke between them and the story was enjoyed by the *Kelly* lower deck. It all stemmed from one Sunday morning when *Kelly* was having a quiet day alongside at Plymouth and the ship's company was assembled on the upper deck, all smartly dressed in the rig of the day awaiting the Captain's arrival to conduct church parade.

One man was not, however, in the rig of the day; Wilkins. He was descending the ladder from his gun deck attired in overalls when Lord Louis spotted him and asked: 'Why aren't you at church?'

'I'm excused sir.'

'But you're not a Roman Catholic.'

Rocky replied: 'No, I'm a Jewish Atheist, sir.'

Wilkins had been told that if a rating wanted to get out of church parade nobody would argue if he described his religion thus. He'd got away with it before. But Lord Louis wasn't to be taken in. He ordered Rocky to get to the church parade double-quick and added: 'And put yourself in my report!' Dressed as he was, Rocky was a real odd man out as he joined his spic-and-span colleagues, and there were lots of sniggers because Wilkins had for once failed.

Wilkins duly appeared at the Captain's 'requestmen and defaulters'. If was 'off caps' and the coxswain read the charge, absent from church parade and out of the rig of the day. Mountbatten looked at the charge and turned to the First Lieutenant, Lord Hugh Beresford, asking him: 'Did you know Able Seaman Wilkins was a "Jewish Atheist?"'

The First Lieutenant, who was a devout churchman and who indeed had two Jewish ratings among the crew, said: 'There's no such religion, sir.'

Said Mountbatten without batting an eyelid: 'Oh yes there is. You are one, aren't you Wilkins?'

'Yes, I am sir,' said Wilkins, equally straight-faced.

'How long have you been a Jewish Atheist?'

'Since I was born,' was the reply. 'My mother was Jewish.'

There was brief silence while Mountbatten thought. 'What I want you to do Number One,' he said to Beresford, 'Is to take Wilkins to this address.'

Wilkins was driven by the First Lieutenant to a synagogue in Plymouth. He never forgot observing the Star of David on the door which was opened by a Rabbi, who was expecting them. Beresford left, telling Wilkins to make his way back to the ship. Wilkins thought this was going to be an excellent opportunity for a little run ashore. The first thing the Rabbi said was: 'Keep your sailor's cap on.' It was said he had strayed from the faith, the Rabbi began to say. Rocky declared that he was not Jewish. 'Yes, according to your Captain you are, and it is my job to bring you back.' Rocky went 'under instruction' for about an hour and he had to go back to the Rabbi three times. It was intended that he should have a week's 'instruction' but before the week was up *Kelly* had to put to sea on patrol. The next time he saw Lord Louis was when he was instructing a young member of the crew at the pom-pom. The Captain said: 'Shalom, Wilkins, Shalom.' It shook Rocky.

'All this was the Captain's way of punishing you. He thought, 'Here's someone trying to pull a fast one over me. I'll play a joke in return.' Lord Louis' style was that an official and recorded punishment could affect a rating's Service career. By doing what he did he decided that no one was going to take the mickey out of him. He'd done his "homework" too, even to the extent of ringing the Rabbi before I got there. What a sense of fun! He always enjoyed the joke and the Jewish greeting "Shalom" became a password between us.'

★   ★   ★

Twenty-five years after they were separated by Lady Louis' death, a memorial to Earl and Countess Mountbatten was unveiled in Westminster Abbey by their nephew, The Duke of Edinburgh, and representatives of the *Kelly* Association were invited by the Mountbatten family to join the congregation of 400. It included the Prince and Princess of Wales, the Queen Mother, Princess Anne and eight other members of our Royal Family; representatives of foreign Royal Families, relatives of the Mountbattens; many of their friends; Service chiefs, politicians, business people and other men and women from all over the Commonwealth and from many organisations which had been served by the Earl and Countess over decades. Leaders of several religions took part in the service.

The memorial through which the Mountbatten couple join the illustrious in the Abbey is a church brass of Belgian fossil marble inlaid with brass and stainless steel, a fine salute to the individual and joint work the couple carried out on behalf of the nation. It is decorated with insignia and badges including, among others, the Royal Navy, the Army, the RAF, Combined Operations, India, the Admiralty, NATO, Supreme Allied Command South East Asia, Chief of Defence Staff, the cyphers of Earl Mountbatten and Countess Mountbatten, the Order of St John of Jerusalem, the Save the Children Fund and — HMS *Kelly*.

During the dedication service the Mountbattens' two daughters placed flowers on the memorial, the Prince of Wales read the New Testament lesson and the Old Testament lesson was read by the famous actress, Dame Peggy Ashcroft. Among those at the service was Dame Peggy's former husband, Lord Hutchinson of Lullington, QC and High Court Judge who, as Lieutenant Jeremy Hutchinson, had been an officer in *Kelly* when she went down. One of the four *Kelly* ratings in the Abbey was Mr John O'Neil of Lewisham, South London, who had been a wireless telegraphist in *Kelly* when she was torpedoed in the North Sea. O'Neil was, at only seventeen, the youngest in the ship. The W/T office was destroyed with several badly wounded men inside. The ship's surgeon could not get through the wreckage to reach the injured men but the teenage O'Neil managed to crawl through the twisted metal and administer morphia. Lord Mountbatten promoted O'Neil on the spot to a higher rate and award of the Distinguished Service Medal followed.

During the long repair work on *Kelly*, O'Neil joined another vessel of the flotilla, *Kandahar*, and was subsequently in Combined Operations in the Mediterranean. He was in special operations vessels working in and out of Yugoslavia. After the war he worked for the Port of London Authority and then went to work at the Queen's Gallery at Buckingham Palace. The fact that he served in *Kelly* helped him get the job, he said. It also gave him the opportunity of discussing the 5th Destroyer Flotilla with the Master of Her Majesty's Household, Vice Admiral Sir Peter Ashmore, who was the navigator in *Kipling* when she picked up *Kelly* survivors off Crete. Mountbatten would have been gratified to know that, among those paying one of the last tributes to him, was his youngest *Kelly* survivor and that, 45 years after the North Sea incident, the sailor was ending his working days in the service of the Queen.

Chapter 26

# *There were critics*

Lord Mountbatten's name has rarely been out of the public eye, even since Bank Holiday Monday, 27 August 1979, when a BBC newsflash stunned Britain and the world: 'Police in the Irish Republic have reported that Lord Mountbatten has been killed in an explosion in his boat off the coast of County Sligo.' Millions of words have been spoken and written and there will be more from new biographers for a long time to come.

Philip Ziegler's brilliant official biography has been hailed by Countess Mountbatten of Burma and her family. In the Navy, some criticisms of Mountbatten implied in the book through Ziegler's research and comments from people he talked to will be discussed for decades. Headlines used in the Press quoting excerpts caused some raised eyebrows, not least from Mountbatten's loyal lower deck men. Rocky Wilkins, who went to the biography launching party at Broadlands, decided to send on to his *Kelly* Association colleagues a Press statement made by Lady Mountbatten, and her praise for the book impressed them.

Nevertheless, not everyone who served in *Kelly* agreed with some criticisms. A most surprising one, which caused a big headline, arose out of a statement credited to Admiral (later Admiral of the Fleet Lord) Cunningham who said to an unnamed officer: 'The trouble with your Flotilla, boy, is that it was thoroughly badly led.' Other impressions referred to Mountbatten's lack of 'sea sense', also that 'by the highest standards he was no better than second rate'.

Criticisms will be reiterated by future biographers digging into the life of Mountbatten the sailor. It may surprise many people to read in generations to come that such verdicts were applied to a man who had such a vast amount of Naval experience for the major part of the twentieth century, who was a Captain D at 38, who as Chief of Combined Operations was prominent in planning the invasion of Normandy, who had naval as well as land and air forces under his command in South East Asia, who, after undertaking his great task in India, all involving absence from the Navy he loved, then returned to command a cruiser squadron, became Commander-in-Chief, Mediterranean, First Sea Lord and finally Chief of the Defence Staff.

Historians should appreciate that, apart from his relatively short spell in command of HMS *Kelly* and as Captain D5, he was deprived of sea time because of the infinitely greater tasks he undertook as Chief of Combined Operations, then in the East. He had scant opportunity of distinguishing himself in personal sea combat with the enemy. It is unrewarding to contemplate how Lord Louis would have fared had he remained afloat and in command of ships throughout the war. *Kelly* was ill-fated, it almost seems, from the beginning. In her two grim commissions, brave and active though she was, she achieved little in the way of damaging the German navy, but this in no way should be taken as a criticism of her Captain. In *Kelly's* wartime, Britain, and notably our ships, bore the brunt of the Nazi onslaught. If we weren't losing the war, we were on our own desperately struggling to avoid defeat. In the Navy, more so in wartime than in peace, a commander could be more easily measured by his success, but for success there had to be opportunity. Opportunity did not much come Mountbatten's way yet, like all his contemporaries as destroyer Captains, he yearned for action and to be face to face with his opponents.

Long after the Navy's débâcle off Crete there were senior officers in the Mediterranean who might have been critical of Mountbatten, not because of his lack of success afloat but because they could not disguise a touch of envy of his position in the Establishment and his influential friends in the highest places. There was unjustified fear that he might be leapfrogging to the disadvantage of Flag Officers who were just as much careerists in the Navy and equally aiming to reach the very top. When Mountbatten completed his tasks in SEAC and India he resumed his Naval career no higher in the hierarchy than he would have normally achieved had he spent the whole five years of the war at sea. It is futile to speculate, but glamorous victories have nearly always accelerated promotion.

Mountbatten gained his 'dashing' reputation in the Navy as much for his handsome appearance and cracking personality as the way he actually handled his own destroyer. He often gave his superiors as well as some of his own officers furrowed brows. Few destroyer captains came into harbour and put their ships alongside faster than Mountbatten. He loved ship handling but he wasn't 'greedy' as some Captains were. Mountbatten let his younger officers 'take over' the ship when it was proceeding peacefully at cruising stations, whereas some Captains never let an officer on watch give a wheel order. When it came to coming into harbour Mountbatten took the destroyer himself, generally proceeding 'terrifyingly fast'. It was admitted by those who served alongside him that he wasn't a 'sensible ship handler' in harbour. But he certainly wasn't alone among Captain Ds with the big black Leader ring around their funnels in adding swank to pride. Crews of destroyers — and *Kelly's* were a proud lot — loved nothing better than their ship coming alongside 'at the rate of knots' and securing swiftly, neatly, 'handsomely'. They stuck their chests out and smiled approval. The crew were also the first to mumble criticism if their Old Man bungled his approach. Destroyers were like souped-up cars and, as Mountbatten said, nifty to handle, and it was tempting to be fast in entering harbour. It was said after Dunkirk that as many as three-quarters of Britain's destroyer force were in for repair and half of this damage could have been avoided with more careful ship handling.

There was no criticism among *Kelly* men of Mountbatten's all-round ability as a seaman and destroyer Captain. He did not lack vanity and was by no means averse to hero-worship but, with the searchlight on his Naval career, before, during and after the Second World War, Mountbatten emerges as a man who was scrupulously fair, straight, dependable, one with a brilliant mind and, so far as the *Kelly* survivors were concerned (including those who went on to be outstanding officers themselves), Mountbatten was a leader under whom they were glad of the opportunity to serve.

Admiral Burnett's views on Mountbatten are important because, during *Kelly*'s early career he was First Lieutenant, and after Lord Louis, he ultimately achieved the highest rank of any of *Kelly*'s officers. He did comment on the suggestion that the 5th Flotilla was badly handled. He would like to have seen more of the context in which Cunningham made the criticism after Crete. Cunningham was Rear Admiral Destroyers when Mountbatten was a Captain in *Daring* and *Wishart* and, if Mountbatten had been 'all that bad', it might have been thought that there would be criticism then. If Cunningham had been discussing Mountbatten's handling of other ships at sea, probably the criticism was justified, but Admiral Burnett rather doubted whether Cunningham would have criticised as he is said to have done because he believed Cunningham and Mountbatten remained on pretty friendly terms with each other. If Cunningham felt as badly as his remark implied when unadorned, he believed Cunningham would have said this on other occasions.

Burnett did not think Mountbatten's handling of his own ship in harbour was good and here he is not on his own, nor is he alone in his belief that Mountbatten was justifiably criticised for his handling of the engagement as Captain D in the Channel when the *Javelin* was beaten by the German assailants who smashed her at both ends.

Admiral Burnett made comments on other incidents during *Kelly*'s first commission where Mountbatten might be unfairly criticised. Mountbatten, after failing to intercept the British vessel *City of Flint* with a German prize crew aboard, was said to have 'pushed on at reckless speed' and that he was ordering full steam ahead 'out of sheer impatience to reach wherever he was heading to start on something else'. 'When he knew the *City of Flint* might have already passed the headland where we were looking for it, he obviously sought to overtake it by going south. By the morning we were within range of enemy aircraft and we wanted to get to hell out of the range, so we turned and went as fast as we could.' The fact that a gale blew up and it became rough shows that Mountbatten should have reduced speed but his decision was not 'impulsive'. Mountbatten wasn't pushing on at 'reckless speed'. He knew there were enemy aircraft about and wanted to avoid being bombed. Nor was it fair to say *Kelly* 'limped back' for repairs. 'We were perfectly seaworthy. All we'd done was lose our boats.'

*Kelly*'s officer of the watch, it was said, could have avoided the collision between *Kelly* and HMS *Gurkha*. It wasn't Mountbatten's fault, said Burnett. 'In a snowstorm quite suddenly you see a ship ahead and you both put your wheel to starboard. Who did it first or who was too slow I don't know but the fact was that both ships were listing to port and *Gurkha*'s X gun deck caught under our port bow. To say it was our fault rather than the other ship's fault is unfair.'

Admiral Burnett also commented about a claim that *Kelly* had sunk a submarine on the first day of the war. 'My memory of it was that Mountbatten thought he'd sunk a U-boat and I couldn't stop him from saying so.' Additionally it is said that, after Namsos in Norway, *Kelly* shot down a dive bomber. 'I simply don't believe that one either,' said Burnett.

Another *Kelly* and 5th Flotilla staff officer, Commander James Turnbull, said: 'Yes, he made mistakes and had his weaknesses, but don't we all? He was certainly better as a strategist than as a tactician and was not an outstanding ship handler, but to say that the Flotilla was badly led is nonsense. Of course 'ABC' (Andrew Cunningham) was not one of Lord Louis' fans but I am surprised that he should make such a comment and I very much doubt that he did.'

Captain Dunsterville, the gunnery specialist in the 5th Flotilla who served in *Kelly* throughout, and was later at Admiralty when Mountbatten was there, considered it necessary completely to separate Mountbatten's performance as Captain of *Kelly* from his performance as Captain D5. 'In the former role he was brilliant as we all know.' From the facts stated by Philip Ziegler it could not possibly be said that Mountbatten was either outstandingly good or even good as a Captain D. There are no facts to conjure up which would show that only the unfavourable ones had been included in Ziegler's biography. Dunsterville also commented: 'It is astonishing that Mountbatten went on to be such a truly great man and lucky that a blind eye was turned to his failures as a seagoing commander.'

*Kelly*'s officers and lower deck men who are still alive have to a man undiminished loyalty and veneration for Mountbatten. Any faults he may have had or whatever strictures might be expressed, whether accepted or not, utterly wither when put alongside the deep respect all these sailors had for the Captain of a warship whose duties, in addition to leading its fighting capacity, were so wide-ranging down to the smallest detail, human or otherwise. It is a Naval legend that Lord Louis had such everlasting affection for *Kelly* that he devoted so much of the second half of his life to the passion and joy provided by the *Kelly* Association.

Mountbatten's qualities as a Naval officer were evident from a tender age. To use some of Captain Dunsterville's words out of context, it is indeed astonishing to his shipmates and contemporaries that Mountbatten should overcome the adversity and tribulation suffered in *Kelly* and emerge to be such a truly great man, as so many have said one of the greatest Englishmen of the century.

When he was at the pinnacle of his post-war military career, the professional presiding over Britain's defence strategy in the 1960s, his most important contribution was to argue in NATO for the right mixture between a conventional and nuclear ingredient. In Whitehall his main effort was to press for greater unification between the Navy, Army and Royal Air Force. He would like to have gone a good deal further than Mr Denis Healey, the Defence Secretary at the time, thought it right to go but Healey gave Mountbatten the credit for being the main force behind such unification as was achieved. Mr Healey said he found it easy to get on with Mountbatten whose sympathies, he said, were more on Labour's side of politics than the other. He recalled that Mountbatten used to like telling the story of the 1945 General Election when he opened his door to a Tory canvasser and said he himself was Labour but he thought that his butler voted Tory. Mountbatten thought the Establishment had been unfair to both his father and his wife but his Royal connection gave him great independence of mind. When Healey was Defence Secretary he and his wife had to hold their first great reception for Service attachés and their wives, about a thousand in all. Mrs Healey complained halfway through that her arm was beginning to ache. Mountbatten looked at her smilingly and said: 'My dear, my aunt the Empress of Russia used to have a blister on the back of her hand as big as an egg at Easter where the peasants had kissed it. She never wore gloves.'

Mountbatten got on extremely well with his American counterparts. From the Pentagon it was said that he was one of the easiest foreigners they had worked with because he had great experience, was respected and admired and he had views they could understand very simply. The aristocratic Mountbatten did not grate on the Americans. On the contrary, they always looked forward to seeing him and where there were differences of opinion they were not unreasonable ones.

A former British Flag Officer said that anyone who served with Mountbatten would say he was an outstanding personality with magnificent brain power — he was top of his term — and with it went a wonderful sense of humour. He was so approachable: 'a man you'd never forget once you'd met him'. His advice and influence on the Normandy landings were widely acknowledged. When Mountbatten was in his South-East Asia command a telegram arrived from British and American Chiefs of Staff, following the successful landings in France, giving full credit to Lord Mountbatten and saying that everyone realized that the landings would not have taken place there in Normandy but for Mountbatten's capacity as Chief of Combined Operations. In South-East Asia, Mountbatten behaved in exactly the same manner as that which endeared him to his crew in *Kelly*. As a member of the Royal family he was never aloof from the men under his command. Much to the contrary, Mountbatten spent a great deal of time going round his vast command to see the troops. There was a lack of formality. He would get on a soap box and say: 'Please break ranks'. Everybody gathered around and he would tell the men exactly what was going to happen in his Command. He achieved marvellous spirit in Asia, then had tremendous success retaking Burma and, but for the 'bomb' being dropped on Japan, he would have had Malaya and Singapore.

Like all other military chiefs who reached the very top, Mountbatten could, of course, be tough. He had to be. Some of the frankest and most hard-hitting comments made about him came from a prominent senior Army officer who served under Mountbatten when he was Chief of the Defence Staff. The Army man said that Mountbatten was a dominant figure. 'Like most Admirals he was a bit of a bully. When you stood up to him you got on well after that. He was slightly inclined to grind people into the dust. When he wanted ideas and advice in the long-term you got the most marvellous treatment from him.' The same officer said Mountbatten was a sophisticated man in a world-wide sense, he was the centre of everything and made a great contribution to defence, which he rationalized and put on a modern level. When the time came for him to give up his CDS desk in Whitehall there was not the slightest thought of 'retirement'. In public he was rarely seen out of his greatly bemedalled uniforms. His proudest moments were with the Queen at the annual Trooping the Colour on Horse Guards. Although he was nearing eighty and often physically tired, his appearance was immaculate.

His activities were prodigious and by no means concerned only with the Services. He was a member of nearly a dozen famous London clubs and he was often to be found in the boardroom of great City organizations, giving directors advice from his great store of knowledge and experience. One of the concerns he visited was the communications company Racal which one of his closest associates, Captain Ernest Dunsterville, had joined after leaving the Navy. Captain Dunsterville was, like Mountbatten, a communications specialist. Being in the same 'trade' in the Navy, they had a lot in common and when Mountbatten went to look up Racal he was an extremely welcome and interesting visitor.

Mountbatten's versatility was displayed the year after he left the top military job in Whitehall and was asked by the Home Secretary to examine into and report on prison security. He shook Whitehall and staggered chairmen of similar sorts of enquiry by the astonishing speed and thoroughness with which his report was completed and presented. Enjoyable tasks bestowed on him included the Governorship of the Isle of Wight and later Lord Lieutenant of the Isle of Wight. It was totally appropriate when, as Governor, he was asked to inaugurate the Radio Solent transmitting station. Mountbatten always got a move on and, in opening the station, he found that air time was on his side so he decided to use the few minutes remaining to him by telling the listeners in the Solent area, which included his home at Broadlands, of his experience in the Mediterranean a long time before the war started. He also surprised Radio Solent's staff. Off the cuff he told how he started specializing in wireless telegraphy in the Navy in 1924 and became Fleet Wireless Officer for the Commander-in-Chief Mediterranean in 1932. At that time Britain had about seventy ships in the Mediterranean and the Commander-in-Chief asked Mountbatten to arrange for every man in the Fleet to hear King George V when he gave his Christmas Day broadcast. It was a tall order. The technical means did not exist. First, Mountbatten had to get a special receiving station rigged up, then a local transmitter to rebroadcast to all the ships; the ships had to build themselves small local receivers then button them on to amplifiers and loudspeakers. It worked. Mountbatten said to his Solent listeners: 'I think we can say we started rebroadcasting for the Forces at that point'.

Just one of the relatively minor contributions Mountbatten made to Britain. What a fantastic all-rounder he was. Some have been so bold as to call Mountbatten 'our man of the century'. Well, the nation will not forget Winston Churchill who was so great he had the greatness to pick out Louis Mountbatten for the first of the immense roles he was to play, Chief of Combined Operations and then Supremo in South East Asia. Few will dispute that Mountbatten went immeasurably beyond being our greatest and most versatile Admiral of the century.

Epilogue

# *Fourth World War would be 'bows and arrows'*

Before I said goodbye to Lord Mountbatten at his house in Kinnerton Street, I asked him if he had any other engagements that day and whether he was returning to Broadlands that evening. It was mid-week and he said he was going back to Broadlands then and there to polish the speech he was due to make that weekend on 11 May. This was clearly uppermost on his mind. He told me the address he was to make was an 'important one' and that he was going back to his home in Hampshire to make final revisions. It was to be about the arms race. Lord Mountbatten added: 'The world is in such a terrible state that someone has got to speak out'. Lord Mountbatten did not indicate any points he proposed making at Strasbourg but told me I would be reading about it in the newspapers. He had been invited to address the Stockholm International Peace Research Institute — he was the only military representative on its committee — so he had an excellent platform. The subject was to be of his own choosing.

I listened to the radio and looked at the newspapers and so far as I knew there was nothing about the speech. I was surprised and thought how disappointed Mountbatten must be. Here was a World War 2 leader who had decided to break a rule and speak on the subject of nuclear arms and war for the first time since he retired as head of Britain's military forces. After losing HMS *Kelly*, Mountbatten had served with great distinction as leader of the South East Asia Allied Forces in an extremely tough assignment. Then, after going to India as the last Viceroy to prepare the way for independence there, he had returned to the military field, concluding his service in the Navy's highest position as First Sea Lord like his father, and finally as Britain's Chief of the Defence Staff. His views as a man of peace on the momentous question of the world going headlong into nuclear war were surely of prime importance. Lord Mountbatten's comments, one thought, would be worthy of prominence in every responsible newspaper in the free world, possibly even in the East and beyond the Iron Curtain. I wondered for some time afterwards whether Lord Mountbatten's address at Strasbourg had been insufficiently reported or whether it had been reported at all.

When, fifteen weeks afterwards, the shattering news of his assassination was broadcast, I immediately thought of his Strasbourg address on peace. Because of the dramatic circumstances of his death in Ireland, Lord Mountbatten's pronouncements on the state of the world were probably more poignant.

I took the trouble to tip off two Sunday newspapers, suggesting that they should get hold of the speech made in May, but they either ignored my suggestion, failed to get hold of the speech or failed to appreciate its newsworthiness. Undeterred, because I considered that someone should get the speech and print it, I rang Britain's new glossy weekly magazine *Now!* whose editor, Anthony Shrimsley, I knew well. Shrimsley was an intelligent and shrewd journalist, former political editor of national newspapers and, on the demise of *Now!*, helped to start the *Mail on Sunday* and eventually became head of Press and Public Relations for the Conservative Party, a post he held during the years of the Tories' tenure of office until he died in 1984 at the early age of 51.

*Now!* acted swiftly and successfully. Anthony Shrimsley was used to daily paper speed and he had collected around him a splendid staff, a mixture of seasoned Fleet Street writers and some bright young reporters. The magazine, alas, had a short innings.

Anyway, so far as Mountbatten's address at Strasbourg went, *Now!* stepped in where the rest of Fleet Street had 'slept in'. The magazine's fourth issue contained such items as an exclusive talk with Mrs Thatcher: 'Where does Labour go from here?', by Shrimsley; Frank Johnson wrote about the Labour Conference that year; there was an article on Fleet Street and the new technology; how the Generals took over in South Africa; and 'A *Now!* exclusive: Mountbatten's Last Testament', words boldly printed on the front cover. In its inside pages the *Now!* documentary was headed 'Lord Mountbatten's Dream of Peace' and included appropriate pictures of Lord Mountbatten 'with his favourite great-nephew, Prince Charles'; on the bridge of HMS *Glasgow* in 1954 — 'He survived the Second World War yet died on his own boat in a quiet Irish bay'; with Lady Mountbatten and Mahatma Ghandhi — 'Two men who spent a lifetime striving for peace'; and one in civilian clothes with Broadlands in the background — 'At home and at peace with the world'.

The article said that Lord Louis wrote a fitting contribution to his own epitaph in a speech earlier that year in which he spoke of his fears of a military confrontation between the nuclear powers which could end in the total destruction of the world in a matter of days. The reporter, a young Scotsman, Thomson Prentice, in addition to getting hold of the Strasbourg speech, wrote that it was one of the most important speeches Mountbatten had ever delivered, 'though he could not know that it would be one of his last'. It remained a remarkable, moving and powerful condemnation of the enemies of peace — and by inference his own murderers. It now fitted with honour into Mountbatten's own epitaph.

'Do the frightening facts about the arms race, which show that we are rushing headlong towards a precipice, make any of those responsible for this disastrous course pull themselves together and reach for the brakes?

'The answer is "no" and I only wish that I could be the bearer of glad tidings that there has been a change of attitude and we are beginning to see a steady rate of disarmament. Alas, that is not the case.

'I am deeply saddened when I reflect on how little has been achieved in spite of all the talk there has been, particularly about nuclear disarmament. There have been numerous international conferences and negotiations on the subject and we have all nursed dreams of a world at peace, but to no avail. Since the end of the Second World War, 34 years ago, we have had war after war. There is still armed conflict going on in several parts of the world. We live in an age of extreme peril because every war today carries the danger that it could spread and involve the super powers.

'And here lies the greatest danger of all. A military confrontation between the nuclear powers could entail the horrifying risk of nuclear warfare. The Western powers and the USSR started by producing and stockpiling nuclear weapons as a deterrent to general war. The idea seemed simple enough. Because of the enormous amount of destruction that could be wreaked by a single nuclear explosion, the idea was that both sides in what we still see as an East-West conflict would be deterred from taking any aggressive action which might endanger the vital interests of the other.

'It was not long, however, before smaller nuclear weapons of various designs were produced and deployed for use in what was assumed to be a tactical or theatre war. The belief was that, were hostilities ever to break out in Western Europe, such weapons could be used in field warfare without triggering an all-out nuclear exchange leading to the final holocaust.

'I have never found this idea credible. I have never been able to accept the reasons for the belief that any class of nuclear weapons can be categorized in terms of their tactical or strategic purposes.

'Next month I enter my eightieth year. I am one of the few survivors of the First World War who rose to high command in the Second and I know how impossible it is to pursue military operations in accordance with fixed plans and agreements. In warfare the unexpected is the rule and no one can anticipate what an opponent's reaction will be to the unexpected.

'As a sailor I saw enough death and destruction at sea but I also had the opportunity of seeing the absolute destruction of the war zone of the western front in the First World War, where those who fought in the trenches had an average expectation of life of only a few weeks.

'Then in 1943 I became Supreme Allied Commander in South East Asia, and saw death and destruction on an even greater scale. But that was all conventional warfare and, horrible as it was, we all felt we had a "fighting" chance of survival. In the event of a nuclear war there will be no chances, there will be no survivors — all will be obliterated.

'I am not asserting this without having deeply thought about the matter. When I was Chief of the British Defence Staff I made my views known. I have heard the arguments against this view but I have never found them convincing. So I repeat in all sincerity as a military man: I can see no use for any nuclear weapons which would not end in escalation, with consequences that no one can conceive.

'And nuclear devastation is not science fiction — it is a matter of fact. Thirty-four years ago there was the terrifying experience of the two atomic bombs that effaced the cities of Hiroshima and Nagasaki off the map. In describing the nightmare a Japanese journalist wrote as follows:

'"Suddenly a glaring whitish, pinkish light appeared in the sky accompanied by an unnatural tremor which was followed almost immediately by a wave of suffocating heat and a wind which swept away everything in its path. Within a few seconds the thousands of people in the streets in the centre of the town were scorched by a wave of searing heat. Many were killed instantly, others lay writhing on the ground screaming in agony from the intolerable pain of their burns. Everything standing upright in the way of the blast — walls, houses, factories and other buildings, was annihilated ... Hiroshima had ceased to exist."

'But that is not the end of the story. We remember the tens of thousands who were killed instantly or, worse still, those who suffered a slow painful death from the effect of the burns — we forget that many are still dying horribly from the delayed effects of radiation. To this knowledge must be added the fact that we now have missiles a thousand times as dreadful — I repeat, a thousand times as terrible.

'One or two nuclear strikes on this great city of Strasbourg with what today would be regarded as relatively low yield weapons would utterly destroy all that we see around us and immediately kill probably half its population. Imagine what the picture would be if larger nuclear strikes were to be levelled against not just Strasbourg but ten other cities in, say, a 200-mile radius. Or even worse, imagine what the picture would be if there was an unrestrained exchange of nuclear weapons — and this is the most appalling risk of all since, as I have already said, I cannot imagine a situation in which nuclear weapons would be used as battlefield weapons without the conflagration spreading.

'Could we not take steps to make sure that these things never come about? A new war can hardly fail to involve the all-out use of nuclear weapons. Such a war would not drag on for years. It could all be over in a matter of days.

'And when it is all over what will the world be like? Our fine great buildings, our homes will exist no more. The thousands of years it took to develop our civilization will have been in vain. Our works of art will be lost. Radio, television, newspapers will disappear. There will be no means of transport. There will be no hospitals. No help can be expected for the few mutilated survivors in any town to be sent from a neighbouring town — there will be no neighbouring towns left, no neighbours, there will be no help, there will be no hope.

'How can we stand by and do nothing to prevent the destruction of our world? Einstein, whose centenary we celebrate this year, was asked to prophesy what weapons could be used in the Third World War. I am told he replied to the following effect:

"'On the assumption that a Third World War must escalate to nuclear destruction, I can tell you what the Fourth World War will be fought with — bows and arrows".

'The facts about the global nuclear arms race are well known and as I have already said SIPRI has played its part in disseminating authoritative material on world armaments and the need for international efforts to reduce them. But how do we set about achieving practical measures of nuclear arms control and disarmament?

'To begin with we are most likely to preserve the peace if there is a military balance of strength between East and West. The real need is for both sides to replace the attempts to maintain a balance through ever-increasing and ever more costly nuclear armaments by a balance based on mutual restraint. Better still, by reduction of nuclear armaments I believe it should be possible to achieve greater security at a lower level of military confrontation.

'I regret enormously the delays which the Americans and Russians have experienced in reaching a SALT II agreement for the limitation of even one major class of nuclear weapons with which it deals. I regret even more the fact that opposition to reaching any agreement which will bring about a restraint in the production and deployment of nuclear weapons is becoming so powerful in the United States. What can their motives be?

'As a military man who has given half a century of active service, I say in all sincerity that the nuclear arms race has no military purpose. Wars cannot be fought with nuclear weapons. Their existence only adds to our perils because of the illusions which they have generated.

'There are powerful voices around the world who still give credence to the old Roman precept — "if you desire peace, prepare for war". This is absolute nuclear nonsense and I repeat — it is a disastrous misconception to believe that by increasing the total uncertainty once increases one's own certainty.

'This year we have already seen the beginnings of a miracle. Through the courageous determination of Presidents Carter and Sadat and Prime Minister Begin we have seen the first real move towards what we all hope will be a lasting peace between Eqypt and Israel. Their journey has only just begun and the path they have chosen will be long and fraught with disappointments and obstacles. But these bold leaders have realized the alternative and have faced up to their duty in a way which those of us who hunger for the peace of the world applaud.

'It is possible that this initiative will lead to the start of yet another even more vital miracle and someone, somewhere, will take that first step along the long stony road which will lead us to an effective form of nuclear arms limitation, including the banning of tactical nuclear weapons?

'After all, it is true that science offers us almost unlimited opportunities but it is up to us, the people, to make the moral and philosophical choices and since the threat to humanity is the work of human beings, it is up to man to save himself from himself. The world now stands on the brink of the final abyss. Let us all resolve to take all possible practical steps to ensure that we do not, through our own folly, go over the edge.'

The words in the speech had been composed by Lord Mountbatten at his bedroom desk overlooking the lush south lawns at his Romsey home. Mountbatten's personal secretary, John Barratt, recalled that the speech meant a great deal to Mountbatten. 'He spent a lot of time on it. He wanted it to be just right, to say exactly what he meant.'

It might have seemed out of place, incongruous to some of those who had gathered in Whitehall to watch the Queen unveil the Mountbatten memorial, under the eyes of great gatherings of eminent people, including military chiefs, that one of the sidelights was a considerable distribution, to the crowds who lined the wet pavements, of copies of Mountbatten's Strasbourg speech.

Certainly some friends of Mountbatten were still unaware of the speech and this was the first time they had read it. It was printed in a four-page folder and given away by the World Disarmament Campaign in association with the United Nations Association. The front page of the leaflet contained this statement made some years previously by President and D-Day supremo Dwight D. Eisenhower: 'Some day the demand for disarmament by hundreds of millions will, I hope, become so universal and so insistent that no man, no nation, can withstand it'. Also on the front page, bold letters announced 'Speech by Admiral of the Fleet Earl Mountbatten of Burma'. This reminded everyone that Mountbatten was an outstanding Commander-in-Chief both by sea and land in the Second World War, and a high authority on all questions of armaments and warfare. Carla M. Wartenburg, the Honorary Secretary of the World Disarmament Campaign, told me that if she had £200,000 to spare she would produce enough copies of the speech to put one through every letterbox in the country. 'And I would put huge ads in the papers, using just some of the magnificent sentences. It took about £21,000 to publish it as one-third pages on 2 November 1983 in *The Times*, *Guardian* and *Telegraph*.'

Lord Mountbatten was a man of peace but certainly not a peacemonger; he was not for peace at any price, not a unilateralist, more a realist. In the many letters he wrote concerning the *Kelly* Reunion Association, he often referred to the past and talked to his former men at their dinners about the state of the modern Navy, but rarely if at all about the current dangerous situation with nuclear weapons.

Mountbatten's views and warnings about the defence situation could not have been clearer, but his friend Lord Zuckerman, who was closely associated with Mountbatten as scientific adviser to British commands, did have occasion two years afterwards to 'put the record straight'. He stated: 'Lord Mountbatten at no time condemned the concept of nuclear deterrence. His Strasbourg statement affirmed the need for the continuation of the present state of mutual nuclear deterrence. At the same time Lord Mountbatten supported the Government in its plea for a balanced reduction in the nuclear armouries of the two sides, and dismissed the idea that field-warfare in which nuclear weapons might be used could ever be contained. Hence he was reasserting a view supported by every other distinguished officer who had held the post of Chief of Defence Staff and who has spoken on the subject.'

His feelings about war were mentioned in an exchange of letters Mountbatten had with a former officer in *Kelly*, Jeremy Hutchinson, who as Lord Hutchinson, QC became one of the country's most distinguished legal personalities. In October 1977 Mountbatten wrote to Rocky Wilkins saying it had occurred to him that it would be very interesting if he could get 'our former RNVR Sub-Lieutenant Jeremy Hutchinson to the *Kelly* Reunion next year, when the Prince of Wales is coming'. Mountbatten suggested that Rocky might be able to 'persuade him to bring his former wife, the famous actress Peggy Ashcroft, with him. But don't press him too hard.'

Eventually Mountbatten himself wrote to Jeremy Hutchinson with a personal invitation: 'I remember how very helpful you were to me in my prison inquiry and I believe this was the last time I had the pleasure of seeing you'. (Lord Mountbatten was referring to October 1966 when the then Home Secretary asked him to examine into and report on prison security.)

Jeremy Hutchinson wrote back: 'Dear Lord Louis, Of course I felt a great sense of guilt upon reading your very kind letter. Of course I will come on 20 May. I gave up attending the Reunion because I have never been one for annual celebrations. To a great extent I have always felt that the past is past, and I've always too preferred to look forward than back. I consider my years in the Navy to have been a great privilege, and I learnt so much from those times. But war was an abomination, and I didn't want to dwell upon it every year — even in such delightful company. So I thought I would quietly slide away.

'I hope that you can understand these feelings, and that you have never felt yourself that my staying away showed disrespect or lack of affection for that wonderful ship, her sailors and her incredibly understanding and distinguished Captain. I look forward so very greatly to seeing you again.'

Lord Mountbatten replied to Hutchinson in a matter of days, thanking him for his letter 'which I read with much interest and sympathy'. He added 'I entirely understand your point of view but there had been a general request among the committee of the Reunion Association that we should try and get you from time to time and see us all. I know they will be delighted to see you.

'I entirely agree that war is an absolute abomination and I am doing everything I can to ensure that there won't be a Third World War by improving international understanding through the United World Colleges. However, the good sides of war were the friendships formed and the happy aspects of a ship's company, so we shall all enjoy seeing you.'

## Acknowledgements

I am indebted to everyone mentioned in this book who generously gave me their time and thoughts and to the sailors who related their experiences in surviving *Kelly*'s sinking and have now passed on. Countess Mountbatten of Burma and Rear-Admiral Burnett were kind enough to read proofs and spot inaccuracies. I am also particularly grateful to Dr Christopher Dowling and the Imperial War Museum; Harry Cox, Chief Librarian, Mirror Group Newspapers; Allan G. Rogers, BBC Radio Scotland; Ron Smith, Director of Swan Hunter; Jeff Chandler for recordings of *Kelly* reunions; ex-RNVR officers William Webb (for help with the Plourivo chapter, and John Hamar Jones; Mrs M. Travis and Mrs M. Chalk for kindness in the archives at Broadlands; and to my wife for considerable girl Friday tasks. Finally my thanks to Rocky Wilkins who entrusted me with Lord Mountbatten's letters and to Gladys Steel for her enthusiastic research and expert typing of the manuscript.

# Appendix

# *Losses aboard* HMS Kelly

Twenty-seven ratings were killed on 9 May 1940 off the coast of Holland by a German E-boat (*E-40*). Nine officers and 121 ratings were lost on 23 May 1941 in the Battle of Crete when HMS *Kelly* was sunk by German aircraft.

## 9 May 1940
Allen, Thomas P., Telegraphist
Amos, Alex, Leading Signalman
Bethell, Edward W., Boy
Boxer, William T. J., Leading Signalman
Camps, Percy, Acting Petty Officer
Cave, William John D., Stoker
Charman, Albert W., Stoker Petty Officer
Clarke, Wallace S., Stoker Petty Officer
Dixon, Joseph W., Stoker Petty Officer
Edwards, Harold B., Acting Leading Telegraphist
Fowler, Gorden, Ordinary Telegraphist
Gough, Victor, Leading Stoker
Jenkins, William J. P., Stoker
Johnson, Jack, Stoker
Kay, Donald, Acting Leading Stoker
Kingsley, Frederick A., Acting Yeoman of Signals
Mires, Arthur D., Able Seaman
Mower, Clifford J., Stoker
Palmer, Albert C., Leading Telegraphist
Peckham, Henry C., Stoker Petty Officer
Pickering, Herbert C., Telegraphist
Prescott, Cyril H., Telegraphist
Pridmore, Leslie, Able Seaman
Richardson, Leslie F., Leading Telegraphist
Waghorn, Edwin F., Chief Engine Room Artificer
Wilkinson, Eric T., Acting Petty Officer Telegraphist
Young, Henry L. W., Able Seaman

## 23 May 1941
**Officers missing, presumed killed**
Beresford, The Lord Hugh, Lieutenant Commander
Brownjohn, H. W. T., Gunner
Cole, E. W., Commissioned Engineer
Money, E. W., Sub-Lieutenant, RNR
Mortimer-Booth, G. R., Midshipman, RNR
Pattison, E. R., Paymaster Lieutenant
Reeder, J. J., Paymaster Lieutenant Commander
Sheridan, V. J. R., Surgeon Lieutenant
Sturdy, M. V., Lieutenant
**Ratings killed (died aboard HMS Kipling)**
Fennemore, Wilfred N., Chief Engine Room Artificer
Hoy, Leonard A., Signalman, Royal Fleet Reserve
Smith, William L., Ordinary Seaman
**Ratings missing, presumed killed**
Abrahams, Harry, Ordinary Seaman
Andrews, Alan A., Ordinary Seaman
Ashenden, Robert E., Petty Officer Cook
Atkins, Leslie J., Ordinary Seaman
Atkins, Joshua W., Chief Stoker
Baker, John R., Engine Room Artificer 2nd Class
Barnes, Lewis H. R., Boy 1st Class
Bell, Stanley A., Stoker 1st Class
Bell, Thomas W., Cook
Blackwell, William E., Ordinary Seaman
Booth, Harry F., Writer
Booth, John H., Stoker
Brown, George, Ordinary Seaman
Burgess, Frederick G., Ordinary Seaman
Campbell, Davis, Stoker 2nd Class
Carroll, George E., Chief Engine Room Artificer
Carter, John, Ordinary Seaman

Chadwick, Frank, Petty Officer Telegraphist
Chapman, George H., Ordinary Seaman
China, George D., Stoker 1st Class
Claiden, Eric C., Leading Steward
Cohen, Ellis, Ordinary Seaman
Collings, Leslie, Able Seaman
Coppard, Reginald D. F., Acting Leading Seaman
Cox, Jack M., Stoker 1st Class, Royal Fleet Reserve
Crawley, Thomas J., Able Seaman
Cripps, Douglas S., Stoker 2nd Class
Dagg, Lawrence D., Assistant Steward
Dent, Herbert T., Boy
Doyal, James, Acting Leading Stoker
Fagg, Thomas A., Boy
Farrer, James, Able Seaman
Finch, Ernest W., Ordinary Seaman
Ford, Alfred J., Ordinary Telegraphist
Goddard, James H., Stoker 1st Class, Royal Fleet Reserve
Goostrey, Phillip L. D., Stoker 2nd Class
Gridley, Lawrence E., Ordinary Seaman
Grimble, Ernest D., Acting Leading Seaman
Guilfoyle, Sidney, Ordinary Seaman
Hale, Robert J., Stoker 2nd Class
Hales, Rhys W. G. J., Chief Petty Officer
Hancock, John A., Ordinary Signalman
Hardwick, Noel R. H., Able Seaman
Harman, Phillip E., Boy
Harrison, Joseph, Able Seaman
Hatton, James B., Assistant Cook
Herbert, Charles H., Assistant Steward
Hewson, George A., Stoker 1st Class
Hide, William F., Shipwright 1st Class
Higgins, Kenneth, Stoker 1st Class
Hollis, John R., Acting Stoker Petty Officer
Holmes, Frederick G., Able Seaman
Hopper, Thomas, Stoker 2nd Class
Howell, Lewis E., Acting Petty Officer Telegraphist
Hurley, Edward, Able Seaman
Jarman, John H., Able Seaman
Jessup, Edwin A., Able Seaman
Jobling, Joseph, Acting Leading Stoker
Jones, Noel W., Engine Room Artificer
Jordon, George H., Able Seaman
Kelsey, William, Engine Room Artificer
Kirby, Christopher, Stoker
Kirk, George, Stoker
Lane, Lionel A. J., Able Seaman
Lemon, Robert, Ordinary Seaman
Livingstone, Herbert, Ordinary Seaman
McCaddon, Norman A. H., Stoker 1st Class
McCann, Peter, Ordinary Seaman
McLeod, Donald, Acting Leading Seaman
Martin, William H., Stoker 1st Class

Maxted, George H. H., Acting Leading Stoker
Miller, Leonard R., Ordinary Seaman
Minter, Sydney G., Able Seaman
Mitchell, William, Stoker
Monks, Walter V., Ordinary Seaman
Morris, Alfred C., Stoker Petty Officer
Newman, Frederick G., Able Seaman
Neve, Sidney G., Acting Leading Stoker
Parker, Frank, Acting Electrical Artificer 4th Class
Parkes, George, Able Seaman
Pay, Reginald S., Stoker Petty Officer
Perkins, Douglas R., Acting Leading Telegraphist
Peterson, Alfred J., Petty Officer Steward
Phillipson, William, Able Seaman
Ransom, George R. L., Chief Petty Officer
Read, Joseph H., Able Seaman
Rendell, Albert B. J., Leading Seaman
Richardson, John F., Able Seaman
Ringer, Walter J., Stoker 1st Class
Rowe, Thomas K., Ordinary Seaman
Sampson, Leonard, Acting Leading Telegraphist
Scarles, Horace W., Ordinary Telegraphist
Scott, Joseph, Able Seaman
Shale, Davis W., Stoker
Sharp, Edward, Assistant Steward
Silver, Fred D., Ordinary Seaman
Skinner, Frank E., Acting Leading Stoker
Small, Hubert A., Stoker Petty Officer
Smith, Douglas J., Petty Officer Writer
Squance, Reginald G., Ordnance Artificer 1st Class
Swallow, Kenneth R. G., Able Seaman
Tailby, Norman F., Ordinary Coder
Tait, James B., Acting Leading Telegraphist
Taylor, Andrew J., Acting Leading Stoker
Taylor, Derrick M., Ordinary Seaman
Tee, Joseph F., Petty Officer Cook
Thomas, Colin H., Ordinary Seaman
Todd, Ernest, Leading Stoker
Turrell, Charles R., Acting Ordnance Artificer 1st Class
Upton, Kenneth E., Acting Leading Stoker
Urquhart, Robert G., Ordinary Seaman
Wallace, Arthur G., Electrical Artificer 5th Class
Ward, Walter A. W., Stoker 1st Class
Wawman, Norman C., Signalman
Williamson, Bernard E., Signalman

## Maltese
Camenzuli, Domenico, Leading Steward

## NAAFI
King, R. B., Canteen Manager
Martin, S. R., Canteen Assistant

Glossary

# Naval words, slang and phrases

**A/A** Anti-aircraft guns, ratings. Ack-ack also used.

**AEC** Used throughout the Navy in World War 2, initials of Admiral Sir Andrew Cunningham, Commander-in-Chief Mediterranean, later Admiral of the Fleet and First Sea Lord.

**AB** Able Seaman.

**A/S** Anti-Submarine.

**Asdic** Apparatus for detecting submarines (and sometimes shoals of fish! When depthcharged, the stunned fish might come to the surface in large quantities, augmenting the ship's diet and, if convenient, delivered to local hospitals).

**Battle ensign** Large flag hoisted by warship going into action.

**Bottle** A reprimand.

**Buffer** The chief boatswain's mate, senior Petty Officer in the seamen's branch.

**Buzz** A rumour, unofficial information or even 'first-news' gleaned by the rating at the wheel with his ear glued to the voice pipe ('buzz pipe') between the wheel and the bridge so he might overhear the Captain and officers.

**Clear lower deck** A pipe summoning the ship's company to assemble on the upper deck to hear an important announcement by the Captain.

**Clubs** Physical Training Instructor.

**CW** CW candidates, recently recruited and war-conscripted ratings chosen as suitable for possible commissioning. They spent a minimum of three months' shore training, three months at sea and crash-courses at shore establishments and 'passed out' as Sub-Lieutenants or Midshipmen.

**Defaulters** Ratings put in report to appear before their divisional officer, or the First Lieutenant and eventually, if justified, before the Captain, alleged to have offended against KR and AI (King's Regulations and Admiralty Instructions).

**Degaussing** Anti-mining treatment of a warship or other vessel.

**Dhobing** Washing one's own clothes.

**D/F** Direction finding, D/F Aerial, etc.

**Draft chit** Form issued to rating going to a new posting, eg, Draft to RN Barracks or draft to warship.

**Drafting Jaunty** Drafting Master-at-Arms in barracks.

**Dockyard matey** Dockyard workman.

**Geordie** A Tynesider (*Kelly* was built at Hebburn on Tyne, by 'Geordies').

**Goodies** Well-behaved ratings, those who never got into trouble and sometimes used for 'temperance ratings' who did not apply for their rum ration and chose lime juice instead.

**Guns** Wardroom nickname for the gunnery officer.

**Guz** Royal Naval Barracks at Devonport.

**Handsomely** Doing a naval job correctly, neatly, ranging from 'bringing his destroyer alongside "handsomely"' to smart handling of ship's ropes and other gear.

**HO** Ratings enlisted for 'Hostilities Only'.

**In and Out** The nickname for the famous Naval and Military Club in Piccadilly which has entry and exit marked in bold letters IN and OUT. It was the home of Prime Minister Palmerstone who, incidentally, had been born at Broadlands.

**Jimmy** 'Jimmy the One', the First Lieutenant.

**Ki** Ship's cocoa, prepared by scraping a block of chocolate, with plenty of sugar and sometimes custard, served extremely thick. Very sustaining and always ready in the galley during the night and dark watches.

**LCT** LC is a prefix for various types of Landing Craft, Landing Craft Tank, Landing Craft Gun, Landing Craft Rocket and so on.

**Liberty boat** And Libertymen, who proceed on leave, either by liberty boat, if the ship is at anchor or moored to a buoy; or down the gangway to a bus or other transport if the ship is alongside.

**Monkey jacket** One of the several types of officers' rig.

**Natives** In addition to local residents, a crew member might be called a 'native' if his ship moors near or in striking distance of his home town.

**Old Man** A warship's Captain.

**OOW** Officer of the Watch on the bridge at sea or officer of the day (OOD) and duty officer if the warship is in harbour or moored.

**Opposition party** To Sid Mosses (see his diary) this was the enemy. An oppo, on the other hand, is a sailor's opposite number or his particular pal.

**Over the side** An expression most commonly used when a man is in a cradle over the side painting the ship. In *Kelly*, when painting had to be done in a hurry, they were all 'over the side' save the cooks, even Lord Mountbatten and the other officers.

**Party** A sailor's girl-friend.

**Piping the side** The boatswain's call or whistle is used for piping aboard HM ships a whole series of distinguished visitors, from the Queen and the Duke of Edinburgh to all commanding officers of RN ships and foreign Naval officers. 'Piping the still' calls the ship's company to attention for a variety of reasons.

**Ping** An echo sound on the Asdic gear when an enemy submarine or submerged object is near. If a ping is confirmed as indicating a submarine, a destroyer immediately goes to Action Stations, puts on speed towards the source of the echo and depth charges are made ready.

**Pom-Pom** Multiple-barrelled, short-range anti-aircraft guns, also nicknamed a 'Chicago piano'.

**Rattle** If a man is in the rattle he is in the First Lieutenant's report for defaulters.

**RNB** Royal Naval Barracks — RNB Portsmouth, Devonport and, in *Kelly*'s days, there was RNB Chatham, now closed.

**Shot mat** Placed to protect a warship's wooden deck from the shell casings falling

out of the breech of a gun after the shell is fired.

**Skates** Ne'er do wells.

**Skimming dish** Or Skimmy dish: a small fast motorboat, easy to place in or lift out of the water, used for urgent transport of perhaps the Captain or the ship's postman.

**Steaming party** Skeleton first party to go to a ship to undertake various duties while the ship is being completed and prior to commissioning.

**Stone frigate** A shore establishment.

**Stripey** A seasoned seaman, usually with three good-conduct stripes.

**MTB** Motor Torpedo Boat.

**Tailor-mades** The manufactured cigarettes from all the well-known firms bought in wartime at 6d for twenty at the ship's NAAFI shop or ashore.

**Tickler tin** The tin containing 'ticklers', the free issue of tinned shag tobacco for rolling into cigarettes by hand (some men on the messdecks, mostly regulars, could roll a cigarette with one hand). Pipe smokers also had free issue tobacco they rolled leaf by leaf, soaked in rum and bound by tarry cord into 'pricks' which, after maturing, were cut bit by bit for the pipe providing a magnificent aroma and (apparently) immense enjoyment by the smoker.

**Tiddly** (or tiddley) Not at all a slang term for drunk, but meaning Smart with a capital S. You could have a tiddly suit or look smart in the tiddly No 1 suit.

**Tinfish** Torpedo, which a destroyer could give and receive.

**Torps** The ship's torpedo officer.

**Up-homers** A regular and welcome visitor to the girl-friend's family, for food and drink and often taking a 'goody' from the ship, a packet of fags or a tin of corned beef. 'Where's Jack tonight?' 'Oh! He's a shore, up-homers.'

**Whaler** A seaboat, with oars. Usable in case of the ship being sunk. Also very much used when the opportunity arose for exercise and a friendly race between destroyers' crews. It was not unusual for the pipe 'Away seaboat's crew' to herald an exhausting row from the moored destroyer at Scapa Flow to the Post Office at Kirkwall or to the grocer's shop...

# Index